GREAT MOMENTS IN BRITISH SPORT

EDITOR
JOHN LOVESEY

DESIGNER
NEIL RANDON

First published in Great Britain 1993
by H. F. & G. Witherby
a Cassell imprint
Villiers House, 41/47 Strand, London,
WC2N 5JE

A catalogue record for this book is
available from the British Library

ISBN 0 85493 229 1

Printed and bound in Great Britain
by The Bath Press, Avon.

GREAT MOMENTS IN BRITISH SPORT

Contents

Introduction

MEMORIES ARE THE GOSSAMER from which dreams are made, and never more so than with sport. And memories are what this book is about. The great games, fights, races and encounters grow in the telling. If what survives today, after a journey in time, comes closer to Arthurian legend than fact, does it matter? If what stirs us is a story of heroism and victory, in which the cast of characters is finally revealed as unblemished and chivalrous to the vanquished, is that not something to be encouraged? Sport, despite professionalism, despite drugs, still has a simple ethos imposed by the rules of competition. Even with the passage of time, stories in this book, most of them culled from contemporary accounts, still have the power to inspire.

The canvas on which sporting exploits are painted is one that everybody can enjoy. If sport also holds a mirror to, say, the skulduggery of the boardroom, at least we can recognize it instantly and come to our own conclusions. There is little else that is quite so open. That is sport's universal attraction and why it should be forever aware of its responsibilities to the young.

At times like football's World Cup, sport today can hold many millions in thrall. It is the one art in whose appreciation all can share. When Geoffrey Green, the former football correspondent of *The Times*, described the sight of Bobby Charlton in full flow on a football field as 'the people's poetry' he put it perfectly. Each of us could see in the flowing figure of Charlton, a wisp of blond hair flying in the wind, the classic British sports hero.

My own first memories of sport go back to afternoons and evenings sitting round the wireless listening to the breathtaking commentaries of Stewart MacPherson on the big fights and Raymond Glendenning on the big races. Nowadays it is strange to go back and read the written newspaper accounts of some of the events they so colourfully and forcefully projected. By comparison the written word sometimes seems lacklustre and turbid. Naturally, the memory may be playing tricks and, of course, newsprint rationing, which continued after World War II, did not allow the extravagance of space which sport enjoys in newspapers today. Moreover, without the omnipotent eye of television revealing the truth to us all, radio commentators had a licence, shall we say, to enhance their reporting without fear of contradiction.

In those days, even of newsprint shortages, it should be said that newspapers sometimes performed functions that they could well repeat now. There was merit in brevity and many of my generation first really learned, for example, about Len Hutton's marathon innings of 364 from small cartoon strips in newspapers. The running feats of Sydney Wooderson were projected in similar fashion, together with many other great moments.

Choosing moments from the whole historic panoply is not easy. Inevitably, the choice is subjective. This book starts, for example, with Denzil Batchelor's summary of the famous prize fight between Tom Sayers and John Heenan. The image of Sayers fighting on and on with one arm incapacitated has stuck with me ever since I first read about it. Thousands of words were expended at the time of the contest and they have continued to be written since. Though great events took place before, the circumstances of the fight and

Forties heroes like Freddie Mills had their feats enhanced by wireless commentaries

the volume of coverage were extraordinary, and it is why this book chooses to start with it. The edition of *Bell's Life in London* that carried the account of the fight sold out virtually as it came off the presses. Five days later the paper reprinted its reporting in the form of a 'Gratuitous Supplement' for its Sunday edition. *The Times* devoted more words to the fight than it would to a world heavyweight championship fight nowadays, and the encounter itself attracted to the ringside many of the great and mighty of the land. It was a media event as well as a legendary, albeit gruesome, sporting contest.

Thereafter many events chose themselves, especially those where seemingly inpregnable barriers have been broken. Only Lester Piggott has two pieces to himself and justifiably so. He is a colossus who came back after one career had ended to raise our spirits again in a second. I make no apology either for including four of my own pieces, three of which reconstruct remarkable moments, one of which is a report written about the Isle of Man TT races and the amazing motor cyclist Mike Hailwood. There are also what may seem oddities, like Walter Lindrum's world record billiards break. Older people than myself will recall the headlines this provoked; but it was a tedious, if miraculous, performance which, in the end, destroyed public interest in the game. Occasionally, an idiosyncratic piece has been preferred, like Danny Blanchflower's highly personal account of the day Tottenham Hotspur achieved the Cup-League double.

Some might argue that climbing Everest was exploration rather than sport, and that Malcolm Campbell's speed attempts were pursuits of technological goals rather than athletic grails. In an era that has admitted darts to the sporting arena such arguments hold little water, and it is interesting to note how the sporting predilections of newspapers have swung. It seems strange now, but in the not too distant past motor racing tended to be a newsdesk rather than a sportsdesk responsibility.

In compiling this collection, I have been helped immeasurably by Richard Wigmore of H. F. & G. Witherby and, more than words can tell, by Neil Randon, the book's designer, whose passion for the whole world of sport matches my own. In the end, though, the moments are my choice. Several of the accounts come from so-called 'popular' sources, and that may raise a few eyebrows. But in my view the popular press frequently captures the essence of an event rather better than the quality papers. Disagree, if you like. As well as providing a bond between people, sport is a debating arena. The important thing to remember and to cherish is Britain's sporting heritage.

John Lovesey
London
June 1993

1860
17 April

Sayers becomes the immortal hero of the prize ring

*The fight between Tom Sayers and John Heenan had its place in history secured by the image of Sayers battling with one arm incapacitated. In his book, British Boxing, **Denzil Batchelor** distilled the essence of a struggle that provided perhaps the first truly great moment in British sport*

TOM SAYERS, a Brighton-born bricklayer, began work as a boy of seven gutting herrings. In appearance he was fit to stand as a model for a Phil May drawing of a London costermonger. Shallow of brow, stubborn of jaw, with fearless dark eyes, only Nat Langham was ever found good enough to blot his record. When Nat turned publican, Tom became unchallenged champion. He was never more than a middleweight, and indeed was formidable inside the welter limit. But at five feet eight inches and eleven stone, he fought and drew the most famous contest in the history of the ring.

This was, of course, his bout with the American, John Camel Heenan, who had been beaten by his country's champion, Morrissey, but had good grounds for considering himself cock of the native walk when the latter evaded a return match.

When the 'Benica Boy' squared up to Sayers, in a meadow near Farnborough in 1860, he dwarfed his opponent by six inches and outweighed him by three stone. Nevertheless, the two special train loads of spectators (each of whom bore a £2 ticket on which was printed 'To Nowhere') believed as fervently in their man as if they were Sunday school scholars nourished on the story of David and Goliath.

The outcome of that meeting was the most ghastly, horrible and glorious in the whole annals of the prize ring. In the fourth or fifth round, Sayers dislocated his right arm. For some thirty-seven rounds thereafter, he fought without being able to raise it for attack or defence. All this while, as if to bluff his opponent into believing that he preferred to lengthen the odds against himself by this sort of accident, he came to the scratch with a laugh of lunatic gallantry on his lips.

In the thirty-seventh round, Heenan, after being drenched in a shower-bath of blood from two smashing blows in the middle of his face, succeeded in intertwining Sayers's neck with the top rope, and then heaving the full weight of his gigantic body on to it. The British champion, black in the face, must have died within a matter of minutes, had not the umpires correctly decided to cut the ropes. But when the men went to the scratch again, there was Sayers laughing his fierce laugh, sending home that hail of pile-drivers with his terrible left hand, and still quick on his feet as a whippet.

In the last round, while the police swarmed about the ring, Heenan staggered forth so blind that when he collected himself to deliver the 'settler', the man he sent head over heels with it was not Sayers, but his own innocent second.

And then came the end. Heenan, barely human in appearance, his face gashed and ghastly, somehow raised a trot to sprint from the field and jump two small hedges on his way to safety. Then he collapsed and was led to the train which carried him back to the darkened room in London, in which he lay blind and in a coma for days to come. As for

The fight between Sayers and Heenan attracted a vast crowd, among them many of the famous

Sayers, he had been smashed down to measure his full length more than twenty times, but he ended the long battle as game as ever, full of fight, with the mad smile still on his face. A draw with a champion's belt for each man was the official end of it all – but there was no doubt to whom the laurel of the day's work belonged. A contributor to Cornhill – it may have been Thackeray – summed up the dreadful affair by reminding a gloating world that prize fighting was illegal, and that the Queen would be in order to send her subject, Sayers, to the treadmill for a month – and to knight him as he came out of prison.

Matthew Webb swims from England to France

*It is hard to credit now but when Captain Matthew Webb first achieved the feat of swimming the English Channel it was barely believable. The following extracts from an account in the **Dover Express** convey the atmosphere of an achievement that many then thought impossible and regarded with awe*

CAPTAIN MATTHEW WEBB has accomplished his great feat of swimming from England to France, having touched ground at Calais Sands at 10.41 a.m., after a swim of 21 hours and three-quarters, during which it is computed that he travelled at the least 50 miles. The start from the Admiralty Pier at Dover took place at four minutes before one o'clock on Tuesday, he having previously been well anointed with porpoise oil, a preparation necessary to exclude the cold and keep up the tone of the body during so long an immersion in the water. The circumstances attending his start were all favourable, the wind was exceedingly light, the seas smooth, and the sky slightly overcast, so that the swimmer was not exposed to trying heat. Having dived from a step at the end of the Pier, Captain Webb,

amidst loud and repeated cheers started, making apparently a direct course to Cap Gris Nez, where he hoped to land...

Captain Webb was accompanied by the lugger Ann, of Dover, and two rowing boats. The persons with the expedition, all told, including the swimmer, were 15, namely: Captain Matthew Webb (the hero of the day), Mr G.H. Ward (cousin of the swimmer), an expert diver named Baker, George Toms (captain of the lugger), John Dodd (mate), and five men, namely, Bowles, Jell, Gates, Decent, and Stanley; five representatives of the press, namely, Mr J. Bavington Jones (editor of the Dover Express), representing the Daily Telegraph; Mr. Warman (reporter of the Dover Chronicle), representing the Times; Mr A.G. Payne (of Land and Water), representing the London Standard; Mr. Wilkinson (of the Field), representing the Daily News; and Mr. Bell, a talented artist, representing the Illustrated London News and the Sporting and Dramatic News. Mr A.G. Payne and Mr. H.F. Wilkinson, being members of the Ilex Swimming Club, were deputed to see that the feat was carried out in a bona-fide manner; and the diver, Baker, was to render service if it should be necessary.

One row boat kept constantly in front of the swimmer to direct his course and supply refreshments; and in the bow of this, for the whole of the 21 hours, sat Mr. Ward, to watch his kinsman and attend to his wants...At 2.30 p.m. a little rain fell, but it speedily passed off, and a quarter of an hour later the swimmer took his first refreshment, consisting of a small cup of ale. He took no solid food whatever while in the water; the only nutriment given him being coffee, ale, brandy, a little cod-liver oil, and beef tea...

The light at Cap Gris Nez became visible at 8.30, and it was then estimated that Webb was ten miles distant from the South Foreland light. The swimmer now took some warm coffee, and was reported to be as well as when he started. Things went on well till 9.30, when Webb called out that he had been stung on the shoulder by a jelly fish, and he asked for some brandy. At that time there was a perceptible weakening of his stroke, and it was feared that

Matthew Webb's sustenance while swimming included ale, brandy and beef tea

ety to those who were watching the efforts of the gallant swimmer, and of perfect torture to Webb, whose pale and haggard face told of thorough exhaustion; but his indomitable pluck would not allow him to give up when the prize was so near; in fact, he assured his cousin, who was anxiously watching him, that he would stick at it as long as he could 'wag a toe.' As he grew weaker the wind and tide became stronger, and still he held on with the most marvellous perseverance, although the seas were breaking over him and obstructing his movements towards land...

Up to the last the excitement was most painful; for even when Webb was within 200 yards of the shore it was feared his strength would not hold out to reach it. In strict accordance with the arrangements, no one assisted him in the least; but every means were used to give him heart. On approaching the shore, soundings were called out rather more favourable than the facts warranted. English and French alike cheered almost constantly, and, as a last encouragement, the rowers pushed down their long oars to show that they could touch the bottom. The excitement increased to the close, and when at last Webb did touch ground, the men in the boats around him jumped into the water and fairly hugged him with delight. The news of his approach had spread in the town, and a crowd ran down the shore to welcome him, while a carriage stood on the margin of the water ready to drive him to his hotel. On landing he was very weak, but, as the boatmen expressed it, 'jolly in his talk' up to the end. He was enveloped in wraps, and driven to the Hotel de Paris, where, after being well rubbed down, he drank three or four glasses of old port wine. He went to bed immediately and slept soundly. There were several medical men ready to volunteer assistance at the hotel, but their services were not needed. On making enquiries I was told that Captain Webb was sleeping.

Both in Dover and in Calais the success of the Captain's feat has created great excitement, as nine out of ten of those who knew anything about the sea felt confident he could not succeed.

eight and a half hours in the water and the chilly air of the evening were beginning to tell upon him. A few minutes later, however, he shouted that he was all right, and that he felt no more of the sting...

Between 3 and 4 o'clock in the morning the hopes of touching the Cape began to fade, for the light seemed to recede. A breeze sprang up in the east, and a ripple appeared on the water. The swimmer's progress was slow...

At 6 a.m. the brave fellow took some beef tea and coffee, and made another vigorous attempt to gain the point; but a stiff breeze had arisen, and both wind and tide drove us towards Calais. An hour of weary watching followed while Webb fought hard to make progress towards land. But the tide and wind were too strong...

[There] were two hours of the greatest anxi-

Bob Fitzsimmons wins world heavyweight title

*England's rare world heavyweight boxing champion won the crown in Carson City, Nevada. Fitzsimmons's victory over Jim Corbett was famously achieved, in large part, with his solar plexus punch and this was how **The New York Times** reported the battle fought, it said, on 'purely scientific principles'*

Bob Fitzsimmons lifted Corbett clean off his feet with a powerful left that made history

AFTER TWO YEARS OF DOUBT and vexatious postponements the heavyweight championship of the world for pugilism was decided beyond cavil today when Robert Fitzsimmons sent James J. Corbett helpless to his knees with a left-hand blow under the heart after one minute and forty-five seconds in the fourteenth round.

The great contest was decided in the simplest manner and the 'knockout' was the result of one unwary move on the part of Corbett. After the first minute of the fourteenth round had been spent in a few harmless clinches and counters Fitzsimmons made a 'fake' lead with his right for the jaw. It was a simple ruse, but it caught the Californian napping. Instead of keeping his body inclined forward and throwing back his head just a trifle to allow the blow, which was of the very lightest kind, to slip by, Corbett contemptuously bent his head and chest backward and thus protruded his abdomen.

Fitzsimmons's small eyes flashed, and, like lightning he saw and availed himself of his advantage. Drawing back his left, he brought it up with terrible force, the forearm rigid and at right angles to the upper arm. With the full power of his wonderful driving muscles brought into play, he ripped the blow up the pit of Corbett's stomach at a point just under the heart. Corbett was lifted clean off his feet, and as he pitched forward Fitzsimmons shot his right up and around, catching Corbett on the jaw and accelerating his downward fall. Corbett sank on his left knee, and with his outstretched right grasped the ropes for support. His left arm worked convulsively up and down, while his face was twitching with an expression of the greatest agony.

Referee Siler threw up his hands on the call of 'ten' and left the ring. There were some cries of 'Foul!' when the referee declared Corbett 'out,' but they were unheeded by anybody as the battle was won fairly and squarely.

The defeat nearly drove Corbett wild. When he was able to feel his feet, after his seconds had helped him to his corner, he broke away from them and rushed at Fitzsimmons, who had not left the ring. A scene of dreadful confusion ensued. The ring was crowded with an excited mob, but Corbett burst through them and struck at Fitzsimmons.

The Cornishman kept his arms by his sides, and with a great deal of generosity, made allowance for Corbett's half demented condition. Fitzsimmons merely ducked under the blow, and when Corbett clinched with him and struck him a feeble blow on the arm the champion only smiled. It was with great difficulty that 'Billy' Brady and the seconds succeeded in quieting Corbett down and getting him back to the dressing room.

The fight was clean and speedy. It demonstrated two facts – that Corbett is the cleverest boxer of his weight in the world, and that Fitzsimmons is able to hit him. The California boy smothered the Cornishman with 'left jabs' in the face and right and left body blows.

Fitzsimmons's most effective attack was a semi-fake left swing, followed with a quick half-arm hook. The first time he tried it, which was in the third round, Corbett threw back his head from the fake, coming forward for a counter when he thought Fitzsimmons's glove was comfortably past his jaw. Quick as a flash, Fitzsimmons doubled back and barely missed Corbett's jaw with the hook. Corbett's smile died away for an instant, and he took no more chances on countering that particular form of lead afterward.

The battle was fought on purely scientific and almost new principles. Corbett made no attempt to bring around his right in breaking away, probably because Fitzsimmons held up his elbows too high.

Corbett's only effort in the way of a parting shot was a full right upper cut, which he brought around very clumsily, and failed to land by at least a foot every time he tried. He did get in one good upper cut in the fourth round, splitting Fitzsimmons's under lip and starting the blood in a thick stream.

'I never saw such a clever man in my life,' said Fitzsimmons. 'He got away from me time and again when I thought I had him dead to rights. I knew I could wear him out, and so I kept coming right along until my opportunity arrived. He was weak in the last round, and all his cleverness could not keep him out of that left punch under the heart. The only blow that really worried me was the one which split my lip. The others I never felt. He fought fair, and hereafter he may have my respect if he continues to merit it.'

Corbett's version of his own Waterloo did not vary greatly from Fitzsimmons's. 'I made a mistake in not keeping away,' was the way he put it. 'Fitzsimmons, I knew to be a terrible puncher, but I never calculated on his being able to reach me. If the sixth round had lasted ten seconds longer I would have landed him to a certainty. His nose was clogged with blood and his legs were wobbling. The gong sounded just as I was about to plug him with my right and end the battle. He recuperated wonderfully, and I stayed away from him until I thought he was about ripe for another drubbing at short range. My neglect in not standing off when he tapped me on the cheek in the fourteenth lost me the championship. That heart punch simply choked me up. I could not breathe or move for fifteen seconds, and it was several minutes before I realised that I had committed a breach of etiquette in trying to follow up my opponent after he put me out. I meant it when I said I would be his friend hereafter. He whipped me fair and square, but I don't think he is the best man yet and we will have another go if money can bring him into the ring.'

1900
5 October

The US Open golf championship falls to Harry Vardon

*It is said that Harry Vardon was one of the outstanding golfers of all time, a forerunner of players such as Jacklin and Faldo. His influence on the game was enormous and he won a record six Open championships and one US Open. His outstanding performance in Chicago was reported on in **The New York Times***

Harry Vardon won his US Open championship by two strokes from another Briton, J. H. Taylor

BEFORE THE LARGEST GALLERY that ever witnessed a golf championship in America, Harry Vardon, former champion of Great Britain, won the United States Golf Association open championship from Great Britain's premier golfer, J. H. Taylor, by the narrow margin of two strokes, on the Chicago Golf Club links, at Wheaton. For two days these wonderful golfers from English links had battled, far in the lead of the representative field of English, Scots, Irish, German and American players, for the title of Champion of the United States. David Bell of Carnoustie, the professional at Midlothian with former champion Willie Smith, gained third place in the championship, with a total of 323 strokes. Bell won the $150 in cash and the gold medal presented by a big golf supply house for the American engaged golfer who finished next to Vardon and Taylor. Laurence Auchterlonie of Glenview, formerly one of the best amateurs at St. Andrew's, Scotland, was fourth, with 327 strokes. Fifth place fell to Willie Smith, whose total was 329.

All the interest in the first round of play centred in the two foreigners. When Taylor turned in a 76 to Vardon's 79, the critics predicted that Vardon would let himself out. This he did in the second round, and made 78 to Taylor's 82, and having one stroke the advantage. Vardon's concluding rounds in 76 and 80, to Taylor's 79 and 78, showed the closeness of the race. It was not until the last hole had been played by Vardon – and he putted so indifferently on the eighteenth green that some feared a tie would result – that the gallery dared cheer the Isle of Jersey man as the victor.

1901

12 September

C. B. Fry scores six consecutive centuries

*People have called C. B. Fry 'Britain's Renaissance Man'. A scholar, he was also an all-round sportsman, who set a world record for the long jump, played football for England and became a public figure. A brilliant batsman, this was how **The Times** of the day accounted for his best known cricket feat*

C. B. Fry, with his many talents, epitomised an envied English insouciance

IN THE LAST MATCH of the season at Lord's, the proceeds of which are to be devoted to the fund for the widow and children of the late Mr. W. Yardley, the old Cambridge and Kent cricketer, the play was full of interest from start to finish. For those who are keen on heavy scoring the cricket must have been gratifying, for it proved a complete batting triumph for the Rest of England against Yorkshire.

During the five hours' play runs averaged over 90 an hour. Mr. Jones laid the foundation of the Rest of England score by hitting up 65 out of 89 for the first wicket; but the batting honours were carried off by Mr Fry and Mr. Jessop. Mr. Fry, who went in second wicket down at 107, was fourth out at 405 to a catch at cover-point. His hundred enabled him to establish two records. It was his 13th score of three figures this season, which beats Abel's 12 of last year. A much more remarkable feat, however, was that it was his sixth successive innings of over a hundred. His last half-dozen scores are 106 against Hampshire, 209 against Yorkshire, 149 against Middlesex, 105 against Surrey, 140 against Kent, and now his 105 against Yorkshire, a truly creditable record.

He was batting some three hours without giving a chance, and his cricket was marked by all his well-known skill. As usual with him, he made the majority of his runs on the leg-side, and his innings included 10 fours. When Mr. Fry and Mr. Jessop were together 204 runs were put on for the fourth wicket in an hour and a half.

(The Rest of England eventually beat Yorkshire by an innings and 115 runs).

Hackenschmidt outwrestles the 'Terrible Turk'

The British showman C. B. Cochran turned a wrestler who grew up in Russia into a British national hero. Hackenschmidt would only wrestle 'on the level' and his matches with Ahmed Madrali made him a national hero.
John Lovesey *wrote about the 'Russian Lion' for Sports Illustrated in 1961*

SAMSON HIMSELF could not have created more commotion than a wrestler and strongman called George Hackenschmidt did at the turn of the century. Celebrated as the 'Russian Lion', Hackenschmidt was born in Livonia, Russia in 1877 and at the summit of his fame was feted, admired and privileged as few athletes have been.

He grew up in czarist Russia. From an early age he was a fitness enthusiast. He preferred exercise and sports to studies, and although his mother tried to teach him the piano he never progressed beyond a few elementary tunes. His father was the proprietor of a dye works in Dorpat, but on leaving school Hackenschmidt became apprenticed as an engineer.

Three years later, however, he became the protégé of a Dr Wladislaf von Krajewski. Dr von Krajewski, a physician to the Czar, had taken up weight lifting at 41. He founded the St Petersburg Athletic and Cycling Club, attracting to its membership many aristocrats, including His Royal Highness the Grand Duke Vladimir Alexandrovitch, uncle of Czar Nicholas II.

Hackenschmidt soon developed into a magnificently muscled human specimen. At 21 he stood 5 feet 9 inches and scaled almost 200 pounds. His chest and shoulders measured 47 inches normally and 51 inches expanded, his flexed biceps each stretched a tape over 16 inches, his thighs were more than two feet around and his calves 15 inches.

In 1898 Hackenschmidt entered his first major wrestling tournament, the amateur championship of Europe, which he won.

Two years later, after a period of service in the Preobrashensky Polk (the First Life Guards of the Czar), he became a professional wrestler. He was an instant success. His matches rarely lasted more than a few minutes. Wherever he went, from Scandinavia to Australia, it became routine for him to throw several opponents, one after the other, within a small span of time.

After one of his matches, when it took him nearly three hours to defeat a wrestler called Kara Ahmed in Budapest in 1900, the Hungarian audience rose as one to applaud. Ecstatic admirers decked Hackenschmidt in flowers and carried him shoulder high through the streets of the city.

Two years later he travelled to England and made headlines at once. Stepping onto the stage of an old London music hall, the Alhambra, accompanied by a Mr Vansittart, an athlete known as The Man with the Grip of Iron, he surprised an American wrestler, Jack Carkeek, with an impromptu challenge. Vansittart staked £25 that Hackenschmidt could throw Carkeek at least 10 times within an hour. The challenge was not accepted – instead, Hackenschmidt and Vansittart were escorted from the stage by the police.

But for the persuasion of the late C. B. Cochran, the king of British show business,

George Hackenschmidt, a lion in the ring, was also a respected thinker

Hackenschmidt might have departed in disgust from England then and there. But Cochran, with the aid of a female photo-journalist who wrote an article entitled Is Strength Genius?, started to build Hackenschmidt into the world's greatest wrestling attraction.

For a time Cochran had his problems. In an autobiography, published almost a quarter century after he first met Hackenschmidt, Cochran wrote, 'To his credit, Hackenschmidt would only wrestle on the level, and the public wanted a show.' Cochran claimed he only succeeded in attracting the paying customers by

persuading Hackenschmidt to toy a little with opponents before defeating them. With Cochran as his agent, Hackenschmidt's most famous matches in England were against Ahmed Madrali, the 'Terrible Turk'. The first meeting between these two took place in January 1904. Cochran recalled: 'London became wrestling mad. The boys in the street were always trying conclusions on the pavement. Supper parties often culminated in holds being discussed and demonstrated.'

A fashionable audience packed London's huge Olympia to see the contest. In his dressing room beforehand Hackenschmidt paced up and down, but once the match started he was calm, confident and quick. Encircling the Turk's body with his powerful arms, Hackenschmidt threw him to the mat. The Turk lay there with a dislocated arm, finished.

From that moment Hackenschmidt was a national hero. As Cochran put it, he became 'a British institution'.

Inevitably a rematch was scheduled. This occurred in 1906, and in the second meeting the Turk at one time had Hackenschmidt down on all fours. But when the Turk released his grip on Hackenschmidt's waist to attempt a half nelson on his right arm, Hackenschmidt obtained a left wrist hold and a leg lock, and with an incredible heave hurled his man clean over. Hackenschmidt won by two out of three falls.

Hackenschmidt amassed a small fortune from wrestling, and since his retirement from the sport has been immersed in research. The Australian athletics coach Percy Cerutty has called him 'the greatest living authority on the relationship between mind and body'. He has written books on such esoteric subjects as Attitudes and Their Relation to Human Manifestations and Man and Cosmic Antagonisms to Mind and Spirit.

'First of all,' Hackenschmidt said recently about his philosophic researches, 'I tried to find out my relationship to my immediate environment, then I tried to clear my relationship between myself and the cosmic energy that carries our physical body. And at last I found the origin of rhythm.'

1920
17 August

Albert Hill upsets form in the Antwerp Games

Never was victory more sweet than for Albert Hill in the 800 metres at the 1920 Olympics. He was 31 and had survived the horrors of the trenches in World War One. After his first great victory, reported on by **W. B. Bennison** *in The Daily Telegraph, he went on to win the 1,500 metres two days later*

ON THIS DAY of blistering sunshine we have witnessed a round of wonders, and we who have come to Antwerp for the Olympic Games have been deeply stirred and thrilled. Englishmen are pardonably proud and happy; experts, for the most part, have been confounded. The victory of Albert Hill, the Herne Hill Harrier, in the 800 metres, exploded form and poked fun at the prophets. This fair-haired, well-knit, stout-hearted athlete, when we were almost sure that Rudd, the Rhodes scholar, wearing the bright-green colours of South Africa, would win; when Americans had only eyes for their magnificent runner, Earl Eby, and when there was more than a possibility of his countryman, Campbell, finishing first; when King Albert and every one of the several thousand people in the Stadium were gripped tight by the desperate, punishing battle for victory, flew to the front not more than thirty yards from the tape, and as he did so a mighty shout went up.

We had scarcely thought of the young Londoner; Edgar Mountain certainly – a well-set-up, strong young man. For Hill, until Rudd took the lead just before rounding the bend for the straight, had occupied no sort of place from which it seemed likely that he would eventually beat all opposition. It is possible that when Rudd kind of wobbled and told plainly of distress, and Eby was almost touching the South African's shoulder, Hill was encouraged to make the effort of his life; until that moment he could scarcely have supposed that he would win.

The condition of Rudd, I am sure, gave him inspiration; in the last few yards of this truly memorable race Hill was as a man who would do or die. With chin held high, jaws clenched, his eyes half-closed, his face distorted by the greediness with which he had already eaten his strength, he forced himself to the first position. But there were more than ten or a dozen yards to go – awful, soul-breaking yards – and Eby, with characteristic grit, challenged Hill to a fight to the last gasp, and this little American, slipping past Rudd, stuck to Hill like some terrier. But Hill never faltered; on he went to break the tape, with the hot breath of Eby on his shoulders. Rudd, on the heels of Eby, was third, and as he passed the post he fell all of a heap, utterly and completely spent. Campbell, a worthy American, also collapsed.

Hill, though he could never have engaged in such a battle before, was by comparison with the others, tolerably fresh, and the while his countrymen cheered and shouted, and everybody roared their admiration for him, he hurried to lend a helping hand to the prostrate Campbell. Great, chivalrous man is Hill. He will never run such a race as he did this afternoon. It was all very wonderful. No athlete ever fought so nobly for his country.

Albert Hill's victory in the 800m had everybody roaring their admiration for him

Policeman on a white horse rescues Cup Final

It was customary once, when people recalled the 1923 FA Cup Final at Wembley, to remember more the policeman on the white horse who helped make the event possible than the final score. Many years later **John Lovesey** *visited the policeman, by then retired, for Sports Illustrated*

THE BRITISH NATIONAL CHARACTER has been mummified in many a genteel novel and drawing-room play as one of reserved emotion and decorous behaviour. Even in sports the true-born Briton is thought of as one who rarely allows himself more than a subdued 'Well played sir!' at a cricket match. But this reticence has its soft underbelly. It is association football or soccer.

England's Football Association Cup Final annually stirs the interest of millions of men and women from all classes. It is therefore a measure of their place in the game's history that a policeman and a white horse are today remembered more vividly in connection with the 1923 Cup Final than the teams which took part.

That year marked a significant step forward in the cup tournament. The Football Association had long needed a larger ground to accommodate the crowd: in 1921 plans were made to build a great stadium in Wembley in the suburbs of north London. Two years later, a mere four days after the last seat had been screwed into place and the final fleck of paint left to dry, the first Final was scheduled to take place there on April 28.

Wembley's huge oval stadium was built to hold 127,000 people, but when the gates were closed to the crowd that first year the rejected multitude outside turned reckless and stormed the place. In their passion to see London's West Ham United play Lancashire's Bolton Wanderers, the soccer zealots made Wembley look more like a battlefield than a site for the nation's greatest sports event. Some of the newspaper reports read like dispatches from the front line.

Estimates of the numbers that turned up at Wembley run as high as 300,000, and some eyewitnesses were certain than 250,000 got in. Iron gates were torn open, barriers broken, and more than a thousand people were injured. The crowd was so dense that some men were able to roll on the heads of the standing spectators down to ground level from the top of one of the terraces.

The mob surged onto the playing field, and by the time King George V arrived, hoping to see the game, Wembley was a chaos. The monarch had to sit for almost an hour while some show of order was created.

The order – such as it was – was largely brought about by Police Constable George Scorey on Billy, a white horse who had a way with people. Scorey, a placid man, sensed the seriousness of the situation before almost anybody.

A veteran of the Boer War and World War I, Scorey lives in retirement in Chislehurst, Kent. 'I saw an opening,' he recalls of that hectic afternoon almost four decades ago, 'and in I went, I told the people to link their arms together and told them to heave, heave, heave. When they got to the touchline I told them to sit down. Billy was on his best behaviour that day.'

The 1923 FA Cup Final may never have taken place without the assistance of Billly, the famous white horse

Inch by inch the field was cleared, the players coming out to help also, and Scorey, with nine other mounted policemen, was everywhere. 'He was never turned from his purpose, this efficient constable,' wrote one reporter. 'He rode from side to side of the ground, and pushed his intelligent mount into the wall of faces.'

The game started 40 minutes late, with human walls as touchlines. Bolton Wanderers won 2-0. It was a crazy mixed-up game. One of the goals was scored while a player on the London team was still lost in the crowd, which had engulfed him as he retrieved the ball. Or so the story goes. It's hard to prove or disprove anything about what happened that lunatic day. The imbroglio achieved the ultimate in status in British controversy: questions were asked in the House of Commons, Sir Oswald Mosley, who later became Britain's most notorious Fascist but was then an independent M.P. for the constituency in which Wembley Stadium is situated, was among those who prodded the Home Secretary for explanations of the disorder. Elderly gentlemen wrote scathing letters to The Times. Ever since, admittance to the Cup Final has been by ticket only.

Amid all the recriminations there was nothing but praise for George Scorey and his horse. Without them the disorder could easily have led to tragedy. When it was all over, Scorey remembers, people patted the horse gratefully. 'We wouldn't have seen the game but for you,' one fan told Billy. The News of the World praised Scorey as the 'Wellington of Wembley.' Sir William Edge, the M.P. for Bolton, paid public tribute to the pair.

Every year Scorey becomes a public figure again, like the first robin. When Cup Final time approaches he is interviewed, photographed – on one occasion in bed late at night – and even asked to appear on television. He keeps a memento of Billy in a place of honour in his bungalow.

When the horse died the Deputy Assistant Commissioner at Scotland Yard ordered that one of the feet be made into an inkpot for Scorey. As he holds it occasionally, George Scorey recalls that he even first met his wife while astride Billy. 'That horse did something for him,' Mrs Scorey says, proudly.

Jack Hobbs scores his 100th century in first-class cricket

*The world's leading batsman between the eras of Grace and Bradman, Jack Hobbs's career extended from 1905 to 1934. During this time he scored 61,237 runs and made 197 centuries. When he scored his 100th century, the writer of the report in **The Times** could not know that the legend would go on growing*

THE FINAL DAY OF THE MATCH at Bath yesterday provided Hobbs with an opportunity to make his hundredth century in first-class cricket. Previously, only two batsmen had accomplished the feat – Dr. W.G. Grace, who made 126 centuries, and Tom Hayward, who made 104.

Hobbs's 116 not out yesterday was an invaluable effort, for Surrey had lost four wickets for 45 in their second innings and still were four runs in arrears, when Hitch joined Hobbs and, by characteristic cricket, assisted in the making of 121 runs for the wicket in a little over an hour and a half. Eventually, Surrey won a most interesting and memorable match by 10 runs.

Hobbs's great achievement makes it worthy of mention that it was in May, 1905, that he first appeared for Surrey, and in his first County Championship match scored 28 and 155. He had previously played for the county against the Gentlemen of England. In the course of his subsequent great career Hobbs obtained centuries in Test Matches in England, Australia and South Africa and, in the season of 1919, for the Players against the Gentlemen, he made 120 not out at the Oval, 113 at Lord's, and 116 at Scarborough. Curiously enough, in spite of his many triumphs against the large majority of the counties he had not, until yesterday, played a three-figure innings against Somerset.

Surrey had batted so badly on the previous day that Somerset had secured a lead of 49. Furthermore, Surrey, at their second attempt, had before the drawing of stumps on Monday lost Sandham and scored only 23 runs. Surrey did not improve matters yesterday, when, without any addition to the overnight total, Ducat, who on the previous day had saved the side from utter collapse, was run out. This disaster was the result of a brilliant piece of fielding on the part of Hunt, who threw down the wicket. In spite of the position of the game, and this warning that no liberties could be taken with the Somerset fielding, Hobbs and Shepherd, when they had been together a little while, attempted a sharp single and promptly paid the penalty. A smart return, by Mr. Considine this time, accounted for Shepherd's wicket. The score was then 36. For the moment, the Surrey batsmen seemed quite to have lost their heads, for, with Mr. Fender in, Hobbs started for a run which his captain would not have, and must have been out if Mr. McBryan had not blundered. The total, however, had only been advanced to 45 when Robson got Mr. Fender leg-before-wicket, and Surrey, with four men out, were still four runs to the bad.

Fortunately for Surrey, Hobbs found a most confident and active partner in Hitch. The two batsmen soon settled down to a lively and effective game. Hobbs reached his 50 in two hours, while, at luncheon time, the score had been advanced to 121, Hobbs being 56 and Hitch 43.

After the master batsman Jack Hobbs made his 100th century, almost as many were still to come

Afterwards, Hitch completed his 50 after batting for an hour and a quarter. The need of further assistance against the clever bowling of Mr. White and Robson was, however, strongly emphasised, for, with the total at 153, a catch at the wicket disposed of Hitch. Hitch's share of a partnership of 121 was 67, which included ten 4's. Joined by Harrison, Hobbs continued to bat in a masterly manner, and he reached his hundred in three hours and five minutes, having made his second 50 runs in 65 minutes. When 112 Hobbs was let off at silly point by Mr. Daniell, who, in that position, had caught him so brilliantly on Monday. A little later, however, with the total at 216 for five wickets, and Hobbs not out for 116, Mr. Fender declared the Surrey innings closed.

Steve Donoghue wins third successive Derby

*Steve Donoghue won the Epsom Derby six times but there was never a more acclaimed victory than his on Papyrus. The jockey's day was best captured in Donoghue's own book Just My Story in a contribution provided by **Beverley Baxter**, then managing editor of the Sunday Express.*

IT IS WITH SOME DIFFIDENCE that I become momentarily the Boswell of Stephen Donoghue, but except for the time he was actually riding I was with the great little jockey from five o'clock Wednesday morning until six o'clock Thursday morning when I went to bed, and Stephen went on somewhere to have bacon and eggs.

It was nearly twelve o'clock when we started in the closed car for Epsom. Traffic was huge, and grew more dense every few hundred yards, but there was hardly any delay. Thousands of people were on the road, but none of them recognised the hero of the day, who looked at them through the glass with all the interest of a small boy at a circus.

The Derby! There was nothing else that mattered. The second race was won by somebody and lost by somebody else. Donoghue was back with the losers. The moment it was over, pandemonium swept the ocean of humanity. The Derby was next.

'Steve' had asked me to join him in the weighing-room before the great event, and with much difficulty I reached there through the crowd. To my horror Donoghue met me with an eye that was brutally discoloured. Obviously he was in pain and he looked correspondingly weary. In answer to my question, he told me that in the first race a stone sent flying up by the leading horse's hoofs had struck him. He had sent out for some raw beef, but it could not be found. Five million pounds depended on how the Derby was won, and the man who was to win it could not get a piece of raw beef for love or money.

Fortunately the pupil of the eye was not touched. But had the stone which must have been small and sharp-pointed, struck him one fraction of an inch higher, Donoghue would have been practically blinded for the great race. Even then he was quite unruffled. He pointed out the various jockeys (all of them strangely quiet), and exchanged a dry joke with Stokes, who seemed vastly amused that he was to ride a horse with a name like Safety First. As he came in last a few minutes later perhaps the humour was justified.

While we were chatting an official passed. 'Eighteen, Donoghue,' he said. 'Thanks,' said Steve, without any comment. Yet his brain must have been working like lightning. It meant that he was drawn on the outside all but one. Even to a novice like myself I could see how it lowered his chances. 'It's a bad draw, isn't it?' I asked. 'It's not good,' he answered, 'but a lot better than being right on the inside. You watch and you'll see that I will get right off at the jump and not hold back. In about four furlongs I'll be fifth or sixth. If I'm not' – and he smiled that amazing Peter Pan smile – 'you'll know that something has happened.'

Donoghue had had a bad season. Again and again he had failed to win. People were saying that he was finished. Supposing Papyrus went badly in the race? Supposing Donoghue's mount was among the also-rans? It would have

After a bad season, Steve Donoghue, riding Papyrus, came first past the post to win the Derby

been a case of 'The King is dead, long live the King!' And there was not a tremor in his voice nor a movement of his fingers that showed any signs of nervousness.

At last the calm of the paddock. Papyrus was as gentle as ever and walked calmly in the parade. The Prince of Wales leaned forward as Donoghue passed on Papyrus. 'Who is going to win?' he asked 'I am, sir,' replied Steve. But most of us were wishing Papyrus was not quite so gentle – most of us with the exception of its rider. We followed them out of the paddock, and they disappeared down the track. I was struggling through the crowd on the edge of the track to get through to our box, when suddenly there came a thunder of hoofs. The horses were galloping towards the starting tapes.

At last I reached our box. There were five minutes of muffled suspense, and then that roar like thunder, 'They're off'' followed by the dismal clanging of the bell, like a warning on a rocky coast. We could see nothing. Every second seemed an eternity. My heart was pounding as if it would burst its confines. The silence was awesome. Then we saw them round the first bend, silhouetted against the grey sky – a thin streak of horsemen almost invisible in the mist. A well-known politician behind me put his glasses to his eyes. 'Donoghue is riding sixth!' he cried. All my pulses leaped at the

words. Then the something had not happened. He was riding according to plan. But how would he go to the front? Again they disappeared and reappeared above Tattenham Corner. At breakneck speed a horse shot down the hill and took the turn at a vicious angle. It was Papyrus, and Donoghue on him was out in front with Pharos alongside.

Together they came along the stretch, while the roar of the crowd shattered the air like a barrage of thunder. Pharos drew ahead. We shrieked to Steve, thousands of us. We were mad. We yelled to him to come on, to come on, to come on, forgetting that the idea might have occurred to Steve himself. 'Steve! Steve! Steve! Steve!'

The word kept time to the flying hoofs. And we saw the little fellow show his whip, but not use it. Papyrus knew. He had known all day. His beautiful muscles responded. The jockey's magic hands seemed to lift the horse and give it new strength. Slowly it passed the gallant Pharos and went out in front, never to be headed again.

The reception given this jockey as he rode in after winning was amazing – unforgettable – creating a scene to live in one's memory for all time. At six o'clock Steve and I started back for town in the car. An immense crowd saw him off, but the whole way in no one recognised him. His pockets were stuffed with telegrams, but only one seemed to excite him much. It was from his little daughter, saying that she and her whole school were very glad.

1923
2 July

Segrave becomes first Briton to win a Grand Prix

Sensational! It was the only way to describe some of the extraordinary happenings in the French Grand Prix at Tours where Sir Henry Segrave finished first. A far cry from the technological vista of today's GPs, **The Autocar** *wrote of an event veritably awash with drama*

AFTER A RACE tingling with excitement from the first to the last lap, in which the lead changed eight times and the final result was in doubt until almost the last moment, the French Grand Prix 500 miles road race for 2-litre cars was won at Tours by H. O. D. Segrave, driving a six-cylinder Sunbeam. The British car's time for the 35 laps was 6h. 35m. 19 3/5s., equal to 75.3 miles an hour average.

Second place was secured by Albert Divo, on a similar Sunbeam, in 6h. 54m. 25 4/5s. K. Lee Guinness, after being in third place on the penultimate lap, accidentally stopped his engine in cornering on his last round, which enabled Ernest Friedrich, who had run consistently throughout on an eight-cylinder Bugatti, to capture third place, his time being 7h. 0m. 22 4/5s. K. Lee Guinness (Sunbeam) was

fourth, in 7h. 2m. 3s. Ultimately, Segrave, who had been running very consistently in third place from half-distance, shot to the front and captured the French Grand Prix for Great Britain for the first time in history. Thus the complete British team survived the gruelling race. Actually, the Sunbeam team was the only one to finish complete. Bugatti finished with one car in third place; Voisin had one car running at the end, a long way behind the others, and the remainder failed to cover the entire distance. Of the seventeen starters, only five survived – an illuminating sidelight upon the strenuous nature of the event.

The seventeen competitors comprised three British, three Italian, and eleven French. A quarter of an hour before the starting hour, the competitors were grouped in lines of two, about two hundred yards down the course, with a racing motor cycle ahead to act as pacemaker as far as the white line in front of the timers' box. Promptly at 8 o'clock M. René de Knyff, Chairman of the Racing Board, dropped his yellow flag, and the pack shot away. It was a breathless sight, seventeen 100 m.p.h. cars unleashed at once, and spurning the dust as they dashed ahead.

At half distance it was still anybody's race, for after sixteen laps Giaccone failed to appear to schedule, and after a delay came in slowly, pulled up at the pits, and in a most methodical manner changed all his plugs, his rear tyres, and filled up with petrol and oil. The work was done with an entire absence of excitement and without a single false movement. Before Giaccone had got away, his team mate, Salamano, pulled up, and in wild excitement, contrasting with the calm of his companion, changed wheels and filled up with oil and petrol.

Another lap, and Giaccone was in the pits again, working for a long time at the carburettor, and attempted to re-start with the mechanic pushing. The engine fired intermittently, but petered out, and ten minutes later the driver withdrew, having discovered a broken exhaust valve. Thus only one Fiat was left in the race.

One of the most exciting incidents of the

race occurred at the end of the thirtieth lap. The Sunbeams had planned to fill up twice with petrol, and when Divo, the leader of the trio chasing the solitary Fiat, came in for the fourth time it was noticed with something like consternation among his supporters that the filler cap would not come off. First a hammer was used, then a chisel, a wrench, a hack saw, but the obstinate cap refused to budge. Every possible method was attempted, all without avail, and after a spare tank had been handed up, with the suggestion that a complete change should be made, it was decided to go away and run on the emergency tank under the dash. During these galling moments, when the public groaned in sympathy with the driver and mechanic, the Fiat was increasing its four-minute lead to such an extent that, with only five more laps to cover, its position seemed impregnable.

A lap later Divo had to stop again to fill up his dashboard tank with a tiny funnel, with his engine running and petrol overflowing all over the car. Salamano thus, to all appearances, had

Henry Segrave, played a waiting game at Tours, to clock up a first for British motor racing

the race in hand, when the coup de théâtre of a most sensational day was sprung upon the public. The leading Fiat failed to appear to time, and before any official announcement could be made regarding it the mechanic was seen on the crown of the hill in the distance sprinting towards the replenishment pits. As one man the spectators rose to their feet and cheered the runner. He reached the pits fagged out after his sprint of about one and three-quarter miles, and, acting on precedent in French races, it was decided to replace him at this point by a fresh mechanic, who would carry the can of petrol back to the stranded car.

To the wild cheering of the crowd the new mechanic started up the road with a big red can in his hand. He had covered fifty yards when the jury decided that this was contrary to the rules, and amid the hisses and cat-calls of the spectators, a marshal ran after the mechanic and ordered him back. Then a bicycle was handed over for the use of the original mechanic, again in accordance with precedent in French races. After covering a few yards, however, the cyclist was stopped, his bicycle taken away from him, and orders given that he must accomplish the journey afoot. The excitement at this moment was really indescribable, the entire sympathy of the crowd going to the unfortunate crew of No. 14 Fiat.

These sensational eleventh hour incidents changed the entire complexion of the race, and the ultimate result was still in doubt. While Divo had to repeat the filling process each lap, he was all the time risking the loss of his second place.

Guinness continued to dash past the stands regularly, though misfiring now and then; the Voisin was consistent if in the tail of the procession, and Friedrich was monotonously regular. When Segrave came round regularly as ever, with Divo at the pits and having seen No. 14 hung up by the roadside, he took the lead on the 23rd lap, a position he never lost. Segrave had held third place from half distance, and, never challenged again, he romped home a winner of the 1923 French Grand Prix at an average speed of 75.3 miles an hour.

Liddell triumphs for God and Great Britain

The moving story of the Scottish sprinter who would not run in the Olympics on a Sunday was immortalised in the film Chariots of Fire. Liddell switched from the 100 metres to the 400 metres and won it. This account by **W. B. Bennison** *was published in The Edinburgh Evening News the following day*

ERIC LIDDELL is today's Olympic hero. For Great Britain, after an electrifying race, he won the 400 metres in 47:3/5 secs. Enthusiasm was unbounded when this fair Scotsman broke the tape, men and women of all the nations cheered him unrestrainedly, and when the British flag was run up the mast in token of his mighty achievement the thousands of folk who had come to the Stadium at Colombes jumped to attention. The scene, on an afternoon radiant with sunshine, was one of immense splendour. We Britons had dared but only to whisper hopes that this flying Scotsman, who, as you know, because of religious scruples, refrained from taking part in the sprint last Sunday, would capture the prize. We knew him to be fit and well. On many occasions he had given ample proof of his fighting qualities.

Liddell is of the do-or-die breed, but that he would put up a world's record-breaking performance scarcely entered into the calculations of even the most optimistic of us.

It was fast approaching seven o'clock when Imbach, Liddell, Fitch, Butler, Johnson, and Taylor, the finalists, were called to the track. The going was appreciably better and faster than on the preceding day. So much had been demonstrated earlier, and I would here set out the extraordinary fact that in the heats of the 400 metres the record was broken three times. First Imbach, the Swiss, did 48 secs: then Fitch, United States, followed with 47:4/5 secs: and Liddell in the last stage of the semi-finals covered the distance in 48:1/5 secs, all of which times were in advance of that previously set up. B. G. D. Rudd, the famous South African and Oxford University athlete, did but 49:6/10 secs at Antwerp four years ago, and small wonder was it that we ached for the coming of the last battle.

Happily the start was as perfect as any start could be. Every man was off his mark simultaneously and as if they had been shot out of their holes by some machine. Liddell set up a terrific pace. He ran as if he were wild with inspiration, like some demon. And as he flew along, to the accompaniment of a roar, we experts fell to wondering whether Liddell would crack, such was the pace he set out to travel. 'Liddell', was screamed; 'Imbach' was thundered by the Swiss; 'Taylor' was shouted by a finely drilled American claque; 'Butler', 'Fitch', in turn was yelled. Liddell, yards ahead, came round the bend for the straight, and as he did so he pulled the harder at himself, for Fitch was getting nearer. There was Butler, too, and Imbach to be reckoned with.

It was the last 50 metres that meant the making or breaking of Liddell. Just for a second I feared that he would kill himself by the terrific speed he had set up, but to our joy he remained chock full of fight. Imbach, perhaps 50 yards from the tape, fell; the little man was out of it. It was then Liddell or Fitch. The Scotsman had so surely got all his teeth into the race that the American could not loosen his hold, and Liddell got first home by what,

400 METRES FINAL

1. Eric Liddell (GB) 47.6
2. Horatio Fitch (USA) 48.4
3. Guy Butler (GB) 48.6
World record remained Ted Meredith's
47.4 for 440 yards)

considering the formidable opposition, was almost a remarkable margin. Butler was third, Johnson next, and then Taylor, who had the bad luck to stumble a yard or so from the finish.

All round the banked area, people were on their feet cheering madly, and as if by magic, hosts of Union Jacks appeared above the heads of the raving crowd as Liddell ripped through the tape and into the arms of the Britishers who were waiting for him. For a moment the cheering lasted, then from the loudspeaker came: 'Hello, hello. Winner of the 400 metres: Liddell of Great Britain. The time 47:3/5 is a new world's record.' Again the great roar of cheering went up, and there were long minutes before the announcer could convey that Fitch, of America, was second, and that Butler, who ran second in this event to Rudd, the South African, at Antwerp, was third and Johnson, of Canada, fourth. Thrill followed thrill, for the flags went up, a big Union Jack in the centre, a little one to the left, and a little Stars and Stripes to the right, and again came that hush as all the spectators stood and the bands played. Then came crash upon crash of applause as Liddell walked across the grass and vanished down the stairs to the dressing rooms.

On his return from the Paris Olympics, Eric Liddell was carried round the streets of Edinburgh

England's cricket team regains Ashes after 14 years

*With victory in the Fifth Test match at the Oval, England ended a lean period versus Australia, their cricketing arch-rivals. The bowling of Rhodes, and the second innings partnership of Hobbs and Sutcliffe, sealed an historic win. As the cricket correspondent of **The Times** made clear, it was a moment for rejoicing*

ENGLAND, 280 and 436; Australia, 302 and 125. We have won! And after all the lean years we were more than half-pleased. We began to cheer when the Australians' innings were little more than half over, and at the finish we charged, ten thousand of us, across the ground, and massed ourselves in front of the pavilion, where we shouted for the 11 men who had won the game, and for the Chairman of the Committee which selected them. We shouted even more loudly for Mr. Collins and the members of his team. We wanted them to know that we appreciated the high standard of keenness and honourable conduct which they have set up and maintained in this and all their other matches.

This final Test match has been an extraordinarily interesting game. There were grounds for fearing that England had missed a golden opportunity by omitting to make at least 400 on the first day, after Mr. Chapman had won the toss on a perfect Oval wicket. But the Australians declined the offered chance. In fact their later batsmen had to extricate the side from a nasty hole. Still it seemed likely that we should have to pay for Saturday's comparative failure in batting. The thunderstorm of Monday

The fielders close in. Hobbs is not to be thwarted and gets one away, to bring the Ashes in sight

ENGLAND
First Innings

Hobbs b. Mailey...37
Sutcliffe b. Mailey..76
Woolley (F.E.), b. Mailey 18
Hendren, b. Gregory.......................................8
A.P.F. Chapman, st. Oldfield, b. Mailey.........49
G.T.S. Stevens, c. Andrews, b. Mailey...........17
Rhodes, c. Oldfield, b. Mailey........................28
Geary (G.), run out...9
Tate, b. Grimmett...23
Larwood, c. Andrews, b. Grimmett.................0
Strudwick, not out...4
b 6, lb 5...11

Total...**280**

Second Innings

Hobbs, b. Gregory......................................100
Sutcliffe, b. Mailey.....................................161
Woolley (F.E.), lbw, b. Richardson.................27
Hendren, c. Oldfield, b. Grimmett.................15
A.P.F. Chapman, b. Richardson......................19
G.T.S. Stevens, c. Mailey, b. Grimmett...........22
Rhodes, lbw, b. Grimmett.............................14
Geary (G.), c. Oldfield, b. Gregory...................1
Tate, not out...33
Larwood, b. Mailey...5
Strudwick, c. Andrews, b. Mailey....................2
b 19, lb 18..37

Total...**436**

AUSTRALIA
First Innings

W.M. Woodfull, b. Rhodes............................35
W. Bardsley, c. Strudwick, b. Larwood............2
C.G. Macartney, b. Stevens..........................25
W.H. Ponsford, run out...................................2
T.J.E. Andrews, b. Larwood............................3
H.L. Collins, c. Stevens, b. Larwood..............61
A.J. Richardson, c. Geary, b. Rhodes...........16
J.M. Gregory, c. Stevens, b. Tate.................73
W.A. Oldfield, not out...................................33
C.V. Grimmett, b. Tate.................................35
A.A. Mailey, c. Strudwick, b. Tate....................0
b 5, lb 12...17

Total...**302**

Second Innings

W.M. Woodfull, c. Geary, b. Larwood..............0
W. Bardsley, c. Woolley, b. Rhodes...............21
C.G. Macartney, c. Geary, b. Larwood..........16
W.H. Ponsford, c. Larwood, b. Rhodes..........12
T.J.E. Andrews, c. Tate, b. Larwood..............15
H.L. Collins, c. Woolley, b. Rhodes.................4
A.J. Richardson, b. Rhodes.............................4
J.M. Gregory, c. Sutcliffe, b. Tate...................9
W.A. Oldfield, b. Stevens.............................23
C.V. Grimmett, not out....................................8
A.A. Mailey, b. Geary......................................6
lb..7

Total...**125**

night, followed by hot sunshine on the following morning, produced a wicket on which 200 was a remarkably good score against first-rate bowling. Hobbs and Sutcliffe made more than that number between them and raised the aggregate of their combined scores in the last ten Test matches against Australia to something like 2,300. Every moment that has passed since they were parted has emphasized the magnitude of their performance. England's last nine wickets fell at rather frequent intervals and when the Australians went in to make 415, they were put out for 125.

The explanation is simple. We had Rhodes on our side. Larwood, Tate, Geary, and Mr. Stevens all bowled well. Larwood, in particular, rendered valuable service. But these bowlers might possibly have been worn down.

From the moment that Rhodes went on the match was over. Rhodes has learnt no new tricks since he used to bowl one end for nearly half the time that England were in the field, and his length is not so regular as it was. Yesterday he sent down a full toss and two long hops to leg, balls which he could not bowl in his palmiest days. The unbowlable ball has had some very distinguished victims in this match. Hobbs, Mr. Macartney, Mr. Bardsley, and Mr. Andrews have all given away their wickets to it. The specimens released by Rhodes were all properly hit for four. Otherwise they found themselves playing forward when they would have played back, and he used the spin which his fingers impart to the ball to make it break back sharply, leaving those who will to swerve.

1927
4 February

Malcolm Campbell sets world land speed

*Bluebird and Campbell became synonymous with record attempts on land and water. Malcolm Campbell begat Donald, who was equally absorbed. This account from **The Times**, on the third occasion the father broke the world land speed record, hauntingly harks back to the seeds of a speed dynasty*

CAPTAIN MALCOLM CAMPBELL beat the international speed 'records' for the flying Mile and the flying Kilometre in his Napier-Campbell car (450 h.p. Napier-Aero engine) on Pendine Sands yesterday. His mean speed for the Kilometre on the best set of runs up and down the course was 174.883 m.p.h., and for the Mile 174.224 m.p.h. The previous 'records,' created by Mr. J.G. Parry Thomas, driving his Higham car at Pendine in April, 1926, were 172 m.p.h. for the Kilometre and 170.624 m.p.h. for the Mile.

With its apparently customary eccentricity, the weather at Pendine, which on the day before had been sufficiently evil to destroy the reputation of the best of seaside resorts, was suggestive of the Riviera in its mildness, the blueness of the sky and sea, and the gentle-ness of the wind. At an early hour many people were engaged in removing sea shells from the selected course, and a farm tractor was employed to cut deep furrows on either side of the course. The immediate result was the drying of a wide expanse of sand on the wrong side of the course, but it is probable that there was actually some improvement in the already firm sand over which Captain Campbell had to drive.

At about 2 o'clock Captain Campbell ran the car down the slipway upon the sands and into a pool in which it promptly showed signs of sinking. From this peril it was pushed by the spectators, and at 2.25 he made his first easterly run. A quarter of a mile from the starting point he stopped his engine, because of a difficulty in changing speed. It was restarted and, without returning to the arranged starting point, he continued to run, thus losing a little of the distance which is so valuable in getting up speed. In this run Captain Campbell covered the Kilometre at a speed of 176.37 m.p.h. and the Mile at a speed of 179.158 m.p.h. In this run he covered a distance between the end of the Kilometre and the end of the Mile, a distance of .37 of a mile, at a speed of 183.2 m.p.h. From this increase at the end of the run it may be assumed that with a longer stretch of sand or road he could very easily exceed three miles a minute.

In the return run Captain Campbell's goggles were blown off when he was in the middle of the measured distance, an incident which possibly caused a reduction in speed. He covered a kilometre at an average speed of 173.029 miles per hour and the mile at a speed of 169.550 miles per hour. The 'record' breaking figures quoted before are mean of these speeds.

About half an hour later Captain Campbell made a second set of runs, but his speeds in both of these were lower than in the first period and are not worth quoting.

Captain Campbell's attempts to increase the short 'records' to 180 miles an hour or more have ended for the present; but he is still determined to persevere. His plans in some degree depend on the result of Mr. J. G. Parry

Speed king and pioneer, Malcolm Campbell was driven by record–breaking dreams

Thomas's next attempt to recapture the 'record,' an attempt which he will make on February 14, at Pendine, in his Higham car.

Captain Campbell says that he has learned much from his several attempts on the 'records'. There is, according to him, no greater difficulty in driving at speeds of 180 miles an hour than there is at 150 or 130. His car was perfectly controllable throughout its range of speed, except when local conditions added to driving difficulties. He found that sinking in wet sands was more alarming than any of the troubles which necessarily beset racing drivers. Yesterday's conditions had so greatly improved that he was able to maintain a perfect course, and he was not troubled either by skidding or sinking, nor did the surface water, never really absent from the sands, cause him trouble. He spoke with praise of his Napier-Aero engine, which had stood up well to a task for which it was not designed.

Except that it had high compression, it differed in no way from the engine used in commercial aircraft of the British Air Lines. Each of these high-speed 'record' attempts provides data for the improvement of the type of car supplied to the public. Plugs, engine, frames, tyres, and the mass of parts which go to make a car are, under such conditions, put to trials which reveal quickly any inherent defects. In the removal of these defects the whole industry is interested.

Lindrum's world record billiards break of 4,137

Once upon a time billiards was followed avidly. Reports were carried in The Times and, to the aficionado, Thurston's in London's Leicester Square was Mecca. It was there that the Australian player Walter Lindrum achieved billiards' most famous break, reported as if on tablets of stone in **The Billiard Player**

ALTHOUGH Walter Lindrum has not yet succeeded in realising his ambition of recording a 5,000 break, such a feat cannot be ruled out of the bounds of possibility, after his performance on January 19 and 20, during his match with J. Davis, at Thurston's, Leicester Square. In approximately two hours and fifty-five minutes, spread over three sessions, Lindrum surpassed his standing record break of 3,905, made against McConachy at the same place last season, with one of 4,137.

It is a curious fact that before entering upon the break, the opportunity for which occurred when Davis failed at a screw loser along the cushion while using his left hand, Lindrum had been quite out of sympathy with his game. He had been troubled by a new cue-tip, and had experienced considerable difficulty in keeping the balls in a true course, especially when playing slow shots at the spot end. But in the break itself, his execution was faultless, if his last scoring stroke – a middle pocket red winner – be excepted. In making this, which was admittedly from a rather awkward angle, Lindrum left the cue ball almost dead in line with the two objects, and white being just behind the red on the spot. He was compelled to use the rest and attempted a cushion cannon off the white, and failed to connect with the red by about two inches. The stroke could not be harshly criticised, however, as Lindrum was, not unnaturally, showing signs of fatigue.

Taking possession of the table at 4.15 on Tuesday, January 19, Lindrum scored 701 unfinished in the half-hour that remained, and continuing the break in the evening, carried it to 3,151 unfinished, the time for this number of points being 2 hours. He was thus within striking distance of his existing record, and there was much resultant enthusiasm among billiard lovers, hundreds being unable to secure admission to the hall on the afternoon of Wednesday, January 20. Upon arriving at the scene, Lindrum expressed himself as feeling fit and confident, but wished he had a better shot to resume with. The position of the balls was fairly favourable, the red being placed for a middle-pocket winner – not quite straight from any part of the 'D' – with the white hard under the top cushion near the spot. Lindrum made the winner perfectly, but experienced a few anxious moments, the balls being inclined to be unresponsive. After adding 18, he made a run-through kiss cannon, which resulted in nursery position, and from that point he was apparently the least concerned person in the room.

Hundred after hundred accrued, and it soon became certain that Lindrum would set up new figures, and when, at length, '3,905' and then '3,907' was announced, the spectators released their pent-up feelings in a prolonged burst of applause. Lindrum was not allowed to proceed until he had responded to calls of 'speech,' and in a few words he modestly said he was gratified at having beaten his own record, which was only possible with the assis-

Towards the end of his feat Walter Lindrum was reported as showing signs of fatigue

tance of the very friendly welcome and appreciation he always received in London.

In the course of the break, Lindrum scored no fewer than 2,590 points by means of recorded sequences of cannons, these numbering fifteen. They were 75, 38, 58, 94, 135, 132, 51, 48, 88, 101, 97, 112, 123, 78 and 65, the first two runs being made in the first stage, the next nine at the second and the last four at the third. It was while he was engaged upon the 78 when he had his new record, and subsequently had 65 cannons.

Upon the completion of the break, Davis congratulated his great rival and immediately settled down to establish a further record by playing out the remainder of the time with a break of 1,131, which he carried to 1,247 in the evening before failing at a forcing loser. When he reached four figures, Davis was complimented by Lindrum, and acknowledging the plaudits of the onlookers, remarked, 'Well, I've had a good tutor, anyway.' Never before had 5,384 points been scored, by orthodox billiards, in two hands.

1934
23 March

Gold Cup hero Golden Miller wins Grand National

Dorothy Paget's Golden Miller is the only horse to have won the double of the Grand National and the Cheltenham Gold Cup. In fact he won the Gold Cup five times, making him arguably the greatest steeplechaser ever. His Grand National triumph was reconstructed by **Gregory Blaxland** *in his book on the amazing horse*

A QUARTER OF A MILLION PEOPLE converged on Aintree racecourse. They came in special trains from all over Britain, they came in cars, charabancs and tramcars, and they came in aeroplanes, which kept droning in to land on an improvised runway all the morning; and at the docks of Liverpool and London the departure of liners was delayed to allow their passengers time off to see the race.

The scene was enshrouded by a mist, and around lunchtime it seemed determined to obliterate completely the view that hundreds of thousands had spent so much money and exertion to obtain. And then, showing the same sense of occasion as when the Spanish Armada threatened, a breeze arose and scattered the mist, opening the whole course to the eye with wonderful clarity...

A buzz of excitement went up from the stands as Golden Miller began to emerge as the winner in the approach to the final dog-leg bend of the long run-in. In the press box one voice rose high above all others. 'What a horse – what a horse – what a horse!!' it yelled frenziedly, drawing the eyes of many correspondents from the horse to his trainer, Basil Briscoe, who happened to have been watching from there. Briscoe rushed down the steps and then stopped. 'No – he hasn't won it yet,' he shouted at the same high-pitched shriek. And then, 'Yes, he has, he's done it!' And off he dashed to meet him, shrieking 'What a horse – what a horse – what a horse!' at a pitch that was audible even above the great roar that greeted the victory in a mounting crescendo. Golden Miller's stride seemed to echo the cry of his trainer, bleeping out the message 'What-a-horse, what-a-horse, what-a-horse!' as he swept sublimely on to the winning post, maintaining the same magnificent rhythm with which he had cantered down a quarter of an hour earlier. He again pricked his ears as he passed the post, and his jockey, Gerry Wilson, had to lean hard against him to slow him down.

Game to the end Delaneige followed him in, keeping up the gallop that would have given him victory in nineteen years out of twenty. He was adjudged to be five lengths behind at the post, and as pictures show, they were giant-size lengths, as was appropriate. Thomond, the marvellous Thomond, finished five lengths further away in third place, showing that his strength had been neither crushed by his 12 stone 4 lb nor sapped by the 4-mile gallop; it was reckoned that a baulking had cost him as many lengths as he lost by, but it was also conceded that The Miller could have increased the distance if he had been asked to. Forbra was fourth, a distant fourth but an honourable one, especially when added to his first and sixth of the previous years.

The stragglers did not receive much attention as they came bravely toiling in. Most eyes were on the winner, and the view holloas kept ringing out for him long after he had passed the post.

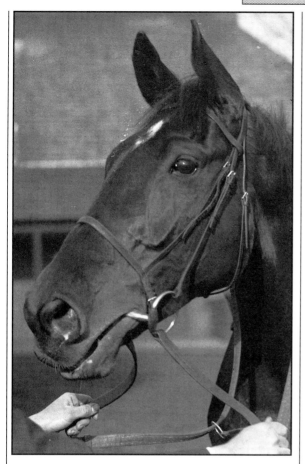

In winning the Grand National Golden Miller became 'a god on four legs'

Briscoe, as was predictable, led the rush to greet him, and The Miller for once showed some of the excitement of those around him, throwing his head high in the exhilaration of achievement. Gerry Wilson panted and grinned, and he grinned from joy and from wonder and amazement. He expressed his amazement to his associates, as much by gesture as word, which vividly conveyed his incredulity that any horse could have won with such ease and distinction after twice being so nearly on the ground. But all he would admit to reporters was 'two slight mistakes at Becher's'.

Miss Paget marched up purposefully, her face looking paler than ever above the beaver collar and wearing a wan smile of victory that could have been mistaken for a scowl. She took over hold of the bit, and set off with the same purposeful stride to carve a passage, and with the aid of a mounted policeman on either side, through the host of excited people surging down from the stands.

Her father put his arm through hers but rather than acting as shield he was tugged along behind her.

Golden Miller had by now lost some of his animation and responded to the tornado of cheers and whistles around him with his usual calm. All the experts were quite certain that no winner had been accorded such a fervent reception since Ambush II had won the race for the Prince of Wales in 1900. This was not so surprising, for as the headlines in next day's Sporting Life proclaimed, Golden Miller was the 'Finest Chaser of the Century', and the witnesses of his greatest win wanted to make the most of their good fortune in being there. A touch of hysteria was in the air. Golden Miller, as Sidney Galtrey put it, had become a god on four legs. Certainly the sense of awe was there, even if it may seem eccentric to give such boisterous tongue to reverence.

The cheering continued while he was being unsaddled, and it grew in volume as word went round that despite the softer state of the going he had knocked almost 8 seconds off Kellsboro' Jack's record. The Sporting Life timekeeper, who was the nearest there was to an official one, made it 9 minutes 20.4 seconds, and others made it a fifth of a second faster. There was a shout of 'Three cheers for Dorothy Paget', drawing a din that appeared to appal the person cheered, although she managed to make an awkward gesture of acknowledgement. Then came a shout of 'Three cheers for Basil Briscoe', and this drew an even louder din which set Briscoe off bouncing once again. The only people not cheering were the bookmakers, who had been very hard smitten indeed. Much was made in the papers of Briscoe's information that Golden Miller had been given plenty of milk, and some wag added the comment that the bookmakers had better start drinking it too, as it would be a long time before they could afford anything stronger.

Henry Cotton annexes the Open at Sandwich

During what proved to be a halcyon few days for British sport, at Sandwich and Wimbledon, the most illustrious English golfer of his generation, Henry Cotton, won his first Open championship. His masterly feat was recorded by The Times's golf correspondent, who was then **Bernard Darwin**

ALL'S WELL THAT ENDS WELL, and T. H. Cotton won the Open Championship at Royal St. George's yesterday by five strokes from S. F. Brews, but there were moments of agony in the last round which no tongue can tell, and no man ever came nearer to cracking completely. Neither did any man ever pull himself together more bravely when he was nearly gone. If his last round of 79 looks, on paper, a little disappointing it was, in fact, infinitely to his credit that it was not well over 80.

If ever a man deserved to be a champion it is Cotton, for he has toiled unbelievably to perfect his methods and to school an unruly temperament. He is where he ought to be, and where a Briton ought to be, at the head of British Golf. Brews's long-drawn spurt, which thrust him into second place, was a magnifi-

cent effort, and South Africa has every reason to be proud of her adopted son. The play started at 8 o'clock, but nothing seemed very important for full two hours and three-quarters after that, Cotton being due to begin at 10.48. If he did not break down, then all the waves of golfers were 'mainly breaking some painful inch to gain.'

Cotton had a big crowd and a perfect partner and pacemaker in C. A. Whitcombe, when he set out on his last lap but one. He was out in 35. Nobody could have gained anything perceptible on him. He was well into his stride and had begun to break the back of his day's work.

The 10th is always perilous, and he passed that milestone in 4. The 18th was mildly exciting. Cotton's second was a little pushed out; as he played his chip an intrusive lady snapped her camera at him and he hit the ball off the socket and was still not on the green. He did not kill the lady (as we should all have liked to do), but laid a lovely run-up nearly dead, got his 5, and with it his 72. Here are his figures:-

Out	4	4	3	5	4	3	5	3	4
Home	4	5	4	5	5	4	2	3	5

Whitcombe, who had played his part to perfection, was round in 74.

The world seemed to stand still till Cotton went out again at a quarter to 3. Cotton at once put our hearts in our mouths at the very first hole of his second round, for, after a fine tee shot, he messed about so sadly that he was four yards from the hole in four shots. Down went a brave putt and we said that this would put him right, but he missed his drive at the second, and, 10 yards away in 3, down went the putt, and this time we were sure he would settle down. A 3 and a 4 for the next two holes confirmed this soothing belief, and then came horrid things. A badly hooked second to the fifth found a sand crater, and he took four more to hole out. He missed quite a short putt for a 3 at the Maiden, and at the seventh ran out of holing down the wind from five yards away, missed coming back, and there was another 6. A 3 at Hades was refreshing, and so was a 5 at the ninth, but only on the ground that this was after three thoroughly bad shots,

Henry Cotton, driving from the 4th tee of the Open in 1934, dominated the championship

and, with the ball by no means on the green, a 6 seemed far more likely. That was 40 out, and that turn of the course brought no turn of the tide.

Cotton was rightly cautious with his second to the 10th, but he was sadly short with his third, and the power of holing the saving putt was in abeyance again. He was short, and short again, at the 11th, and the 4's he wanted would not come. A fine tee shot gave him an apparently easy chance of a 4 at the 12th, but out came his cloven hook and down went the ball to the left of the green. Three 5's, and the long holes to come.

We knew now that Brews, playing like a lion, had finished in 71 for 288. Cotton wanted 83 to beat him, and might not be able to do 83. Then at last came a ray of hope to lighten the darkness. A good chip and a 7ft putt gave Cotton a priceless 4 at the 13th, and now he would have the wind to blow him homeward. From that instant he was a changed man, and his long game suddenly became as impressive as it had been in his first rounds.

A drive and an iron reached the 14th green. He was short with his first putt, but holed the next like a true man. At the 13th the loveliest second gave him a 5ft putt for a 3. He missed it, but victory was now in sight. When he escaped the jaws of all the bunkers at the 16th with a dead straight shot we could breathe freely. He nearly had a 2 there; he nearly had a 3 at the 17th. Now the Championship was over, and he wanted a 4 to beat Sarazen's record Championship score of 283. His second to the home hole was just pushed out and bunkered. He played a great shot out within 12ft but the putt would not drop, and so with cheering and laughter ended a round that must have seemed to Cotton by far the longest he has ever played. This was Cotton's Championship from beginning to end.

1934

6 July

At Wimbledon, Fred Perry picks up the crown

*A swashbuckling tennis player, Fred Perry was that rare animal, a Briton who could win Wimbledon. In fact, he won it for three years in succession. On the first occasion, in 1934, **Helen Wills Moody**, herself a former great champion of Wimbledon, wrote this account in The Daily Telegraph*

FRED PERRY WON THE CHAMPIONSHIP yesterday because he was the better player. He could have defeated a stronger player than Crawford. Perry was exactly at the top of his game. His serving, driving, volleying, and smashing were equally good, and his forehand drive down the line was definitely the best ground shot seen at this year's Wimbledon.

Crawford was perhaps not so steady on his backhand as usual, but this may have been because the opposition was so strong. There are some followers of tennis who believe that the Australian played his best tennis last year at Wimbledon, when he won the title. However, since then he has been defeated by Perry both in the American championships last September and in Australia early this year.

Without doubt Fred Perry is the best singles player in the world today. One did not have to look up his record of the past year to be aware of this. The match on the Centre Court yesterday was complete proof. There has never been a more marked contrast in personality between players in a final match at Wimbledon than there was between Crawford and Perry. Perry was dark, dynamic, highly strung, aggressive in his tennis. Jack Crawford was calm, reserved and with such a quiet manner of playing that he seemed scarcely to be trying.

However, hidden beneath the players' smiling and imperturbable faces as they faced a battery of eighteen cameras before the match were the feelings which fill the hearts of competitors before the intensely moving experience of a final match on the Centre Court.

After the preliminary rally the play started in a manner which predicted the course of the game, in that the volleys were steady, brilliant, and intensely interesting. Here were two champions. Line balls, corner shots, exact placing filled the first game, which Crawford won after deuce was repeated several times. Another game of the same kind followed, which Perry won. Spectators settled down to enjoy a highly delightful final.

The only fear had been that Perry might strike one of the days when he was unsteady. But it was evident that he was 'on' his game. In the third game both players were very consistent. It went to deuce. Each was eager to win this crucial lead. Crawford, after an exchange of several shots, forced Perry to send a forehand drive into the net. In the fourth game Perry had an unsteady patch and Crawford led at 40-0, but Perry, serving, pulled up to deuce with an extra effort.

The match could not have been closer. Deuce four times in the second game and then Crawford calmly persisting in his play to win the game and to achieve a lead of 3-1. Perry did not waver, however, and won the next game to make the score 3-2, Crawford still leading. In the next game, on his serve, Perry led 40-0. His serve so far in the match had been very strong and consistent.

Three all now in the first set. This was a

Fred Perry (left) beat Jack Crawford in three straight sets, 6-3, 6-0, 7-5, only a week after Henry Cotton won the British Open golf

very crucial stage in the play. Both players realised it. Perry was the aggressor at this important moment. His drives seemed to be going even more smoothly. At deuce Perry was playing Crawford's backhand assiduously and forced him to net the ball. Perry won the next four points to lead at 4-3, first set. It was Perry's serve, and this was distinctly to his advantage. He won this game.

At 5-3, Perry was leading, it seemed that the first set was assured for the Englishman. Perry led 40-0 on the last game of the first set. So far he was distinctly the dominating figure on the court. His serving had been splendid, his ground-work accurate, and his cross-court drives devastating. Also he was on his toes and was keen for every shot.

There may be days when Perry is not so accurate, but this was certainly not one of those days. And there is never a day when Perry is dull to watch. He ranks with Borotra for possessing a tremendously interesting presence on the courts.

Racing ahead in the second set Perry led at 40-0, two games to love. Would it be a love set? Now it was 4-0 for Perry, who was brilliantly consistent and could do no wrong. Not many players have been able to take a love set from Crawford. 15-40 set point. A severe rally followed and then a short forehand volley for Perry to win this set 6-0. Two sets in a row had been won by the Englishman.

At one all in the third set there was a curious lapse of interest on the part of onlookers, who had decided that Perry was going to win in straight sets – that he was playing so awfully well that there could be no opposition. But Crawford seized this opportunity. A super rally occurred at 30-15, Crawford serving and (Perry leading 3-2) the Australian won the game to even the score at 3 all. If Crawford were to win this set he must fight for this game. But he made several errors and at the same time Perry hung on tenaciously.

However, to even the score at 4 all Crawford sent drive after drive to Perry's backhand. On his next serve Perry advanced to the net and a forehand drive of Crawford's licked the netcord and passed Perry. This was the perfect example of how freak shots seem to occur always at crucial moments. This ball gave Crawford the lead at 5-4.

In the next game there occurred several super rallies, and the score see-sawed around deuce. But Perry added pace to his drives and evened the score to 5 all. So far Perry had been practically unbeatable on his serve. At this important point in the game it was unfortunate for Crawford that he was serving.

He led 40-15, but could not take advantage of this splendid opportunity. On Perry's advantage, Crawford made a double fault, and the match and championship were Perry's.

The winner threw aside his racket and raced to the net, leapt over, and shook hands with the Australian. After being photographed, they gathered their rackets and left the court together amid thunderous applause.

1936
4 January

Prince Obolensky scores two historic rugby tries

The All Blacks did not expect to be outshone 13-0 when they played England at Twickenham but they were, by a Russian prince, first with one try and then with another so brilliant it has been recalled uncounted times since.
Howard Marshall *vividly recounted the match in The Daily Telegraph*

SO ENGLAND HAVE BEATEN New Zealand at last! A clear-cut decisive victory at Twickenham by a dropped goal and three tries to nil, and the 70,000 spectators will remember it for the rest of their lives.

Again and again this great match will be discussed. As we talk of it, smoking our pipes, we shall see once more the white figure of Obolensky, running gloriously, and Peter Cranmer, smashing his way through the centre, and the English forwards, solid as a wall against which the black waves of New Zealand broke in vain. It does not greatly matter that this is the first time any combination of English players has beaten a New Zealand team. What does matter is the quality of the game itself, and this was higher than we had any reason to expect.

Our selectors said these New Zealand forwards must be pounded and shaken – and pounded and shaken they were. The tight scrummaging ran fairly level, but the tearaway loose rushes of New Zealand were steadily controlled and held and worn down by the strength and weight of this grand English pack.

With the sting thus taken out of the New Zealand attack, the next problem was for England to score and Cranmer was the man to find that gap in the New Zealand mid-field defence. Twice he found it, and went thundering up the centre to pave the way for tries, and once he checked suddenly and dropped a beautiful goal. The rest is Obolensky.

New Zealand must have been painfully surprised by the brilliance of Obolensky's running, though they had played against him on a miserably wet day at Oxford. I shall never forget how Gilbert raised a hand helplessly, with a look of almost comical resignation on his face, as Obolensky lengthened his stride and raced round him to score England's first try. Obolensky has a genius for the game, or I am much mistaken.

The instinct which took him inwards from the right wing to run diagonally across the field and score his second try in the left corner showed the real player. Here is no mere sprinter, but a footballer who uses the weapon of exceptional speed with intelligence and precision. Obolensky has the most deceptive change of pace. He fades past his opponents like a ghost, and how refreshing it is to see a wing three-quarter in full cry for the line!

We settled ourselves down and England were hard pressed indeed, but a penalty kick gave them relief, and then Obolensky struck his first blow. England heeled from a loose scrum, Gadney whipped the ball across to Cranmer, and in short, sharp passes it went from Gerrard to Obolensky. Here was a chance surely, for Obolensky was 10 yards out from touch and near the half-way line. He leapt into his stride, going right-handed as Gilbert raced in to cut him off. For a moment we thought he must inevitably be crowded into touch, but just as Gilbert shaped for his tackle Obolensky changed pace, swept past and was running like

The mercurial running of Prince Obolensky brought a look of almost comical resignation to the face of one All Black

a hare clear for the line, with Gilbert watching him in sorrowful bewilderment.

That was beautiful running, and the crowd cheered as I never heard a Twickenham crowd cheer before, though a moment later New Zealand came perilously near to making the scores level. So 38 minutes passed, and then suddenly the ball came to Cranmer, who checked, shot swiftly through the centre for 30 yards and passed to Candler, whose path was blocked by Ball and Gilbert. This was Obolensky's inspired moment, for he saw that there was no hope down his own wing, dashed inwards, took a pass from Candler, flashed through a barn-door gap, beat Mitchell by that subtle lengthening of stride and scored in the left corner. A remarkable try which was not converted – our place-kicking was lamentable

– and at half-time England led by six points to nil.

A fine effort, but we wondered whether England could last the pace. We should have been happier if those tries had been turned into goals, and we shivered as New Zealand piled into a ferocious, roaring, head-long attack, with Hadley nearly over and Mitchell swinging alarmingly through the defence, and Tindill and Gilbert both dropping at goal. And then came Cranmer's chance, for the ball reached him quickly after a scrummage and he checked, glanced at the posts, let fly, and that was another four points to England.

Fine work, and England kept at it, gradually taking control of line-outs and tight scrummages, packing 3-4-1, banging away at a brave defence. New Zealand did escape into the England half, but there the ball went loose, Candler picked it up, Cranmer broke through gloriously again, and Sever took an awkward pass, beat a couple of men, and raced round behind the posts.

The last few desperate minutes what I chiefly remember is the giant Clarke hurling himself through the line-outs, and the England pack, the whole side indeed, holding steadily to their winning lead, unflurried, certain of themselves, content to wait for the final whistle which would bring to an end 80 minutes of superb rugby football history.

ENGLAND

H.G. Owen-Smith (St Mary's Hospital); A. Obolensky (Oxford University), P. Cranmer (Richmond), R.A. Gerrard (Bath), H.S. Sever (Sale); P.L. Candler (St. Bartholomew's Hospital), B.C. Gadney (capt.) (Leicester); D.A. Kendrew (Leicester), E.S. Nicholson (Leicester), R.J. Longland (Northampton), C. Webb (Royal Navy and Devonport Services), A. Clarke (Coventry), E. Hamilton-Hill (Harlequins), P.E. Dunkley (Harlequins), W.H. Weston (Northampton).

NEW ZEALAND

G. Gilbert (West Coast); N.A. Mitchell (Southland), C.J. Oliver (Canterbury), N.J. Ball (Wellington); T.H.C. Caughey (Auckland), E.W. Tindill (Wellington); M.M.N. Corner (Auckland); A. Lambourn (Wellington), W.E. Hadley (Auckland), J. Hore (Otago), S. Reid (Hawke's Bay), R.R. King (West Coast), J.E. Manchester (capt.) (Canterbury), H.F. McLean (Auckland), A. Mahoney (Bush Districts).

Referee: J.W. Faull (Wales).

1937

30 August

Tommy Farr goes 15 rounds with Joe Louis

In Yankee Stadium, Tommy Farr proved the experts wrong by not only going the distance against the amazing Joe Louis in the American's first defence of the world heavyweight boxing title but battling savagely against the champion. **James P. Dawson** *in The New York Times was clearly impressed*

JOE LOUIS, DETROIT'S FAMED Brown Bomber, retained the world heavy-weight boxing championship last night at the Yankee Stadium in fifteen fast, bruising rounds against Tommy Farr, but he caught a tartar in the British Empire titleholder.

Before a gathering of about 35,000 wildly cheering men and women who came to see Louis in his first defence of the title he won two months ago, Farr confounded the critics who conceded him little or no chance against the Bomber. He befuddled Louis, he stayed fifteen rounds with him, he stood up under his battering blows, he fought back savagely, furiously, contemptuously at times in a glorious offensive against tremendous odds, and he ended by going longer with the Bomber than has anybody else.

On only six occasions has Louis gone ten rounds or longer. He has five ten-round battles in his marvellous record, four of them won on decisions, the other on a knockout. He went twelve rounds against Max Schmeling – and was knocked out. So that Farr, though he was beaten last night, battered and bruised and pounded with staggering force at times, won glory in that he attained the unique distinction of surviving fifteen full rounds against the master puncher of the day.

Of him it can truly be said he was beaten but not disgraced. He soared to heights hitherto unattainable for him when he fought Louis through fifteen rounds, surviving not by strategy, nor by disorganised retreat, but by fighting every inch of the way, a style of fighting, too, that made Louis look bad. The champion retained his title but suffered a loss of prestige. Louis entered the ring a prohibitive favourite to win at odds as short as 1 to 10. They were betting even money Farr would not come up for the bell starting the sixth round. That reflects the margin of superiority conceded Louis over his foe before the bell sent them on their forty-five-minute journey.

Louis won the battle by no such margin. He was harassed and menaced at every turn, even when he had Farr jarred and staggering. The champion found a man with a granite jaw, an iron will and great courage, one who regarded him not as a superman but merely as another fighter and acted accordingly. Face to face with such a foeman, Louis disappointed as he has on one or two occasions before. He won, but it was a hollow victory.

Following the battle Louis asserted he hurt both hands and thus was handicapped. He said he hurt the right in the third or fourth round and the left in the seventh. The injuries were bruises which were painful, but even this would not explain the slump in Louis's stock, for he came closest to a knockout in the thirteenth round, supposedly with bruised and painful hands.

Farr, too, said he had an injured right hand, hurt in the fourth round. But the doughty British Empire champion declined to detract from Louis's victory with this excuse. 'I done

Tommy Farr, a straight left well in evidence, ended his fight against Joe Louis bloody but unbowed

the best I could,' said Tommy through bruised and bleeding lips as he left the ring. 'He's a tough man to fight. He's the hardest puncher I ever fought.'

Appearances supported the Welshman's statement. He was cut under both eyes, his nose was bashed and bleeding, his lips were ripped and his head had red welts where Louis's fists landed. Louis was unmarked, save for a 'mouse' under his right eye, mute testimony of Farr's pumping left jabs and swishing left hooks, and a slight bruise under the left eye.

As a cold matter of fact, Louis won this battle not by his punching in the sense of paralysing hitting but by boxing – by expert use of a stiff, punishing, flawless left jab. This was the one weapon of attack he found most successful against the fighting Welshman. This implement of warfare won Louis the round with which he clinched the battle. On the two occasions when he gave promise of living up to expectations this left jab led up to punches which menaced Farr's consciousness.

Having tasted Louis's punching power Farr

boxed cautiously or aggressively as the battle's developments dictated thereafter, until near the end of the thirteenth round. Two minutes of the session had gone, with Louis sticking that left of his in Farr's face, drawing fresh blood with every thrust, until suddenly the Bomber saw an opening. Like a flash he shot a left hook to the jaw as Farr leaped in with a roundhouse right that was wild. Tommy's knees buckled under the blow. His body sagged. It seemed for a moment he would crumple there on the ring floor.

Louis didn't know his punch had hurt Farr for he made no move to follow the advantage until Farr blindly sought a clinch. Then Louis hooked another left to the jaw as Farr lurched forward just as the bell rang. And from the effects of this blow Farr staggered to his corner on uncertain legs. These two rounds held the highlights provided by Louis – the only exhibitions of punching prowess he flashed. Through the battle Farr provided highlights as he stormed at the puncher for whom he had only contempt. This contempt reached a stage in the fourteenth round, where Farr deliberately stuck out his chin, leering at his foe as if inviting him to do his worst. And Louis was powerless to do anything about it.

Len Hutton smashes records at The Oval

With a marathon score of 364 by Hutton, England eventually beat Australia at The Oval by an innings and 579 runs in history's most one-sided Test match. But the day Hutton achieved the record total, everything else was secondary, as **Howard Marshall** *made clear in The Daily Telegraph*

RECORD-SMASHING TEST

HUTTON established a world's 'endurance' record for the longest individual innings – 13 hours 20 minutes. His 364 beat Bradman's 334 at Leeds in 1930, the previous highest in an England-Australia Test; passed Hammond's 336 not out against New Zealand at Auckland in 1933 (formerly the biggest innings in any Test), and made a record for The Oval, exceeding Bobby Abel's 357 for Surrey v Somerset in 1899.

Hutton and Leyland, by putting on 382, set up a record for the second England wicket in a Test against Australia. They beat the 188 by Sutcliffe and Hammond at Sydney in 1932. Hardstaff, who scored his first Test century against Australia, and Hutton, in adding 215, created a new record for the sixth England wicket, beating the 186 by Hammond and Ames at Lord's in 1938.

England's total of 903 for seven (declared), exceeding their 658 for eight (declared) at Nottingham in June, was not only their highest against Australia but the biggest in any Test. Australia's highest is 729 for six (declared) at Lord's in 1980. The England total is also the biggest made in a first-class match in their country, beating Yorkshire's 887 v. Warwickshire at Edgbaston in 1896.

Three Yorkshiremen (Hutton, 364; Leyland, 187, and Wood, 53) obtained 604 of the score in an innings lasting 15 hours and a quarter – the longest in Test history.

HUTTON MAKING HIS RECORD SCORE of 364 in the final Test match at The Oval, Bradman being carried off the field with a fractured shin bone, England declaring at the phenomenal total of 903 for seven wickets – these were the outstanding events in one of the most remarkable days' cricket ever played.

That Australia lost three wickets for 117 after tea seemed entirely unimportant. The match is over, to all intents and purposes, and all that remains is to add up the records. Records do not make cricket, however, and we can only hope that these fresh ones will prove to be eight stout nails in the coffin of timeless Tests played on wickets which turn a great game into a farce.

First of all, though, let us praise Hutton for his tremendous exhibition of concentration, endurance and skill. He gave point and purpose to the early hours, for the excitement was intense as he slowly and surely approached Bradman's record of 334, the previous highest individual score in Test matches between England and Australia.

We could almost feel the huge crowd willing Hutton to succeed, and when, with a beautiful square-cut, he hit the decisive four off Fleetwood-Smith, a roar went up which must have shaken the Houses of Parliament across the river. Bradman raced up to shake his hand, and while drinks came out and all the Australians toasted him in the middle of the pitch the crowd cheered, and sang 'For he's a jolly good fellow,' and cheered and cheered again.

An astonishing scene, and Hutton richly

deserved this wonderful ovation. When at last his concentration wavered and he was caught at cover by Hassett off O'Reilly, he had batted for 13 hours and 20 minutes, and hit 35 fours, 15 threes, 18 twos and 143 singles. A prodigious effort, and if Hutton's innings was

A remarkable spot in cricket history is Hutton's as he leaves the field at The Oval

immensely prolonged, it was also logically and strictly in accordance with the conditions imposed by such a wicket and such a match.

ENGLAND

Hutton, c Hassett, b O'Reilly	364
Edrich, lbw, b O'Reilly	12
Leyland, run out	187
W. R. Hammond, lbw, b F.-Smith	59
Paynter, lbw, b O'Reilly	0
Compton, b Waite	1
Hardstaff, not out	169
Wood, c and b Barnes	53
Verity, not out	8
B 22, l-b 19, w 1, n-b 8	50
Total (7 wkts. dec)	**903**

AUSTRALIA

C.L. Badcock, c Hardstaff, b Bowes	0
W.A. Brown, not out	29
S.J. McCabe, c Edrich, b Farnes	14
A.L. Hassett, c Compton, b. Edrich	42
S. Barnes, not out	25
B 4, l-b 2, n-b 1	7
Total (3 wkts)	**117**

Wooderson takes European 5,000m and then drops

Superman could not have managed so many transformations from sober solicitor to record-breaking runner as Sydney Wooderson. And his place in the hearts of the British was already secure when he won his last great race.
Stanley Halsey *reported from Oslo for the Daily Express*

SYDNEY WOODERSON WON THE LAST RACE of his international athletic career at the European Games in Oslo tonight a week before his 32nd birthday. Then he collapsed ten yards beyond the tape.

It was his supreme race. Roared home by the cheers from a crowd of 21 nations, running with his usual great judgement and exclusive finish, he beat the much fancied Finn, Viljo Heino, to win the 5,000 metres (3 miles 188 yds) in 14mins 8.6secs.

For the first time in his long, successful running career Wooderson showed signs of distress.

He had to be carried from the track by other runners. He was pale, limp and breathing painfully. But to those who went to congratulate him he murmured: 'I intended this to be

Sydney Wooderson was both an unassuming solicitor and a famous runner (inset), who became a favourite son of athletics

my last big competition race. I gave it all I had got.'

He certainly did that. It was the second fastest time ever recorded for the 5,000 metres – and within two-fifths of a second of the time he had set himself for the race. But he was still thinking about running for he said: 'I am going to finish the season and my first-class career by having a shot at the two-mile record.'

Wooderson was helped by his previous trackside stopwatch study of Heino. He knew exactly what he was up against and ran a fine tactical race. As the field began to string out he was so dwarfed by the other competitors that a Norwegian asked me: 'Where is Wooderson?'

He was there running about fifth place.

Heino started off at a pace intended to break Wooderson, as he broke all other opposition in the 10,000 metres. But Wooderson responded cheerfully, moving up so that he was always within striking distance. He tripped and faltered over the wooden verge of the stadium at one point. But he recovered and avoided bumping by choosing an outside position for most of the race.

At 3,000 metres tension began to spread. Durkfeldt, a Swede, was close to Wooderson, while Reiss the Belgian and Heino made the running. The first cheering began at 4,000 metres when Wooderson moved to second place while Heino, obviously broken by the pace, trailed away to finish fourth.

Suddenly there came a new challenge. Slykhuis, the Dutchman, streaked ahead of Nyberg, the Swede, who came third – and the real race began. Wooderson stepped off into one of his great finishes and chased the flying Dutchman. As he drew near – to win by 30 yards – the tension was so great that, when I looked at my programme later, I found it a ball of crumpled paper in my hand.

● In 1942, Gundar Haegg, the Swede, did the 5,000 metres in 13mins 58.2secs, [then] still the world's record.

Blower conquers swimming's most awesome challenge

Within the realms of the possible there is no more terrifying challenge in swimming than the North Channel of the Irish Sea. In 1947, Tom Blower did it in conditions resembling a Norse saga. After his death **John Lovesey** *pieced together the details of the heroic feat for Sports Illustrated*

FROM DONAGHADEE in Northern Ireland to Portpatrick in Scotland is a fraction under 21 miles. Between the two land masses the sea rages in swollen tides and hungry eddies. Out in the centre a man could sink some 100 fathoms in places before touching the dark bottom. The water is so painfully cold that to swim in it is to feel as if one has a steel band around his forehead that gets tighter with each stroke. This is the deadly and cruel North Channel of the Irish Sea. To long-distance swimmers it makes the English Channel look like a wading pond. The first swimmer to make it across was Tom Blower.

Not many others have even dared to try the crossing. The American Florence Chadwick made two unsuccessful attempts – in 1957, when her life was in danger for 24 hours after-

wards, and in 1960, when she left the water with a body temperature of 90 degrees. A Greek, Jason Zirganos, died after an unsuccessful try in 1959 despite the efforts of a doctor who cut him open with a borrowed penknife to massage his heart. Tom Blower, who swam the English Channel first in 1937, found the challenge irresistible.

He was a citizen of Nottingham, on better terms with the authorities than Robin Hood but a match for the legendary outlaw in bold charm. A blond and jovial giant (6 feet 1 inch, 252 pounds), to his native city's youngsters he was always Uncle Tom, who helped crippled kids to swim, was devoted to youth clubs and gave exhibitions for charity. But when people contributed money, in turn, to one of his long-distance attempts, he said it felt like swimming with £500 in halfpennies around his neck and refused such help ever after.

After the war he made two tries at swimming the North Channel of the Irish Sea. The first, early in the summer of 1947, was called off when the water became so rough that exhausted crews could not manage the boats that accompanied him. On July 27, 1947 he made his second attempt. As he kissed his wife goodbye he said, 'I'm not getting out for anybody this time.' And he did not.

When Blower slid into the water there was a forecast of 15 hours of perfect weather, but his wife was already beset by a feeling of disquiet. 'The sea looked smooth,' she recalled recently at her home in Nottingham, 'but it was a sort of slimy smoothness. And the sky was too red.' It was evening when Blower splashed away, accompanied by an armada of boats and an army of well-wishers who gradually drifted away into the night until he was left with only those directly concerned with the swim. He was at last almost as alone as a flyer in the sky. Around his waist he had tied an old, cherished and much-darned pair of swimming trunks with a piece of string.

The water temperature dropped as low as 49 degrees. He wallowed across fields of floating seaweed. Shoals of herring at one time surrounded him so thickly that they nibbled his feet. The sea looked like a carpet of silver, and

Popular with children, Tom Blower was a jolly giant with the courage of a lion

the pilot's boat propeller churned up fish. One observer from the Irish Amateur Swimming Association, who accompanied him in the water for an hour, came out so cold that he had to thaw out his feet by putting them, wrapped in a blanket, in a cooker oven. For eight hours Blower swam in comparative quiet.

But the morning after the start, one of the most spectacular thunderstorms Scotland has ever known swept through large areas of the country. Towns and villages were plunged into twilight as lightning struck and rain fell. Streets were flooded, bridges swept away, flowers and crops destroyed. Out at sea it took two men to hold the stove on which Clarice Blower cooked food for her husband. It was impossible to reach him with the food, however. Blower

occasionally disappeared completely from sight, swamped amid the waves. Then hail fell in harsh lumps as big as eggs.

Some wanted to take Blower from the water, but his wife, obeying his instructions, would not allow them. For a brief time he changed from the trudgen, a combination of overarm strokes and a scissors kick, to the breast-stroke. Then he appeared to lose strength in one arm. Later, when his arm was moving again, his legs seemed to drag. At one time Blower swam for four hours without making a mile. The Irish Sea eventually grew quiet. Two fishing tugs, chugging by, sent out across the swell that eerie salute of sailors everywhere, the sound of a ship's horn. Blower was going to make it, come thunder, lightning, wind and hail, badly bruised and torn though his body was.

As he swam into a small Scottish cove the sky seemed to clear. He climbed agonisingly out of the water onto the rocks, and raised his clasped hands, shyly, above his head. 'I can't tell anybody how I felt,' said Clarice Blower. 'I'd been every yard of the way with him in my mind. I just burst into tears with joy. But when I looked round everybody else was crying – 21 men and me, one woman.' It had taken Tom Blower 15 hours and 26 minutes to make the historic swim. In Nottingham a proud lord mayor interrupted a city council meeting to tell members of Blower's exploit.

As Blower came limping ashore at Portpatrick the first man to clasp his hand was a Scottish policeman. 'You're the first one to do it, lad,' he said, 'and you'll be the last.'

Blower became a national figure and need never have done any more. But as long as there was a difficult swim to be made he wanted to make it. No amount of bitter cold, exhaustion, cramps, seasickness, sore mouths, puffed faces, arm ache and stinging jellyfish ever seems to deter such men. 'They get the bug and it kills them in the end,' said Clarice Blower.

After the Irish Sea swim, he swam the English Channel twice more – in 1948 and 1951. Then, in 1955, at the age of 41, he died suddenly of a heart attack in his home.

Freddie Mills fights his way to the very top

Older British memories of Freddie Mills are coloured by the wireless accounts of his fights, and none impinged on the imagination more than the courageous battle between Mills and America's Gus Lesnevich. Mills got the verdict and the world championship. **Boxing News** *was cock-a-hoop*

FREDDIE MILLS BROUGHT OFF the greatest triumph of his astonishing career when he gained the referee's verdict at the conclusion of his fifteen rounds contest with Gus Lesnevich at the White City on Monday night, and so won the light heavyweight championship of the world.

He owed his victory to the magnificent attack he made in the 10th round, after the referee had asked both men to put more action into their work. Hefty punches to the chin had the American down for eight, and again for a nine count. Many thought that Gus had failed to beat the count, but he got up to fight back and foil all Freddie's attempts to drop him for the full count.

Then, with fortunes fluctuating for the next four rounds, Mills came out for the final session to demonstrate how to use a straight left.

He jabbed Lesnevich round the ring with a succession of punches that had the champion beaten to a standstill, and at the finish the referee had no hesitation in naming the Britisher as the winner.

That he was fit as a fiddle was plain from the manner in which he was able to take the American's best punches, especially some smashing rights to the chin. Freddie took these, and innumerable left stabs to the face, with almost nonchalance, whereas when he caught Lesnevich with a real punch he hurt him.

Mills deserves every credit for his great victory, as he boxed with planned confidence from the start. The contracts call for a return match, and on Monday night's form we would back Mills to retain his newly-won crown.

One surprising feature was the protective cover put up by Freddie at long range. He held his gloves high and he kept them up in every round and they saved him many a punishing blow. He did swing wildly on a few occasions, but generally he was going back from a methodical left jab that Lesnevich made the feature of his attack, and countered with long lefts to the mid-section and two-fisted spurts that had the champion on the jump.

The damage caused to the American's eyes in the first 20 seconds of fighting did not materially affect the issue. His handlers knew how to look after his injuries and although the right eye was opened in successive rounds, it was eventually patched up and did not cause Lesnevich the slightest bother.

Age has told on Gus more than it has on Freddie, and it was this factor that made us think highly of our champion's chances.

In the Britisher's dressing-room after the fight there were naturally very high spirits and someone suggested that Mills would now tackle Joe Louis, if the latter wished to continue his career. Freddie scotched this idea, but expressed himself anxious for Bruce Woodcock's return to action.

Freddie Mills owed his victory over Gus Lesnevich (left) to his magnificent attack in the 10th round

The night Sugar Ray was defeated by Randolph Turpin

*It was the result that was never expected, despite the faith of **Tom Phillips** in the Daily Mirror, who wrote this report of Randolph Turpin's lifting of the world middleweight crown from Sugar Ray Robinson. Sixty-four days later Turpin lost the title back to the superstar of American boxing*

TWENTY THOUSAND BRITONS cheered at Earls Court, London, last night as the hand of a young English lad was raised in victory in one of the most dramatic moments in sporting history – Randolph Turpin, 23, of Leamington had defeated the hitherto invincible Sugar Ray Robinson, of America, and won the world middleweight championship on points over 15 rounds.

And their cheers resounded around the British Isles as listeners-in everywhere heard the result. What a great moment it was! Some of us were in tears at the ringside as Mr. Eugene Henderson, the referee, unhesitatingly gave his verdict.

In the dressing-room there was even greater drama, for Mr. George Middleton, Turpin's manager, was crying unashamedly, and so were Randolph's brothers, Dick and Jackie, and his sparring partners, Mel Brown and Ted Morgan.

As soon as Turpin could tear himself away from the mobbing which the enthusiastic crowd had given him, he went straight to Robinson's dressing-room and said: 'Sorry, Sugar.' Robinson grasped his hand and replied: 'Don't worry Randy. You were real good like I thought you were.'

Robinson took his defeat like a great sportsman. 'Randy was a better man than I tonight,' he told me. 'It was a tough fight, if not my toughest. Randy sure can punch.'

George Gainford, Robinson's manager, said: 'No alibis. He was beaten. That's all there is to it. There's always the return fight, for which contracts were signed in the event of Turpin's winning. This is due to take place in New York on September 26.'

At the end of the fight Turpin looked down and said to me: 'Tom, come into the ring. Thank you for your faith in me, all through.' I always believed in him when other people had said Turpin should wait twelve months before meeting Robinson. That was one of the reasons George Middleton wept tonight. He had so much correspondence – telegrams, letters and telephone calls – saying he was wrong in putting a callow boy against such a ruthless bruiser.

Long before the fight was announced I wrote in this newspaper that Turpin would win if he got the chance. On the eve of the bout I expressed the view that his big punch would finish Robinson off early in the contest. I was wrong. Turpin outboxed, outclassed and out-punched Robinson.

From the sixth round when Turpin cut Robinson's left eye he was always the master. Turpin bobbed and weaved and took body punches like an old-timer. This is all we had hoped for. English boxers in the olden days went to America and showed them the art and science of this craft. And for decades the Americans have thrown it back at us. Last night Turpin showed them how to do it better.

So many people had believed that Turpin could not do fifteen rounds. Quite rightly.

Because he had never done fifteen rounds before. But from the first bell it was obvious that Turpin, who many of the experts thought had only a forlorn hope, was master.

Turpin did everything we would wish to see an English boxer do. He left-jabbed, piercing Robinson's defence. He was always the aggressor. He took everything on the chin and everything the great Robinson could fire to the body. And yet throughout those fifteen rounds, he came through unmarked. Like a great artist he moved inside the punch, making his opponent miss. And he swayed away from the punch, also to make him miss.

You could sympathise with Robinson. For every now and then, as his brain was adding up how the fight was going, he counterattacked, mostly to the body. When he did so,

For once, the great Sugar Ray Robinson (left) had met a boxer, Randolph Turpin, who was prepared to defy the odds

with the left side of his face bleeding badly, Turpin just took it, allowed him to clinch, and in the clinch counter-punched so easily that Robinson was wondering what he was up against.

What was he up against? A bit of old England. A bit of old England that did not care for Cadillacs, dwarfs, professional barbers, golf professionals and what have you. It was just an English lad, Randy Turpin, who showed the world that he had guts, science and skill to shoot down a very good, a very gallant American.

Jeanette Altwegg becomes queen of the Olympic ice

*The skater Jeanette Altwegg excelled in the compulsory figures, and it was from a commanding lead in that part of the Winter Olympics competition that she serenely went on to her figure skating gold medal and, in due course, was awarded a CBE. This report of her great moment appeared in the **Daily Mirror***

JEANETTE ALTWEGG won Great Britain's first gold medal of the winter Olympics, with a near perfect exhibition in the free figures event of the women's figure skating in the Bislett Stadium, Oslo, last night.

A great roar of welcome from the 30,000 crowd greeted her as she took the ice in a brilliant red and gold costume, with a red rose in her hair above her left ear. Jeanette, already holding a commanding lead in the compulsory figures, took no risks and performed a series of difficult pirouettes and loops without mishap.

And when she finally came to a graceful halt, the crowd didn't wait to hear the official result. Photographers swarmed on to the arena and had to be removed by police before Jeanette, who is now World, Olympic, European and British champion, could leave the ice.

Jeanette's points for the free skating were 63.938 – her aggregate, 161.760. Jacqueline du Bief, of France, scored 67.513 in the free skating, but she was way behind Jeanette on aggregate (158.000) and finished third behind sixteen year old Tenley Albright, of America, who had an aggregate of 159.133.

The last time Britain won this event was in 1908.

Graceful Jeanette Altwegg, perfect in compulsory figures, won her gold medal to a roar of acclaim

Stanley Matthews – at last an FA Cup winner's medal

The amazing Matthews played his first full season in Stoke City's senior team in 1932-3 and his last first-class competitive football in 1965 at the age of 50. His only FA Cup winner's medal came from Blackpool's 4-3 win over Bolton in 1953. **Stanley Halsey** *reported the moment in the Sunday Pictorial*

IN WHAT MUST RANK as the most exciting Cup Final finish in Wembley history, Blackpool emerged from early disaster to dramatic Cup-conquering triumph with two goals in the last three minutes. So Stan Matthews, Blackpool wonder winger with the world copyright style, was presented by Queen Elizabeth with the Cup Final winner's medal which has eluded him throughout so many seasons of soccer stardom.

It was to Matthews that Blackpool turned as to the skipper of a sinking ship, when 3-2 down, and time ticking away in the second half, they seemed doomed to Cup Final defeat for the third time since the war. Matthews diddled and dazzled in the old tantalising fashion. But backing the fancy football was a tremendous drive. And gallant ally of Stan Matthews

in this epic comeback against a tiring, strained and injury-hit Bolton was that other Stan of kindred fame – Mortensen.

Three minutes from time Blackpool were losing 3-2. Bolton despite defensive disorganisation caused through injuries to left half Bell and left back Banks, were still stoutly holding their goal lead. Then Mudie, Blackpool inside left, was fouled. Skipper Harry Johnston signalled Stan Mortensen to take the kick.

Bolton formed the routine barrier which has blockaded the ball in many League matches. But Mortensen spotted a gap between the tallness of Barrass and the shortness of the player alongside him. From around thirty yards range, with all his fire and fury, Morty cracked the ball through that gap to the net.

In the last seconds, Matthews brought a vivid climax with a perfect pass which brought the victory goal. Manoeuvring the ball and outwitting defenders as only Stan can, he passed to Perry who, with the crowd around crazy with excitement, found the necessary coolness to kick it into the net.

George Farm, Blackpool's Scottish international goalkeeper, struck the most disastrous moment of his career one and a half minutes after the start. Nat Lofthouse, Bolton's centre forward, pounced on the ball and sent it out to right winger Holden. Holden sent it back to Lofthouse who hooked the ball from about fifteen yards. Farm reached the ball as one expected a goalkeeper of his class to do. Alas, it spun away from his grasping right hand and rolled into the net.

I must fault Farm again for Bolton's second goal in the fortieth minute which gave them another gift lead after Blackpool had managed to equalise. Langton swung the ball into the goalmouth. Moir jumped to head. His sudden dart at the ball put Farm off and a flick of his head completed the defensive chaos and sent the ball to the net.

It was Mortensen who prompted Blackpool's first goal. He sent in a hard cross shot which seemed to ricochet from Hassall, Bolton inside left, back in defence, to the net. In the fifty-fifth minute, Holden beat his man and crossed the ball. Bell, hobbling on the wing, headed it

Stanley Matthews, his hand finally on the FA Cup, and Blackpool's captain Harry Johnston (left), are chaired by their Blackpool colleagues

grandly to the net. When Bell became a limping hero some twenty-five minutes after the start, Bolton's chances certainly slumped. They were also hard hit when Banks was hurt and Hassall had to move to left back. It seemed an unlucky day for Wembley goalkeepers. Hanson might have let the ball go wide but he tried to stop it, and Morty flung himself at the ball and practically went into the net with it for Blackpool's second goal.

At this stage Stan Matthews stepped on to the scene with his shimmering display.

BLACKPOOL: Farm; Shimwell, Garrett; Fenton, Johnston (capt.), Robinson; Matthews, Taylor, Mortensen, Mudie, Perry.

BOLTON: Hanson; Ball, Banks; Wheeler, Barrass, Bell; Holden, Moir (capt.), Lofthouse, Hassall, Langton.

Referee: Mr. B.M. Griffiths (Newport).

1953

29 May

Mount Everest conquered by Hillary and Tensing

It was the dawn of a new Elizabethan Age. The news of the climbing of Everest, sent by coded message, had arrived in time to be revealed on the day of the Queen's Coronation. A few days later this account bylined Our Special Correspondent, who was **James Morris**, *appeared in The Times*

IN THE PYRAMID TENT, over an omelet served on an aluminium plate, Hillary told the story of the final climb. The tent was uncomfortably crowded. Newspapers were all over the floor. The climbers sat around on packing-cases, groundsheets, and bedding rolls. From time to time the flushed face of an excited Sherpa would appear through the tent door with a word of delight.

Hillary's account began with the events of May 28, when he, Tensing, and the support party – Gregory, Lowe, and a tough young Sherpa, Ang Nima – left South Col to establish Camp VIII on the ridge below the South Summit. Colonel Hunt had already dumped most of the necessary stores at about 27,500ft during the first 'reconnaissance-assault'. Now the camp was to be established at a point as high as possible so that the next day Hillary and Tensing, relying in large measure on their limited oxygen, would not have so far to climb. It had been planned that two Sherpas would accompany the party but one was sick and as a result the amount of oxygen carried had to be reduced.

The party left Camp VII on the South Col, about seven, and set off up the back-breaking steepness of the ridge to find a suitable camp site for climbers carrying 50lb to 65lb each and Sherpas 40lb to 45lb. It was a difficult climb. For what seemed hours no possible site showed itself, and the ridge was covered with difficult snow. Oxygen began to run short, and Gregory and Ang Nima had to use some from the assault cylinders. Tensing remembered a possible tent site just below Lambert's Point. Successive ridges in the rock proved impracticable, but at last the place was found at an estimated 27,800ft. Camp VIII was established – incomparably the highest camp ever put up on a mountain – and Gregory and Lowe, their mission brilliantly accomplished, returned to the South Col.

Hillary and Tensing were left alone in their eyrie. They spent the next two hours pitching a tent on the snow-covered rock, but were handicapped by the lack of rock pitons. The tent platform was on two levels, with a step in the middle. Tensing sat in the lower half, Hillary in the top.

As darkness gathered they took a little sleeping oxygen, but throughout the night they sustained themselves with sardines and biscuits – 'paradise' is Tensing's word for them. It was a calm night though a cold one – the temperature at one time was minus 27deg Centigrade. At four in the morning they thawed their boots over the Primus stove, and half an hour later looked out of the tent. It was a glorious clear morning, calm and peaceful. They could see far down the valley to the monastery of Thyangboche, the expedition's original rear base, on its lofty wooded hill.

They were away from camp by six o'clock on May 29, and started up through deep, crusty, powdered snows towards the South Summit. There were no signs of tracks left by

Bourdillon and Evans and they had to cut steps constantly, taking it in turns to break the trail. They kept going steadily, but Hillary describes this climb to the South Summit as the hardest part of the day. At nine they were on the South Summit, the little knoll of snow-capped rock about half a mile from the summit proper, and were seen by the exhilarated watchers on the South Col. They spent 10 minutes there, and took off their oxygen masks without any sudden reaction. Nevertheless their main worry was their shortage of oxygen supplies. To economise, when they moved off again they reduced their flow of oxygen from the normal four litres a minute to three.

They were now on the final ridge of Everest, never reached before. Hillary describes it as 'technically good, interesting Alpine work.' They moved along the west side of the ridge, characterised by difficult cornices, with occasional glimpses of this camp, an infinity below. They crossed safely the one major obstacle on the ridge, a difficult rock step, almost vertical. At every moment they expected to see the summit, but time and again minor elevations deceived them. It was at 11.30 a.m., May 29, 1953, that they stepped at last on to the snow-covered final eminence of Everest.

Hillary described this as 'a symmetrical, beautiful snow cone summit' – very different from the harsh rock ridge which is all that can be seen from below. The view was not spectacular. They were too high for good landscape, and all below looked flat and monotonous.

To the north the route to the summit on which pre-war Everest expeditions pinned their hopes looked in its upper reaches prohibitively steep. Tensing spent the fifteen minutes on the summit, eating mint cake and taking photographs, for which purpose Hillary removed his oxygen mask without ill effects. Tensing produced a string of miscellaneous flags and held them high, while Hillary photographed them. They included the Union Jack, the Nepal flag, and that of the United Nations. Tensing, who is a devout Buddhist, also laid on the ground in offering some sweets, bars of chocolate, and packets of biscuits.

At 11.45 they left the summit on the return climb, keeping a careful check on the oxygen gauges. Because of the shortage of oxygen supplies they dared not stay at the ridge camp, and they moved straight down towards the South Col, the going being reasonably good. Above the South Col they met Lowe and Noyce. Noyce was the leader of a rescue or reinforcement party which had come up from Camp IV; it was Noyce's second climb to the South Col. By 4.30 all four were back at Camp VII, and yesterday morning, May 30, they made their way down the face of Lhotse to the Cwm.

Hillary and Tensing seem in astonishingly good form, with none of the desperate fatigue that has overcome Everest summit parties in the past. Nor have they any other than modest pride in their achievements, and more still in the wonderful success of the expedition as a whole. The heroic quality is undoubtedly in them, as it is in most of this fine team, but yesterday afternoon, after the first flood of emotion, it was agreeably shielded by the aura of not very good omelets (eaten indigestibly fast), untidy tents, high spirits, and home thoughts from abroad.

For within a day or two the expedition will be down at the base camp at Khumbu Glacier on its way home. One obstacle remains before it – the icefall has now changed beyond recognition since the centre of operations moved into the Western Cwm. Three weeks ago it had a certain stark and nasty grandeur; now under the pressure of the thaw, it resembles nothing so much as a gigantic squashed meringue. It is as if the mountain, thwarted of its isolation, has prepared one last hazard for its climbers, and there is certainly no member of the expedition who will not feel a deep relief when this danger is passed.

Setting foot on the base camp again will be a symbol, undramatic perhaps but vivid, that implacable Everest's sting has been drawn at last.

On the roof of the world, Hillary photographed Tensing with a string of miscellaneous flags held high

1953
6 June

Sir Gordon Richards wins his only Derby

In the week of the Queen's Coronation a victory for Her Majesty's Aureole in the Derby, held on the Saturday, would have added the final touch. Instead Gordon Richards, knighted in the Coronation Honours, won his only Derby on Pinza. **Cyril Ray** *captured the exitement in The Sunday Times*

IT COULDN'T have been more exciting. We wanted the Queen's horse to win, or Gordon Richards's, and there they both were in front, all the way down the straight, their colours gleaming in the sun, and the silky flanks of the horses, too, and the biggest crowd I have ever seen cheering its head off.

They had cheered the Queen's arrival, with the Duke of Edinburgh, Queen Elizabeth the Queen Mother, Princess Margaret, and a royal party of a couple of dozen or more. They had cheered them again as they went to the paddock to see the horses saddled, and they had cheered Sir Winston, in a grey morning-coat and grey top-hat, busy with binoculars and a big cigar, and with him General Marshall, a tremendous silk hat pressed firmly on to his ears.

'Royal weather,' somebody had said to me as I reached the course and everything was lit and glorified with it. The sunshine and the happiness spilled over and drenched us all. But now it was the race of the day that was irradiated, and the cheering poured down the course, alongside and ahead of the galloping horses, like a river in flood.

I was pressed against the rails of the unsaddling enclosure, and I could glimpse the horses coming and hear the thumpety-thump of their hooves; with a twist of my head I could look at the Royal Box above me, where the Queen, a trim figure in smoky blue, was up and down in her seat with excitement, her black-gloved hand right on the rail.

'Gordon,' the crowd was shouting. 'Come on, Gordon!' and I think some were ahead of the accolade and calling out 'Sir Gordon!' Then it was over and we rushed to the grass ring to greet the winner. Gordon Richards was the calmest man there. Everyone else was either cheering or calling out his name, or, even if silent, had a flicker of excitement in his face. The Queen was looking down, her face alive, and around me there was a forest of raised grey toppers.

Gordon Richards's Derby victory on Pinza made the Coronation Week complete

1953
19 August

England recapture the Ashes after two decades

*The last time England had regained the Ashes was the Bodyline Tour of Australia 1932-3. Following four drawn Tests, the series was decided at the Oval. There, the final celebration followed hours of anxiety. In the Manchester Guardian **Neville Cardus** delivered his verdict*

Compton, quintessential English hero, hooks a ball from Johnston to leg

IN SUNSHINE WHICH MIGHT have come to us from an August at Kennington Oval more than a quarter of a century ago, a victory for England over Australia was vociferously celebrated today. The result on paper suggests that after all the prize came to us fairly comfortably, but as a fact every run to the end needed hard work and determination to get. The Australians fought vehemently until a boundary hit or two would settle the issue. Then Hassett bowled like a gallant captain and opponent who chivalrously chose to be the first to present the laurel wreath.

Had the gentlest wind of chance blown Australia's way the finish would have unsettled the nerves and, possibly, unseated judgement. W. A. Johnston, Australia's only spin bowler, missed taking important wickets by inches, for several mis-hits from him eluded a field which on the whole appeared as omnipresent as avid and brilliantly safe. But though no patriotic spectator dared take events for granted, the die was all the time cast against Australia. Ably and manfully though Johnston worked away, over after over, the wicket called for spin at the other end of the pitch as well. England needed too few runs with no need for hurry. No single bowler not a genius in his class could have won the match by dint of his own arm in the circumstances which challenged and brought the best out of Johnston, as splendid and sterling-hearted a cricketer as Australia ever sent to us.

Hassett, in a humorous speech to the crowd, paid his generous tribute to England. He has the philosophy to ask himself, now the

AUSTRALIA

1st Innings

A.L. Hassett	c Evans b Bedser	53
A.R. Morris	lbw b Bedser	16
K.R. Miller	lbw b Bailey	1
R.N. Harvey	c Hutton b Trueman	36
G.B. Hole	c Evans b Trueman	37
J. de Courcy	c Evans b Trueman	5
R. Archer	c and b Bedser	10
A.K. Davidson	c Edrich b Laker	22
R.R. Lindwall	c Evans b Trueman	62
G.R. Langley	c Edrich b Lock	18
W.A. Johnston	not out	9
Extras	(b 4, nb 2)	6
	Total	**275**

2nd Innings

	lbw b Laker	10
	lbw b Lock	26
	c Trueman b Laker	0
	b Lock	1
	lbw b Laker	17
	run out	4
	c Edrich b Lock	40
	b Lock	21
	c Compton b Laker	12
	c Trueman b Lock	2
	not out	6
	(b 11, lb 3)	14
	Total	**162**

ENGLAND

1st Innings

L. Hutton	b Johnston	82
W.J. Edrich	lbw b Lindwall	21
P.B.H. May	c Archer b Johnston	39
D.C.S. Compton	c Langley b Lindwall	16
T.W. Graveney	c Miller b Lindwall	4
T.E. Bailey	b Archer	64
T.G. Evans	run out	26
J.C. Laker	c Langley b Miller	1
G.A.R. Lock	c Davidson b Lindwall	l4
F.S. Trueman	b Johnston	10
A.V. Bedser	not out	22
Extras	(b 9 lb 5 w 1)	15
	Total	**306**

2nd Innings

	run out	17
	not out	55
	c Davidson b Miller	37
	not out	22
	Extra (lbw 1)	1
	Total (for 2)	**132**

battle is done, if he did not make a mistake in going into action at the Oval in so crucial an engagement with inadequate reserves of spin.

Edrich's unbeaten innings of 55 was worth framing in gold. He controlled the bridge on a voyage by no means sailed in smooth and entirely charted waters. Throughout my comments on these Test matches, I have taken the view that the collective ability of the two teams was so evenly balanced that the merest straw of chance would sway the scales. England have won because they commanded in Lock and Laker the bowlers suitable to the wicket on which Australia had to bat when the issue was anybody's. One lesson of the rubber should already find the Australians at least receptive. So long as wickets are covered in Australia so long will England win matches against Australia in this country whenever rain and sun or wearing turf call for batsmen experienced against spin. It was England's turn, as they say, and every cricketer will be mightily pleased that all's well that ends well, for Hutton's sake. With heavy weight of responsibility on his shoulders he has done his job with unwavering patience and determination. England, and – as important – all Yorkshire, may be proud of him, more than ever.

The joy of England's cricket fans runneth over, and Hutton and Hassett shake hands on the balcony at The Oval after the final Test

Piggott becomes the youngest Derby winner

When Lester Piggott, at 18, won his first Derby on the American-bred Never Say Die, he was almost certainly the youngest jockey ever to win the Classic. In the Daily Mirror **Peter Wilson** *captured the cocksure calm of a young man destined to scale even greater heights*

SO A 33-1 OUTSIDER that nobody tipped, ridden by the youngest jockey in the race and owned by a 78 year old American who was 3,000 miles away, yesterday beat the cream of the world's horses in the Derby, the world's greatest race.

The jockey in this youngest-oldest partnership was pale-faced, fair haired Lester Piggott, 18, from Lambourn, Berks. The owner is retired New York businessman Robert Sterling Clark. The horse was the chestnut colt Never Say Die, which won from Arabian Night and Darius.

Piggott is probably the youngest jockey ever to win the Derby, and he will go down in Turf history as just about the coolest. Self-possessed ('cocky' some say) and unexcited, he smiled his thanks amid the shower of congrat-ulations. In answer to eager questions about his victory, he was as unemotional as a Boy Scout who had just got his badge for woodcraft. Yes... he had always been in the first five... No, he had had no difficulty...Yes, he was sure of winning once they came into the straight.

'I took one quick look behind me a furlong from the post, and then I knew we were home,' he said. They came to invite him to appear on television. 'Not interested,' he said. Later, he did say that 'Never say die' was a motto he would remember. But then quietly, almost as an aside, he added 'Why all the fuss? After all, the Derby is just another race...' So that is

what the summit looks like when you are only eighteen!

Piggott was asked what his ambition is now. 'Why to be champion jockey of course,' he said. 'But that may take a lot longer to achieve...'

Cocky? Well, confidence is easily mistaken for cockiness. When he was sixteen and already a brilliant jockey, Piggott said: 'Maybe it's because I'm young that some people think I'm cocky. What should I do when I win? Hang my head and blush, and say how surprised I am to come in first? I ride to win! That's what I get on a horse for.'

This philosophy, and a natural zest for rid-

Lester Piggott took 'one quick look behind' a furlong from the post and, he claimed, knew then that it was in the bag for Never Say Die

ing, have led to plenty of fireworks in the short racing career of the boy who was born on Guy Fawkes Day. Only seven weeks ago he was suspended for the fifth time in four years. The suspension lasted only two days. There were proud smiles on the faces of Piggott's parents as they watched him win yesterday. But there was just a trace of regret, too.

'We didn't back him,' confessed Mr. Piggott, a former jockey and now a trainer.

Roger Bannister breaks the 4-minute mile

*A mile in four minutes was once the Holy Grail of athletics. Numerous accounts of how it was achieved have been published but, away in America, **Arthur Daley**, a Pullitzer prize-winning columnist of The New York Times, succinctly put the feat into its historical perspective and world-wide importance*

IT FINALLY HAPPENED. The 4-minute mile no longer is an impenetrable barrier. Roger Bannister of England burst through it and beyond with his electrifying 3:59.4 yesterday under conditions that would seem to make its acceptance as a world record a formality. From an athletic standpoint this is as historic as the breaking of the sound barrier.

In the enthusiasm of the moment, there is a tendency to rank Bannister's exploit as the most important sports achievement of this century. Yet it may still hold that stature even after sober and profound reflection. Casey Stengel's pet adjective fits it perfectly. It is truly 'tree-mendous'.

To foot racers, the 4-minute mile was what Mount Everest was to mountain climbers, a defiant peak that could not be successfully assailed. But someone finally reached the top of Everest and someone also has scaled the peak of the 4-minute mile.

The surprising aspects of this feat are two in number. In most ratings of the world's best milers, Bannister was third on the totem pole behind John Landy of Australia and Wes Santee of the United States. The Aussie had done 4:02 and had five other performances under 4:03. The Kansan had done 4:02.4 while Bannister's best official mark was 4:02.6, since his paced mile of 4:02 had been disallowed. Yet the paced effort demonstrated that the ability was there and that trackdom's Holy Grail was within his reach.

The second surprise developed in the circumstances of the race. The experts had insisted all along that the 4-minute mile could be surpassed only under perfect conditions. The track itself would have to be perfect. So would the weather and so would the running of the race itself. But reports from Britain reveal that a strong cross wind blew across the track and that sullen clouds hung overhead. 'Conditions are stupid,' remarked Bannister beforehand. Yet they didn't seem to trouble him.

About the 'cross wind' item... when a race is run around an oval track, it has no effect on the acceptability of a record. It blows against a runner just as much as it blows behind him. Technically speaking, the buffeting he gets from a wind takes so much out of him that the helping tailwind cannot compensate.

However, the competition was ideal. Chris Brasher set a blistering first half and then faded while Chris Chataway, the top-flight British Olympian, challenged the rangy medical student enough to force him all out on the final lap. No time was wasted in jockeying or manoeuvring for position, a significant consideration. Thus was Gunder (the Wonder) Haegg's mile record of 4:01.4 sunk without a trace.

Almost two months ago, a feature story from Stockholm appeared in this newspaper. In it Gunder the Wonder was quoted as predicting that Bannister was his choice to be the first to crack the 4-minute mile. Some of his quotes are worth repeating:

Roger Bannister crosses the finish line, the 4-minute mile barrier is broken, and his feat sends ripples round the world

'Bannister has brains. That's something you can't say about all runners. He doesn't over-train the way most runners do. You don't see Bannister burning himself out, running twenty and thirty miles a day. He's a miler, a middle-distance man. That's the way he trains. He makes his daily session as much like a mile race as he can.'

However, Haegg erred slightly in saying that the Briton would need stadium walls to block off any wind. But he was correct in declaring that the runner must not be 'psychologically tied down – afraid of the mighty 4-minute mile.'

That's why it was a trifle disconcerting to have Landy, the Australian, express those fears when he arrived in Stockholm the other day for a competitive tour. 'It will be very hard to run a mile in 4 minutes or less,' he said. 'It's just that last little bit that matters.' Landy obviously was wearing those psychological fears Haegg mentioned. Bannister was not. So he broke the record.

Somehow or other a feeling of smug satisfaction follows the news that mile supremacy has returned to Britain, where it originated. They don't have the coaches over there that we have here, and the sports attitude in general has been 'jolly well done, old chap'. English casualness is almost alarming to intense Americans. That makes the Bannister achievement a monumental personal accomplishment. It was his first race of the year and he did it all himself with typical British doggedness. Being a medical student, he had to steal his training hours where he could find them.

There will be many miles henceforth under 4 minutes. The impossible no longer is out of reach. Even Bannister's record will be broken some day. But never will it be forgotten that he was the first to reach into the realm of fantasy and surpass the 4-minute mile.

Chris Chataway beats Vladimir Kuts at the White City

The antithesis of the ascetic Soviet athletes who came to the White City in 1954, Chris Chataway beat the iron man of the USSR in the 5,000 metres. His feat had the crowd in the stadium and a TV audience in a nail-biting frenzy. In the Daily Mirror **Peter Wilson**, *in a front page story, knew it was time to cheer till we dropped*

CHRIS, THE MAGNIFICENT. That's all that mattered at the White City, London, last night. Forget Moscow's overwhelming victory in both the men's and women's athletic matches over London. Just throw your hats into the air, cheer till you are hoarse, like more than 40,000 of us at the White City did last night – and as millions more must have done in their homes as they watched the race on TV – when Chris Chataway won the 5,000 metres (3 miles 188 yards) in the new world record time of 13m 51.6s.

In beating the record Chris beat the man who outfoxed him in the European championships, Moscow ex-sailor Vladimir Kuts, and in five seconds better time than the Russian made at Berne. This wasn't just the greatest race I've ever seen it was just about the most exciting spectacle in my whole panorama of sport which has lasted for a quarter of a century.

Picture the scene: As they crouch under the diamond-bright lights on the blood-red track, there are just four of them – Chataway, Kuts, young Peter Driver and Vladimir Okorokov. But you know that for all it matters Driver and Okorokov could drop out. The pistol bangs and blond Kuts leaps into the lead. Chataway who in the European Championships was fooled into thinking the Russian would crack is making no such mistake this time.

He's on the heels of the Russian sailor, his red hair sleek, his face flour white, in the flood-lighting. Driver follows Chataway and the other Russian is last. For over a mile they stay that way, and then Kuts cracks on the pace. Chataway stays with him. They pull away from Driver, who in turn leaves Okorokov. In the seventh lap Kuts tries to play it smart. He would sprint for several strides and then slow down to a comparative dawdle. Chataway stays with him.

Then they get into the belly of the race. Kuts with his muscular, padding stride looks as strong in the eighth lap as he did in the first – and in the ninth, tenth and the eleventh. And Chataway stays with him.

Now the crowd is chanting rhythmically 'Chat-a-way, Chat-a-way,' but the two runners seem to be joined with some kind of umbilical cord of the cinder track. Kuts leads by the same margin that one arm of a windmill leads the next. And Chataway stays with him.

The interval times – 4m. 24.4s for the mile, 8m 54.6s for the two miles – tell us that the time is going to be a cracker. But who cares about time now? The old enemy has ceased to matter. Time stands still. The only movement in the roaring pandemonium is out there on that blood red track where the scarlet vest still leads the white one. But Chataway stays with him.

You can see an official thrashing a bell madly. It might have had a rubber clapper for all the hope it had of being heard above the surging, monstrous howl and roar of the crowd. So you know that it's the last lap – just

Chris Chataway beat the Iron Man of Soviet athletics and the whole nation was on its feet cheering

400 metres left with 4,600 metres having been swallowed up by the blond fighter and his red-topped rival. Kuts is still leading. But Chataway stays with him.

Three hundred yards to go and the position is the same. Two hundred yards and it's unaltered. One hundred yards left and still they haven't varied their place or their pace. Fifty yards and now, it must be now, yes, yes, yes... Chataway is moving up on the outside. They are level – there are thirty yards to go. Now only twenty and Chataway makes his effort. He's ahead – and Kuts can't stay with him. He's past the tape, is Chris. He's won. He's won. He's done it!

And now madness takes over. Chataway half collapses into a confetti-cloud of officials. Hats are sailing into the air... Yes, literally. I mean it. I find I can't begin to type because I have banged my hand so hard on the wooden bench in front of me that it is numb. Chataway the world's sparring partner, the man who helped Roger Bannister become the first man to break four minutes for the mile, the man who then spurred John Landy on to break that record again, the man who beat Zatopek but was out-guessed by Kuts, Chataway, the gay blade from Oxford who will smoke a cigar and drink a glass of stout with the best of them has proved that we've still got it in us to turn in with non-chalance a world-shattering performance, an epic with a grin.

Out of the ruck of hysteria which was going on on the green lozenge in the centre of the track – and don't think it wasn't happening in the stands, too – the white shoes and the white vest, topped by the red head came trotting out. His face was very pale, but it was still smiling, and when at last he vanished into the depth of the dressing rooms it was to the loudest, most sustained, most sincere roar that I have ever heard a sports crowd give to any man.

For if they had not cheered I swear that many would have cried – I was not so far off it myself – in a moment of the highest emotion. This... this, well this was something that you see only once in a lifetime. Chataway will not run again for six months and will run no 5,000 metre races next year. 'But I should like to try to win the Olympic 5,000 metres in 1956' he said. Mr Sergei Pushnov, leader of the Russian party, said: 'It was a beautiful race – Kuts and Chataway helped each other to break world records.' For Kuts's time for three miles was a new world record of 13m. 27s.

The Mille Miglia race falls to Stirling Moss

The now abandoned Mille Miglia was held on public roads in Italy and the year Stirling Moss won he broke all the records over the 1,000-mile course. He had prepared himself 'scientifically' with **Denis Jenkinson**, *his navigator, who wrote an enthralling account for Motor Sport. This brief extract conveys the mood*

BEFORE starting I had a complete list of our more serious rivals and also the existing record times of every control point round the course. We had privately calculated on an average of 90 m.p.h. – two miles an hour over the Marzotto record. Mercedes gave us no orders, leaving the running of the race entirely to each driver, but insisting that the car was brought back to Brescia if it were humanly possible.

Stirling and I made a pact that we would keep the car going as long as practicable, having decided at which point we could have the engine blow up and still coast in to the finish and how many kilometres we were prepared to push it to the finish or to a control. There were Mercedes pits at Ravenna, Pescara, Rome, Florence and Bologna, completely equipped with everything that might be required...

Starting positions were arranged by ballot, and this was quite important, for the later starters had the advantage of knowing what was going on ahead of them. They could, at their pits, secure exact information of the times of their rivals while the early starters in the fast group could not tell what was going on behind them and had to be a jump ahead for real information. For example, with Taruffi, a greatly fancied driver, starting later than us, we would have to wait until Pescara before we could know our relative positions at Ravenna.

Among the important men who started ahead of us were Fangio and Kling on Mercedes S.L.R.s like ours, Peter Collins (Aston Martin) and a group of Ferraris headed by Maglioli. Our big worry was not so much those ahead as those behind. Thirty seconds before our starting time, 7.22 a.m., Moss started the engine, which roared into life and then, as the flag fell, we were off to a surge of acceleration and up to peak revs, in first, second and third gears, weaving our way through the vast crowds.

We had the sun shining full in our eyes which made navigating difficult, but I had written the notes over and over again and gone over the route so many times in my imagination that I almost knew it by heart...

On one straight, lined with trees, we had marked down one hump as being 'flat out; only if the road was dry.' It was, so I gave the appropriate signal and we took it at 7,500 revs, in fifth gear. For a measurable amount of time the vibro-massage you get sitting in a 300 S.L.R. at that speed suddenly ceased, and there was time for us to look at each other with raised eyebrows before we landed again. Even if we had been in the air for only one second, we should have travelled 200 feet, and I estimated the 'duration of flight' at something more than a second. The road was dead straight; the Mercedes made a perfect four-point landing, and I thankfully praised the driver because he did not move the steering wheel a fraction of an inch, for that might have been our end...

We were certainly not wasting any seconds anywhere, and Moss was driving right on the limit of adhesion all the time, sometimes over the limit, driving in that awe-inspiring narrow margin that you enter just before you have a crash, unless you have the Moss skills...

The last six miles [into Rome] were an absolute nightmare. Normally we would have been doing 150 or more miles an hour, but the crowds of spectators were so thick that we had to slow down to about 130 m.p.h., and that was pretty hectic through the dense crowds. It seemed that all Rome was out to watch the race, all oblivious of the danger of a high-speed racing car....

[We] led at Rome, and Moss drove off with every intention of breaking down the superstitious tradition that whoever leads at Rome will not win at Brescia...

Up the Radicofani we stormed, with the car bucking and slithering about to such an extent that I should have been frightened but for my complete faith in the masterly driving of

Stirling. Previously he had been pointing to the front of the car, indicating that a brake was beginning to grab on occasions, and it happened on a sharp left-hander. Without any warning, the car spun round and there was just time to think what a desolate part of Italy this was for a breakdown when I realised that we had stopped almost in our own length and were gently sliding into the ditch. It didn't seem so bad, and looked as though we could push it out, but as I was about to get out of the car, Moss dropped into bottom gear and out she came, with a dented tail. It took us two turns into reverse before we could point the car in the right direction, and as I fiddled about with the safety-catch on the reverse position, we poked our tongues out at each other in mutual derision.

At the Siena control, we had no idea whether we were leading or not, but we knew Taruffi was on our tail, and Moss had no thought of relaxing. He continued to drive what I think must have been the most superb race of his career, twirling the steering wheel this way and that, controlling slides with per-

Stirling Moss and Denis Jenkinson, faces blackened but joyful, after an epic victory in Italy's Mille Miglia road race

fect judgement or alternatively provoking slides so as to make the car change direction bodily. On the winding road from Siena to Florence, physical strain began to tell on me, but I gave myself renewed energy by looking at Stirling, who was seated beside me, perfectly relaxed, working away at the steering as though we had only just left Brescia instead of having driven for nearly 700 miles in a broiling sun...

Now Moss had really got the bit between his teeth; nothing was going to stop him winning, I thought; he had rather a special look of concentration on his face and I knew that one of his greatest ambitions was to do the section Florence–Bologna in one hour. The road crosses the heart of the Apennines, by way of Futa and Raticosa Passes, in about 60 miles, but it is like a Prescott hill climb all the way...

Moss left Florence as though at the start of a Grand Prix, and as he looked at his wrist-watch I realised that he was out to crack the hour to Bologna. 'This is going to be fantastic!' I thought as we screamed up the hills from Florence; 'he is going to do some nine-tenths plus motoring.'

He did, while I gave him occasional signals and leaned to the left as far as possible away from Moss, for he was going to need all the room possible for his whirling arms and for stirring the gear-lever about. Up into the mountains we screamed, occasionally passing other cars. Little did we know that we had the race in our pocket...

At the top of the Futa Pass there were enormous crowds all waving excitedly, and on numerous occasions Moss almost lost the car completely as we hit patches of melted tar coated with oil and rubber from the cars ahead of us...On we went, up and over the Raticosa Pass, plunging down the other side in a series of slides that to me felt completely uncontrolled, but which to Moss were obviously intentional. By sheer good fortune we missed the stone parapet on the outside of the corner. Down off the mountains we raced, into the broiling heat of the afternoon, and dashing into the Bologna control at nearly 150 miles an hour...

The hard part was now over, but Moss did not relax, for it had now occurred to him that it was possible to get back to Brescia in the round ten hours, which would make the race average 100 m.p.h. Up the long straights through Modena, Reggio Emilia and Parma we went, not wasting a second anywhere, cruising at 170 m.p.h., cutting off only where I indicated corners or bumpy hillbrows. Looking up I suddenly realised that we were overtaking an aeroplane, and then I knew I was living in the realms of fantasy; when we caught and passed a second one my brain began to boggle at the sustained speed. They were flying at about 300 feet, filming our progress, and it must have looked most impressive.

This really was pure speed; the car was going perfectly and reaching 7,600 r.p.m. in fifth gear in places, which was as honest a 170 m.p.h. plus as I'd care to argue about. Through Cremona we went, and now we were on the last leg of the course, there being a special prize and the Nuvolari Cup for the fastest speed from Cremona to Brescia...

The final miles into Brescia were sheer joy, and after we had passed my final direction indicator, I put my roller map away and thought: 'If it blows to pieces now, we can carry it the rest of the way.' We took the last corner into the finishing line at well over 100 m.p.h., still not knowing that we had made motor history, but happy and contented at having completed the race. On the way to the official car park, Stirling said 'Do you think we've won?'

We were soon informed that we had actually won, and we clasped each other in delirious joy. Then we were swept away amid a horde of police and officials. Our total time for the course was 10 hours 7 minutes 48 seconds, an average of nearly 98 m.p.h. From Cremona to Brescia we had averaged 123 m.p.h. As we were driven back to our hotel, tired, filthy, oily and covered in dust and dirt, we grinned happily at each other's black faces, and Stirling said: 'I'm so happy to have proved that a Briton can win the Mille Miglia and that the legend "he who leads at Rome never leads at Brescia" is finished.'

Jim Laker takes 19 wickets in a Test match

*In this year the spin bowler Jim Laker took no fewer than 46 wickets in the Test series against Australia. This feat included the phenomenal return of 19 for 90 runs in the Old Trafford match. In the Manchester Guardian **Denys Rowbotham** commented on the 19-wicket masterpiece*

A SUPERB PIECE OF BOWLING by J. C. Laker not only brought England victory by an innings and 170 runs in the fourth Test match at Old Trafford yesterday (and continued custody of the Ashes) but created several remarkable records at the same time.

First, by taking Australia's eight remaining wickets Laker became the first bowler ever to take all ten in one innings in a Test match. These ten wickets, added to his nine in the first innings, also gave him more wickets in a single Test match than any other bowler has obtained in cricket's history. Seventeen of his nineteen wickets were taken in succession, which may also be a record. His aggregate of 51 wickets from five matches against the Australians this season seems unlikely also ever to have been beaten.

Significant records rarely are broken unless the performance is worthy. But a record which derives from an aggregate may be achieved luckily, with the willing connivance of a partner, or with a performance at the crucial moment below the record-breaker's best. More than once, one suspects, ten wickets in an innings have been taken because the bowler at the other end has 'soft-pedalled' for the last few overs or minutes.

Yesterday, however, Laker's records were achieved in the highest tradition. To the end of the day at half-past five Lock used every stratagem to take even one wicket which would have quickened England's victory. Field placings, even after the ninth wicket had fallen, were adjusted subtly to enable him to take it had Johnson made only a single error. So that when Laker finally had Maddocks leg-before and the crowd burst into rounds and rounds of cheering he knew that the proudest distinctions had never been gained more genuinely.

Laker's performance becomes still more outstanding when it is emphasised, as it must be, that yesterday's wicket was never strictly sticky. Until about a quarter of an hour before

When Jim Laker achieved his records, the mighty feat was accomplished in the highest tradition

ENGLAND

First innings

P. E. Richardson	c Maddocks b Benaud	104
M. C. Cowdrey	c Maddocks b Lindwall	80
D. S. Sheppard	b Archer	113
P. B. H. May	c Archer b Benaud	43
T. E. Bailey	b Johnson	20
C. Washbrook	lbw b Johnson	6
A. S. M. Oakman	c Archer b Johnson	10
T. G. Evans	st Maddocks b Johnson	47
J. C. Laker	run out	3
G. A. R. Lock	not out	25
J. B. Statham	c Maddocks b Lindwall	0
Extras	b 2, lb 5, w 1)	8
Total		**459**

AUSTRALIA

First innings

C. C. McDonald	c Lock b Laker	32
J. W. Burke	c Cowdrey b Lock	22
R. N. Harvey	b Laker	0
I. D. Craig	lbw b Laker	8
K. R. Miller	c Oakman b Laker	6
K. D. Mackay	c Oakman b Laker	0
R. G. Archer	st Evans b Laker	6
R. Benaud	c Statham b Laker	0
R. R. Lindwall	not out	6
L. V. Maddocks	b Laker	4
I. W. Johnson	b Laker	0
Extras		0
Total		**84**

Second innings

	c Oakman b Laker	89
	c Lock b Laker	33
	c Cowdrey b Laker	0
	lbw b Laker	38
	b Laker	0
	c Oakman b Laker	0
	c Oakman b Laker	0
	b Laker	18
	c Lock b Laker	8
	lbw b Laker	2
	not out	1
	(b 12, lb 4)	16
Total		**205**

lunch the ball turned slightly but exasperatingly slowly and never with a hint of bite or nip. Then the wicket still was a mud patch.

Within 45 minutes of the start at 11.40 in fact Laker was replaced by Oakman, and fifteen minutes later Lock gave way to Statham. The soft surface helped an accurate Statham no more than it had Laker and Lock. Craig and McDonald had only to keep their heads, make no palpable misjudgement, and sustain a watchful concentration to survive without hint of obvious difficulty. They were able as well to cut and hook anything short with impunity.

All the time a strong wind was drying a wet wicket as amiably as one can well be dried. At 1.10 however, when Laker replaced Bailey at the City end, the sun came out and shone brightly, if not hotly until roughly an hour after lunch. Within ten minutes Laker had made a ball pop and before lunch he was turning the ball markedly more sharply and quickly. Clearly after lunch it would soon be obvious

Jim Laker exemplified, in a single day, 'all the classical conceptions of the art of slow bowling'

whether Australia was to save or lose the match. The answer came more quickly than one had expected. May promptly changed Lock to the City and Laker to the more dangerous Stretford end. Twice in Laker's first over McDonald was in trouble; twice in Lock's first over balls jumped nastily. And fifteen minutes after lunch Craig was out. Laker made an off-break turn sharply from a full length richly flighted; Craig played a half-cock, missed, and was leg before...

At five o'clock it is 198 for eight and England all but home. Laker now is tiring and Lindwall pushes forward and actually gets away with snicks and edges through the leg trap. Another ball curves tantalisingly in rich flight: this time Lindwall's forward shot just fails to smother it, the ball spins, and Lock at close fine leg is hugging the catch delightedly. A last effort by Lock, and now Laker has changed his pace and flight again; Maddocks, too, has played back to a half-volley, the Ashes are England's, and Laker has achieved the performance of a lifetime.

Laker, indeed, has done more. He has done what always must excite the imagination. He has exemplified, in a single day, all the classical conceptions of the art of slow bowling: strict control of both length and direction; the imparting of dangerous spin by technique superbly applied; the variation of spin with the ball that runs straight through to sow doubt as well as prompt error in the batsman; the subtle changes of flight, length, and pace that will induce fatal errors of judgement; and lastly, the cool appraisal of each batsman's temperament and resource, without which right method for right situation can hardly be applied.

S. F. Barnes, who took seventeen for 159 runs against South Africa at Johannesburg in 1913-14, had the best Test match performance before Laker's. Wilfred Rhodes and the late Hedley Verity with, respectively, fifteen for 124 at Melbourne in 1903-4 and fifteen for 104 at Lord's in 1934 were, until yesterday, England's best performers against Australia. All three would have recognised Laker's as bowling of their vintage.

1958

14 June

Christine Truman beats Althea Gibson in Wightman Cup

Nobody could believe it, but it happened. Christine Truman, a 17-year-old, beat Althea Gibson, the mighty Wimbledon champion, in the Wightman Cup. Her triumph turned the tide against America and Britain regained the trophy after 30 years. In the Manchester Guardian David Gray reported with his customary authority

ON A DAY OF DESPERATE EXCITEMENT and mighty jubilation at Wimbledon the Wightman Cup made the journey perilously back to Britain after 28 years in the United States by the narrow margin of four rubbers to three.

Britain had led 2-1 on Friday night, and then Miss Bloomer lost to Mrs Knode – in spite of all the hopes the American is too good a player to play badly for two days in succession – 4-6, 2-6; Miss Truman, possessed, it seemed, by some divine frenzy which made her play a greater and more beautiful game than one had ever seen from her before restored matters with a wonderful 2-6, 6-3, 6-4 victory over Miss Gibson; Miss Haydon won the last and important singles against Miss Arnold, 6-3, 5-7, 6-3; and then Miss Gibson and Miss Hopps gained the consolation of the last doubles for the United States by beating Miss Ward and Miss Shilcock 6-4, 3-6, 6-3.

It was Miss Truman's triumph that turned the tide, for in beating the Wimbledon champion she won a match that Britain had resigned herself to losing long before the start. Before she went on the court, one rubber that might have been won had slipped away as Mrs Knode, using her graceful, forceful backhand to great profit, had steadily worn down Miss Bloomer. If the British player had been able to angle her smashes and volleys the result of that match might have been different. As it was, under the strain of the occasion, she seemed unable to put the ball safely away and many times Mrs Knode, thus reprieved, won points that she seemed to have lost.

And so, with the rubbers at 2-2, to the great match that Miss Truman played. She would have been forgiven if she, too, had been a little nervous at the start. After all, had not Miss Gibson beaten her twelve months ago in a semi-final on the centre court at the cost of only two games? If anything, the nervousness was on the other side of the net. Miss Truman swept into the match and, serving fiercely and hitting her forehand with great hammer-blows, took the first game and broke Miss Gibson's service to love for the second.

After this flying start Miss Gibson looked at her, rather as a champion boxer might look at a newcomer who suddenly affronted him by landing a couple of straight lefts in the first round. She gave a wry and slightly respectful glance of surprise – perhaps she had not expected so much speed from the British girl – and then, assured that the storm would blow itself out, very deliberately and confidently set the powerful machinery of her game in motion. The next six games went to her for the set, but by no means easily, most of them reaching deuce. Miss Truman, it seemed, was in the process of being beaten, and an American victory in the tie loomed largest hereabouts.

But in the crisis Miss Truman attacked splendidly, coming in where before she had tried to play from the back of the court. She volleyed boldly and her forehand drives sped across the court and died away far from the

American's reach. The suspicion that under sustained pressure Miss Gibson was liable to falter suddenly became a fact. One had seen lapses for a game or two before, but no one in England in the last couple of years had ever maintained such an attack as Miss Truman set forward. She led 5-1 in the second set and took it from 5-3, and in the decider she gained a crucial break in service in the ninth game. There was a double fault at match point and

Althea Gibson salutes Christine Truman after the British girl's surprise Wightman Cup win

then a swift rally and Miss Truman had won.

On to Miss Haydon fell the heavy task of winning the tie, and the rubber that she played against Miss Arnold, the youngest of the Americans, was full of long and agonising rallies. She took the first set but, when she lost the second after seeming to have it safely in hand, the Cup, which had appeared to be nine-tenths of the way across the Atlantic, suddenly began to veer slowly back towards the American shore. It hovered there until Miss Haydon broke the sturdy little American's service in the eighth game and won her own from 15-40 down in the ninth.

It was journey's end and the tension was over.

THE WIGHTMAN CUP
Second day

Singles: Miss S.J. Bloomer lost to Mrs D. Knode 4-6, 2-6; Miss C.C. Truman beat Miss A. Gibson 2-6, 6-3, 6-4; Miss A.S. Haydon beat Miss M. Arnold 6-3, 5-7, 6-3.

Doubles: Miss J.A. Shilcock and Miss P.E. Ward lost to Miss Gibson and Miss J. Hopps 4-6, 6-3, 3-6.

Hawthorn becomes Britain's first world GP champion

This was a purple patch for British motor racing, an era when the country's drivers won all but one of the year's 10 Grands Prix. In the end, the flamboyant Mike Hawthorn won the world championship though Stirling Moss won the last race, staged in Casablanca. In a terse first report **Autosport** *trumpeted the news*

SALUTE THE NEW CHAMPION! In one of the most dramatic finales of any post-war motor racing season, Mike Hawthorn won the honour of being the 1958 World Champion at Casablanca on Sunday. The race was won by Stirling Moss who also set up fastest lap to gain maximum points for the event.

After the two days of practice Hawthorn in his Ferrari had gained pole position. Alongside him were Stirling Moss and Stuart Lewis-Evans, both in Vanwalls. The second row comprised Phil Hill (Ferrari) and Jean Behra (B.R.M.).

The tactics of the Ferrari and Vanwall teams with regard to the Championship seemed fairly obvious. Stirling had to stake everything on his incredible skill and the ability of the Vanwall to stay in one piece, for he had to win the race and make fastest lap. Of the Ferrari boys Phil

Hill was to be the pacemaker. It was his job to harry the Vanwall and try to blow it up. All Hawthorn had to do to win the Championship was to finish in second place. So Phil was to try to win the race and Mike would be quite content to finish behind him. However, Moss had the very able backing of Tony Brooks and Stuart Lewis-Evans and it was Tony's job to see that he, too, finished in front of Mike. All this gave promise of a terrific duel on Sunday.

Under a burning sun tempered by a gentle breeze the flag dropped to release the impatient field. Moss and Lewis-Evans shot into the lead. Hawthorn, wary of his clutch which let him down at Monza, took it gently to avoid trouble. As they came past the pits at the end of the first lap Stirling was in the lead with Phil Hill alongside him! Not for long though, for Stirling drew away from the American. Hawthorn took second place for a few laps but then dropped back to let Hill do the work. Meanwhile Tony Brooks had been moving up quietly and on lap 16 Mike found himself being shadowed by the Vanwall. For some laps there was a great fight for third place but then the Vanwall began to lose oil and Mike knew he was safe. Sure enough Tony was forced to retire on the circuit and the danger was over.

On lap seven Stirling set up a new lap record of 2 mins. 24 secs. (117.9 m.p.h.). Phil Hill then replied with 2 mins. 23.3 secs. but on lap 20 Stirling clinched that deal with a time of 2 mins. 22.9 secs. He drew farther and farther away from Hill, eventually returning a fastest lap of 2 mins. 22.5 secs. Hill was then ordered to slow down and a couple of laps later Mike passed him into second place and remained there to the end.

With only 50 miles to go poor Stuart Lewis-Evans had a bad smash. Rounding a bend at about 150 m.p.h. his Vanwall hit an oil patch. There followed a series of hair-raising slides, completely beyond Stuart's control, before the car hit a tree and caught fire. Stuart got out enveloped in flames and ran away from the wreck. He was rushed to hospital where, at the time of going to press, his condition was stated to be critical. Olivier Gendebien also crashed on the far side of the circuit, his Ferrari being

split in two. It is believed he suffered only superficial injuries.

So Stirling won in 2 hrs. 9 mins. 15.1 secs. (116.23 m.p.h.). Mike was second some 75 seconds behind. On the 10.30 p.m. B.B.C. news (Sunday) there was a short interview with the new World Champion. Amid a tremendous hubbub he was asked 'How do you feel?' 'Well, I'm b——y glad it's over!' replied Mike! He was heartily congratulated by Stirling who must have been bitterly disappointed to be runner-up in the Championship for the fourth time!

Tony Brooks, although a non-finisher, retained his third place in the table and Tony Vandervell won the Manufacturers' Championship. Truly a joy day for Britain!

Shortly after he became world champion, Mike Hawthorn was honoured and feted at the Royal Automobile Club in London

MOROCCAN GRAND PRIX

1. **Stirling Moss (Vanwall)** 2h 9m, 15.1s
(116.23 m.p.h.)
2. **Mike Hawthorn (Ferrari)** 2h 10m 31.8s
3. **Phil Hill (Ferrari)** 2h 10m 40.6s
4. **Joakim Bonnier (B.R.M.)**
5. **Harry Schell (B.R.M.)**
Fastest Lap: Moss, 2m 22.5s (118.7 m.p.h.)

England's Billy Wright wins his 100th cap

*Footballer Billy Wright was the epitome of English manliness. In 1959 he became the first player in the world to make one hundred full international appearances, playing at Wembley against Scotland, who were beaten 1-0. The Sunday before the match an interview by **John Gale** appeared in The Observer*

MR BILLY WRIGHT, who – barring accidents – will get his hundredth international cap next Saturday when he captains England against Scotland at Wembley, had an afternoon off last week in his top floor flat in a red-brick house in Wolverhampton within sight of the tall pylons of the Molineux floodlights.

He was wearing a fawn sweater and relaxed clothes, but admitted, as he sat in a purple armchair opposite the television set, that life had been hectic lately, mainly because of the Press. Yet he was calm, helpful and straightforward. He produced a scrapbook, showed his records (from opera to Sophie Tucker, with a good deal of Mantovani in between), and talked about his rug-making. 'I go so mad at it, I want to see the finished product.' His present task is a cream rug with a large rose pattern.

His fair hair was receding a little; few men can have more smile-lines round the eyes.

He said it was quite true his football career nearly ended almost before it had begun: Major Buckley, manager of Wolverhampton Wanderers when Billy joined as a boy in 1938, told him shortly afterwards that he was too small for a footballer, and advised him to try something else. But at the last moment Buckley relented and kept him on.

In his early days with Wolves, Billy played in every position except goal. Finally he settled down at left-half – although his first appearance for England was at right-half, in January 1946, against Belgium. Since then, he's missed only three internationals for England: an astounding record, unlikely to be equalled. The most remarkable thing about his play has been his consistency.

He was first chosen to captain England in October, 1948, against Ireland, and heard about it by chance on a bus when he was coming home after playing for England against Denmark. Playing for England and, particularly, captaining England, he regards as a great honour: 'honour' is a word he uses often, and with great sincerity.

Wright is well known for saying very little to his team on the field.

'I love to be in the game and doing a lot of work,' he explains. 'I do shout occasionally when it's needed. But I'd rather do my work. If they see the captain bawling all the while and not doing anything to help the team, they've got good cause to grieve.' This has always been Wright's philosophy.

But reliability and a good example have not been his only qualities as captain. He has a great football sense and the ability to 'read the game.' His mental awareness seldom allows him to be deceived by new tactics – particulaly – by Continental sides.

The most troublesome centre-forward he's played against in England is Nat Lofthouse: 'We've had some tussles. Then, going abroad, there's big John Charles. And deep-lying centre-forwards, Di Stefano of Real Madrid, and Kopa of Real Madrid and France. Wonderful ball players.'

He thinks the Hungarian side of 1954, which beat England so thoroughly at Wembley, were the best team he ever played against; they were probably the best team ever.

He will never forget the Hungarians against Uruguay in the semi-final of the World Cup in Switzerland in 1954. 'It was played in pouring rain before 63,000 people, and you got wonderful football the whole time.'

Perhaps his most exciting moment was when England beat Austria, then the leading Continental team, 3-2 in Vienna in 1952. Lofthouse scored the winning goal just before the end, and British soldiers ran on to the field and carried off the England players. Other memorable moments were when Wolves beat Leicester City to win the Cup at Wembley in 1949, and when they beat Honved and Spartak under the floodlights at Molineux. There was also last year's lunch at Buckingham Palace. 'It was marvellous,' said Wright. 'A wonderful lunch. I enjoyed it remarkably well.'

Bad moments? 'I think the worst was when the United States beat us in the World Cup in Brazil in 1950. We had all the play but couldn't take our chances. When we came home people said: "How did the United States beat you? They don't play soccer, do they?" It took some living down.'

Last year Wright married Joy, one of the Beverley Sisters. Their baby is due on the same day as his hundredth cap. 'I feel so well towards Joy,' he says. 'She's done so much in coming into my life. We've had a wonderful year. I want to be a good husband – and now a good father.'

Billy Wright is 35. How long can he continue playing in the exacting position of centre-half? He says he enjoys it as much as ever at present – including the training. He'll stop as soon as it gets hard or his play deteriorates. Perhaps in two or three years.

And then? Well, it will be something to do with soccer, which has been his life and has given him his chances – unlike some players, he has never had a trade or business to fall back on. 'I'd like to keep my knowledge in the game.'

Billy Wright, busy rug maker and captain of England, leads the national team out against Scotland for his 100th international cap

1960
21 July

Francis Chichester sets a new record across the Atlantic

*Sir Francis Chichester was a record breaker without equal. He started in the 1930s with solo flights. Now, after fighting cancer, he won the first Plymouth to America single-handed yacht race in Gipsy Moth III. **Keith Morfett** reported for the Daily Mail on the final moments of what was just the forerunner of more feats*

CHEERY, 59 YEAR OLD FRANCIS CHICHESTER, wearing a Sherlock Holmes hat, sailed triumphantly into New York tonight – an easy winner of the first Plymouth to America single-handed yacht race.

He sailed past the Ambrose Light finishing post to be joined in a victory procession by fishing smacks and harbour tugs greeting him into New York. And for the last dozen miles up to the Ambrose his wife, Sheila, was alongside, sitting proudly on the bridge of a fishing smack, waving madly all the way.

Mrs Chichester, in a scarlet bandana hat made specially for her in London just for this occasion, also clutched a leather case containing the victory champagne she was ready to open as soon as her husband's Bermudan yawl, Gipsy Moth III, hove-to. She called to her husband across the 20ft or so of water separating the stern of the Gipsy Moth from the fishing smack: 'Wonderful to see you again, darling.'

Chichester put weatherbeaten hands to his mouth to yell back: 'Wonderful to see you too: it's been quite a trip.'

The Gipsy Moth had been reported 30 miles off the Ambrose Lightship early today at the end of the 3,000 mile voyage. But with barely a hint of a breeze it was hard work covering those last 30 miles. A few hours before she reached Ambrose I found the Gipsy Moth by flying out into the North Atlantic in a seaplane.

As we flew low across her masthead Chichester put his thumbs up in the air, then started waving and shouting. Then he went back to work, pulling down his big Genoa sail

In 1967, Francis Chichester, in a scene evocative of the earlier Elizabeth's reign, was knighted by Her Majesty

to take advantage with his mainsail of whatever wind there was to help him to the winning post. A little later, with 25 miles to go, a breeze came up to help him home – and the black-hulled yawl with the figure one encircled in white on her bows started moving through the swell at a spanking pace.

Now a launch from New York Harbour took up the lead, and fishing smacks closed in from all sides to cheer Chichester home. A great roar from fishermen, tugsmen, and people in tiny motor-boats went up as Gipsy Moth III passed the Ambrose and swung shorewards for the run towards the Manhattan skyline.

The other competitors in the race, 'Blondie' Hasler, of Southampton in Jester; Dr. David Lewis of London, in Cardinal Vertue; Jean Lacombe of France, in Cap Horn and Valentine Howells of South Wales in Eira were all believed to be much farther out, strung across the Atlantic. Mr. Hasler was last heard from five days ago, when he was 600 miles east of New York. The boats left Plymouth on June 11.

In London, Miss Ann Todd the actress, who met Mr. Chichester in a nursing home near Guildford two years ago when he was recovering from a serious illness, sent a telegram of congratulations. 'He has incredible courage, When I first met him he was terribly ill. But all he could talk about was his plan to cross the Atlantic alone in a yacht.'

1961

6 May

Tottenham Hotspur and Danny achieve an historic double

*The League Championship and the FA Cup in the same year became an impossible dream in the 19th century. Then Spurs did it, beating Leicester City 2-0 in the Cup Final, because the belief of their captain, Danny Blanchflower, imbued the team. This was how Danny recounted the day, post-match, to **Bob Ferrier** in The Observer*

I HEARD A DOOR SLAM. I looked at my watch; it was 8.15. I had slept well.

I seemed to hear noises, a baby crying, noises from the crevices of the hotel, but distant, as though deep into a tunnel. I was warm and comfortable and dozed off.

I heard the voice of Ron Henry, and he seemed bright and cheerful. The telephone rang, and the man said: 'It's nine o'clock, sir.' I said: 'Congratulations,' and got up. A bunch of Indians from Burnley cornered me in the lounge and said that after Spurs' semi-final win the Cup was as good as ours.

Coming up the Stadium you hear a trumpet voice demanding: 'Repent in the Lord.' Dixieland jazz from the kerbstones, strange sights and sounds. This is all part of the wonder of football. The Cup Final seems like a fair, or a bazaar or something. There were telegrams on the dressing-room table, the business of preparation, the mixture of noises, some of them distant, some just above our heads. But you cannot reach out and grab tension before it comes to you. Even at Wembley it seemed solidly absent.

I injured an ankle a couple of weeks ago. There was no pain but oddly I was aware of it. I wondered if it might go at some point in the match and if so when. It took us a long time to get a fine touch on the ball. Wembley is a difficult field. The texture of the grass slows everything, and when you have played a full season with a lively, alert rhythm, as we have, you have to adjust.

I think both teams may have been perplexed by this and concentrated hard on it. The ball

Danny Blanchflower (left) instilled the Tottenham Hotspur team (above) with the belief they could win the double – and they did

comes through slowly. You must learn to wait for it. And you are apt to over-compensate by moving the ball on. After four or five matches here I still found it difficult.

I felt we never really had control of the game. But then neither did Leicester. There was never a time when I thought we would lose even if we lost a goal, but in the second half there was a time when I thought we would have to play an extra half hour. I pondered whether to conserve myself or make one big effort then. I kept saying things to the others but nobody paid much attention.

When our first goal came the team recovered faith in itself and began to play with something of its true style and tempo. Before it happened I think we were wondering where style and tempo had gone. I just played the match. The crowd was remote, not intimate as it is at Tottenham. I was caught up in the mechanics of the play and nothing else.

Leicester did not make too many demands on themselves. They played simply as they always do, but they, too, seemed worried by the surface and perhaps by our presence. It's a funny thing, we never have a good game with Leicester. It's as though the chemistry of the teams doesn't mix.

When it ended I didn't seem to have any thoughts apart from having to climb the stairs and take the Cup. For so many people that seemed the point. And when we ran round the field with it, I recognised this tour of honour as part of the day. I didn't like it. I didn't dislike it. I just did it. The whole point to me wasn't in winning the double. It was in believing that we could win the double.

1963
18 June

Gaseous Cassius is sent to the canvas by 'Enery's 'ammer

Britain could hardly have been taken with more surprise, and likewise Cassius Clay, later Muhammad Ali, who was put down by Henry Cooper with a punch that left residues of controversy to be chewed over ever after. In Sports Illustrated **Huston Horn** *described all the fun in an inimitable way*

IN ENGLAND LAST WEEK declamatory verse and vitriol were all the rage. Tory Nigel Birch told the House of Commons that Harold Macmillan, the Profumo-plagued Prime Minister, should resign, and quoted Browning's The Lost Leader ('Let him never come back to us!') in support. Elsewhere in London, boxer Cassius Clay, quoting himself, said, 'It ain't no jive/Henry Cooper will go in five!' And at the Fellowship Inn in Bellingham, in southeast London, the menfolk munched pork pies and lifted their nightly pints of luke-warm bitter in salute to the doggerel posted over the bar by one of the regulars. It made the point that Humble Henry would soundly thrash Gaseous Cassius 'and once again prove that very old adage:/Action speaks louder than strong verbal cabbage!' At the end of the week Macmillan and Clay were still in command of things and the 'Ode to our 'Enery' had been quietly unpinned at the pub. It was about all the men of Bellingham could do for their friend after his brave and ghastly fight. Just as Clay had promised, Cooper went in five.

Not that the outcome of the fight caused much surprise. Least surprised of all, it seemed, was Henry Cooper, who said, when the brutal business was done, "E said 'e would, and 'e did it, and that's 'ow it goes. It can't be 'elped.' It was a typical remark for the stolid

ex-plasterer with battered good looks who faces life with the patient, unrewarded optimism of an English sundial.

Since the last week of May, Cassius had been casting his spell of ballyhoo and, though weary of training, weary of hearing himself talk, he kept at it until the first-round bell rang in Wembley Stadium.

The day of the fight dawned in the best tradition of English summer mornings: cold and rainy. But despite the rain almost 2,000 people queued up that morning to see the weigh-in at the Palladium Theatre. In his dressing room, borrowed from Susan Maughan, a currently popular English singer, Cassius tried on the ankle-length red-and-white satin robe he had had tailored in London for £25. Then, on the sudden inspiration of his attorney, Louisville's Gordon Davidson, Clay sent out to a costumers for a crown to wear into the ring that night. Strutting onto the Palladium stage, Clay held his left hand aloft, his fingers spread in an insolent 'five', and struck Charles Atlas poses while the crowd fairly bounced with hoarse and happy jeers and boos.

Later, preceded by music by the band of the Coldstream Guards and the grand, tumultuous, shouting and shoving entrance of Elizabeth Taylor in a turquoise ensemble, accompanied by Richard Burton in a rosy flush, Cassius Clay made his 9:15 entrance in the damp and lingering twilight. In the best tradition of English evenings, it was cold and rainy. Half a dozen red-tunicked gentlemen in the ring heralded his approach with a fanfare played on three-foot, flag-draped trumpets, and a spotlight glinted off his purple-and-gold crown. While hoots of derision followed his steps a seething BBC announcer snapped that Clay was 'ridiculous' and he 'cheapened the fight game.' But Cassius was smiling. The noise he heard was in direct proportion to the number of tickets sold (35,000) and his cut of the gate (about $60,000).

In the fourth round Cooper, to his eternal glory, found an opening with his left and Clay went down

Characteristically a slow starter with a stand-up old-lithograph style, Henry Cooper confounded Clay by opening the fight fast and furiously. 'I meant to show the writer critics I knew a trick or two,' he said later. Unprepared for Cooper's aggressive rush, Clay reacted by moving away, the worst possible move for a man forced to contend with Cooper's dangerous left hook. Consequently, he was repeatedly hit by Cooper's left and repeatedly driven into the ropes. Something Clay was expecting was Cooper's habit of 'throwing sucker shots' – hitting during the breaks. Cooper later denied he committed such a sin, but Clay got a bloody nose coming out of one unclean clinch. It was the first of his career, and he appealed furiously to the referee 'for justice.' He might better have spent the time meeting Cooper halfway, but he did not and the round went rightfully to Cooper. Dreams of glory went rushing to the heads of onlookers on this 148th anniversary of the Battle of Waterloo.

Back in his corner Clay was scolded by his trainer for moving too much and was inflamed by the blood dripping from his nose. He started the second round as enthusiastically as Cooper had started the first. His jabs were directly on target, his combinations precise. He was carrying the fight to Cooper when, toward the end of the round, blood began to flow from a cut beside Cooper's left eye. For Cooper, notoriously thin-skinned, a cut is the same as a snag in a silk stocking: the unravelling takes care of itself. It is too bad it had to happen, because Clay's eventual win – which he would have had anyhow – was marred.

Corner men are like cosmeticians: their handiwork is often unavailing in the hot light of reality. Thus Cooper came into the third round looking, if not feeling, as good as new. But in moments the cut and another had been opened by Clay, and Cooper said that from then on his vision was a blur through a red screen. Cooper's troubles, however, went deeper than those cuts. Clay had figured out his style and was so confident of beating Cooper that he actually stopped throwing punches. Instead, in a show of bad taste and worse sportsmanship, Clay warded off

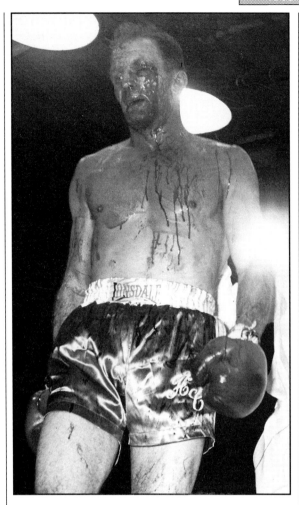

The fifth round lasted 1 minute 15 seconds, a gruesome minute too long for Cooper, before the referee stepped in

kept his hands up in the fourth but continued to prance, and further asserted himself by jabbing casually and by leading with his right hand, a risky and unorthodox procedure. To Cooper's everlasting glory, he eventually found the opening he was looking for and with a lunging, rising left hook tagged Clay's contemptible cheek so proper that Cassius went tumbling into the ropes in a beautiful heap.

'The Kentucky Rooster laid an egg,' crowed the Evening Standard next day, but Clay's brains were not so scrambled that he could not get up. At the count of three or four (the sound of the bell ending the round was lost in the screams of the crowd) he was on his feet, a trifle shaky and very lucky. 'You O.K.?' asked Dundee, pulling him onto his stool. 'Yeah,' said Cassius in one of his classiest lines yet, 'but Cooper's getting tired.'

The fifth round – which lasted one minute and 15 seconds – lasted one gruesome minute too long. Clay flung himself on Cooper at the bell, staggered him with his first punch and thereafter simply overran the man. Cooper's chest became a smear of crimson, his face was sickening to behold as the cuts around his eye discharged blood in sobbing, pulsing spurts. Cooper was fending, not fighting, and the referee, with the crowd (including Liz Taylor) pleading for him to hurry, stepped up to Cooper and said, 'The fight's over, chum.' With the simple eloquence of a very nice, very courageous and very resigned man, Henry Cooper shrugged his shoulders. 'But we didn't do so bad for a bum and a cripple, did we?' he said as he was helped from the ring.

Clay, for his part, showed a rare streak of dignity by refusing to put on the make-believe crown that had rested on a white hotel pillow during the fight. The mob booed him as he went to his dressing room, but when he got there he told the press he had woefully underestimated Cooper, had never fought a better man, had never been hit harder and had been hurt – all of which was polite and true. His showing off in the third and fourth rounds, he said, was not to carry Cooper into the predicted fifth round but to disguise the fact that he was in trouble – which was polite but untrue.

Cooper's lefts and rights by extending his gloves at arm's length, popped his gloves together in Cooper's face, jutted out his chin, daring and defying Cooper to hit it, made foolish faces and literally danced in the ring, his long arms jouncing down by his thighs. 'Contemptible cheek,' one ringsider called it, but good old Henry Cooper said he had not minded. 'I told myself if he keeps this up I'll find an opening and tag him proper.'

Bill Faversham minded and between rounds roared to Angelo Dundee, Clay's trainer, to stop the nonsense. Apparently chastened, Clay

1964
1 February

Nash and Dixon pinch two-man bob by a fraction

When Tony Nash and Robin Dixon won Britain's third medal in the history of the Winter Olympics, national elation knew no bounds. In The Observer **Christopher Brasher** *and* **John Crammond** *took the reader through the techniques behind the victory, including the saucepan scourers on Dixon's boots*

Tony Nash (left) and Robin Dixon, Olympic gold medallists in the flicker of an eye

TONY NASH AND ROBIN DIXON won an Olympic gold medal here by 12-hundredths of a second – the time it takes to snap your fingers – and they won it magnificently. Those are the bare facts: the detail is unfamiliar to even a close follower of sport.

The event is the two-man bobsleigh in which two men sit on a sophisticated metal toboggan and hurl themselves down a narrow ice gulley at an average speed of 52 m.p.h. The front man steers the bob by pulling on two ropes which alter the angle of the front runners, and with this apparently crude, but, in practice, exact, form of control they hurtle down an ice track that is only six feet wide.   On the last run they were to go down third, the Italian No.2 team eighth and the Italian No.1 team, with Eugenio Monti, eight times world champion, in charge, seventeenth.

The start consists of five yards of flat ice. Both men are outside their bob, rocking it gently back and forth to work up a rhythm. And then they heave, trying to throw nearly half a ton of metal over the crest and on to the plunging track. First into his seat is the steersman, reaching for his ropes. The second man still pushes – on ice. To get a good grip, Robin Dixon uses a light pair of soccer boots over which he slides a housewife's saucepan scourer. All was well with Nash until a ferocious bank called the Hexen-kessel, the witch's cauldron, and then Nash tried to hold the bob too high. Time 1min 5.88sec, their slowest run.

The Italians had only to keep their heads to win. Nash and Dixon, disconsolate, retired to a cafe. Fifteen minutes later the Italian second team broke under the pressure. Their time: 1min 6.05sec. Nash and Dixon were in the lead again by twelve-hundredths of a second. But still there was the world champion, Eugenio Monti, to come. Any time under 1min 5.65sec would be enough to win.

Nash and Dixon were routed out of the cafe and as Monti started his run they sat on a bob and waited for victory or defeat. Then came the announcement in German, 'Monti's time one minute zero six point...' The rest was drowned in a roar as Nash and Dixon disappeared beneath a horde of British competitors.

The day the legend of Arkle was born

*Etched firmly in the memory of all followers of jump racing is the day Arkle first floored the mighty Mill House, in the 1964 Gold Cup. A new and glorious chapter in racing history was ushered in, and nobody painted a more moving picture of the occasion than **John Oaksey** writing in Horse and Hound*

Arkle claimed jumping's throne in a famous Gold Cup battle with Mill House

IN MORE WAYS THAN ONE the 1964 Cheltenham Gold Cup defied belief. It was, for a start, almost unbelievable that the race should live up in full to such tremendous advance publicity – and to most of us in England it was quite unbelievable that, barring accidents, Mill House should be beaten by as much as five lengths. Yet both these wonders came to pass and, by achieving them, the Duchess of Westminster's Arkle proved himself beyond question the greatest steeplechaser seen in Europe since Prince Regent.

With so much at stake, so much could have gone wrong – a single slip, a fall, a tiny error of judgement. Any of these might have left a nagging doubt in the mind – but none of them transpired. There can never have been a race more perfect in every way – or a triumph more complete.

One day, of course, perhaps with the help of a pacemaker, Mill House may get his revenge. The man who denies that possibility is a fool. But last Saturday afternoon there was no doubt. England's champion was beaten fair and square and it is the measure of Mill House's greatness in defeat that, to overcome him, Arkle had to produce a display of flawless majesty, speed and power – and a record time to boot.

Everything conspired, it seemed, to set the scene ideally for an historic sporting occasion. The first three races on Saturday were run in blood-curdling cold and intermittent showers of snow. But the last of these had cleared as the rugs came off and, as the four horses in the Gold Cup field cantered past the stands Cheltenham was bathed in hard, clear sunlight.

Trotting calmly back towards the start, Mill House was a sight I shall never forget. So relaxed that Willie Robinson needed but one hand on the reins, he suddenly broke, for a few strides passing the first fence, into an extravagant, extended gait that would have done the High School in Vienna proud. Behind him Arkle, eager to be off, twisted his head impatiently against the bit.

If Pas Seul and King's Nephew knew they were outclassed, it did not show and, as all four turned to inspect the first fence, the atmosphere was electric with a brand of suspense and fascination I never felt before on any British racecourse.

Both champion and challenger, needless to say, looked supremely hard and fit. Save perhaps in height, Mill House is just a size bigger all round, but Arkle, though leaner behind the saddle, has almost equal depth and strength in front.

The tactics, like everything else, lived up to expectations. Mill House swept over the first two fences four lengths clear and although, to begin with, Arkle pulled hard for his head, Pat Taafe, without apparent difficulty, settled him down to dispute second place with Pas Seul. Here – and I think throughout – King's Nephew brought up the rear.

First time round the order never changed, but now, looking back, you can see that in one respect the writing was already on the wall. For although, in the Hennessy Gold Cup, it had been Mill House's tremendous jumping that gained the day, this time it was he who fiddled the occasional fence – while if Arkle made a mistake I personally never saw it.

At the open ditch in front of us, the favourite took off far too close for comfort – but sailed on undisturbed and, as Willie Robinson let out a reef going down the hill, appreciably increased his lead.

Here, against any normal rivals, the race would have been over. Soon after the water Pas Seul and King's Nephew were already feeling the strain, but although Pat Taafe had not yet noticeably moved a muscle, Arkle never let the gap get dangerously wide.

Instead he closed in without effort, and for the first time – even for Mill House's most convinced adherents – the awful spectre of defeat was plain to see.

Turning downhill towards the third from home, the favourite, as we know now – and as poor Willie Robinson must have suspected then – had his last chance to poach an advantage that might neutralise his rival's fearsome final speed.

On the verge of despair, one felt – like a baited bear struggling to loose the bulldog's hold – he threw an enormous leap, and Arkle, rising barely a length behind, matched it with cruel, almost careless ease.

Until the second last, which Arkle jumped the better, neither horse had been asked for his ultimate effort. But ten strides after it, for perhaps the first time in his life, Mill House felt the whip, gave it all he had – and found it nothing like enough.

For now it came in all its glory – that blistering, explosive burst of speed in which, all along, we had known that Arkle's only hope of victory must lie.

Now, well before the last, it was no longer hope but certainty. Mill House never gave up, never even faltered, but, in those few decisive yards, he, of all horses, was made to look like just another beaten 'chaser.

And as Arkle stormed victorious up the hill, though every throat was sore with cheering, in many – mine for one – there rose a choking lump of sadness, too.

The scene that followed – with half Ireland surging off the stands to welcome back their hero – would make most Epsom Derby days look like a Salvation Army meeting. Arkle, patted from head to tail on every side, took it all just as he had the race, with a champion's calm assurance. He did not say, 'I am the greatest,' but it was said for him many times – and it was true.

Now, with all the tumult and shouting only a memory, it is time to attempt some measurement of Arkle's achievement. On time alone, there is no doubt that this was an outstanding Gold Cup, for Arkle won in four seconds less than Saffron Tartan three years ago over the same course on even faster going. This, I think, disposes at once of the theory that Willie Robinson should – or could – have set a more testing pace on Mill House. Neither Fulke Walwyn nor anyone else able to judge gives this as an excuse for the favourite's defeat.

To my mind, Mill House was beaten largely because he hardly ever succeeded in outjumping his rival. If anything it was the other way round, for Arkle, with the incentive of another horse to lead him almost throughout, never lost an appreciable amount of ground in the air and never made a single serious mistake.

Ann creates her own fairy-tale victory in the 800 metres

*In the 1964 Tokyo Olympics Ann Packer was a leading contender for the 400-metres title. She was narrowly beaten in the final but then went on to contest the 800 metres. The final of this event produced an unexpected result, reported on by **John Rodda** in The Guardian*

EVERY BRITON in the National Stadium here this afternoon watched in fascinated disbelief as the slim form of Miss A. E. Packer took the swift strides to an Olympic gold medal in the 800 metres in the world-record time of 2 mins 1.1 secs. It was the most excitingly startling result of these Games and a hard search through Olympic history would be needed to find one more surprising.

Had Miss Packer found fairies at the bottom of her garden she could have looked no more startled than when she pressed the medal to her cheek after winning a race in which, at one point, she did not want to take part. The coaching that D. C. V. Watts planned for her during the past two years was devised to win the gold medal in the 400 metres. Racing over two laps was an afterthought, a part of that training programme. On a wet May night at Leyton this year, she ran her first 800 metres: today's golden triumph was the seventh – three of them in Tokyo. Only when she learned that the longer race would be after the main event did she get down to the task of achieving the qualifying standard, in September.

Three hard races, and the acute disappointment when she finished runner-up in the 400 metres, left her mentally exhausted. She just got into a semi-final and looked a little happier

The magic of a surprise victory casts a smile on the face of Ann Packer as she leaves her rivals standing in the 800 metres final in Tokyo

800 METRES FINAL

1. Ann Packer (GB).............................2:01.1
2. Maryvonne Dupureur (France)......2:01.9
3. Marise Chamberlain (NZ).............2:02.8

stepping, with hair flopping, led the field at a momentum designed to scatter the weak. A gasp went up when the 400 metres time was announced as 58.6 secs. Miss Packer was in the middle of the string, and Miss Smith, whose moment this should have been, already was beginning to tail off. In the back straight the pace eased, the bodies closed up, and most eyes were on the easy flowing movement of Miss Dupureur, and the tall girl in black, Miss Chamberlain of New Zealand.

But then, at the crown of the bend, the pattern of the strides was broken: Miss Packer had suddenly dislodged herself from the inside position and was moving faster than everyone else. She strode past Miss Chamberlain, Miss Gleichfield, Miss Szabo. Still she was moving faster than the rest, and, with half the straight still left, she glided past the French girl. With every stride she moved farther away, every stride looked so much easier than the one before and she swept through the tape.

The athletic world will dissect this performance for many years, and two theories that will be propounded are that, of all the competitors, Miss Packer was the most relaxed, and that many athletes, particularly some in Britain, do not compete in their proper events. Few get Miss Packer's opportunity to experiment.

Miss Packer began running over 200 metres, but was not fast enough: she moved up to 400 metres, and was fast enough bar one.

Today she displayed both stamina and sprinting power to which the rest had to bow. It will remain a point of conjecture, but even Miss Sin Kim Dan of North Korea would have been pressed to cope with the finishing power that the British girl revealed in the final straight.

the next day when recording 2 mins 6 secs. But by Monday morning she wanted to shut athletics out of her life and had decided to scratch from the final. Only at five past three, after 'Rob', her fiancé, had failed to win the men's 400 metres, did she decide she had to run.

In the final, Miss Szabo, of Hungary, high

Jim Clark bestrides the Indianapolis 500 in a Lotus

*It was the reward for crusading endeavour. Colin Chapman, the creative, driving boss behind Lotus, and Jim Clark, the cool Scottish driver, chased the Indy prize with unrelenting zeal until they won in what was a 'most lopsided victory' the description of **Roger Huntingdon** in his authoritative account for The Autocar*

JIM CLARK IN HIS TINY LOTUS-FORD walked away with the Indianapolis 500-mile race on 31 May – at an average speed of 150.69 m.p.h., over 3 m.p.h. faster than last year's winning speed. His winning margin over second place Parnelli Jones of nearly two minutes was the most lopsided victory at Indy in recent years. Clark's win was clear, quick and decisive. Clark and his boss Colin Chapman have beaten the Americans at their own game in three short years!

Actually, Clark led the race for 190 of the total 200 laps, and picked up over $28,000 just in lap prize money! He out-accelerated pole man A.J. Foyt on the flying start, to lead him into the first turn, and through the first lap. Foyt squeezed by to lead the 2nd lap; but then Clark passed him again on the 3rd – and was not headed again until he made his first pit stop. Foyt held second through those early laps in a reworked '64 Lotus-Ford; Dan Gurney ran third in a '65 Lotus, Parnelli Jones fourth in another reworked '64 Lotus, and rookie Mario Andretti came up into fifth with a new rear-engine Brawner-Ford. Clark was lapping in the 157 m.p.h. bracket, and pulled out a 10-second lead over Foyt by the 40th lap.

Colin Chapman's brilliant race strategy became obvious quickly. He divided the race into three equal segments of 67 laps each, because of the new rule requiring two mandatory pit stops and maximum fuel tank capacity of 75 U.S. gallons (actually reduced to about 67 usable gallons by the internal baffling). But Chapman was one of the very few who took advantage of the new rule requiring gravity fuel feed from the pit refuelling tanks – which were set up in such a way that it required an average of about 20sec to load 25 gallons of fuel. While most of the rest of the boys used methanol fuel and loaded 40 to 60 gallons on three stops, Chapman converted to gasoline-base fuel, and loaded only around 30 gallons on two stops. The 10 per cent loss in power with gasoline fuel cut his lap speed potential by 3 or 4 m.p.h.; but he saved a lot of time – not only the time of one complete pit stop, but

Jim Clark (left) led the Indianapolis 500 for 190 of the total 200 laps, and crossed the finish line (above) giving the thumbs up. He and Colin Chapman had pulled off an incredible coup

his time in the pits for his two stops averaged only 24sec.

The alky-burners were spending twice that much time loading fuel, plus the extra stop. And they couldn't make up the difference in higher lap speed. Clark could stay with anybody on the track. Several times coming off corners he out-accelerated Foyt who was said to be running a methanol-toluene blend. And nobody in the race approached the fantastic qualifying lap speeds of 160-161 m.p.h. (which were mostly done with 10-20 per cent nitromethane in methanol!).

So the race unfolded like clockwork. At the half-way point it was Clark, Foyt, Jones, Andretti and Bud Tingelstad in the first five places, the latter driving a new Lola-Ford. The average speed at this point was 152.19 m.p.h., with only six minutes at low speed under the caution flag. Clark had a lead of 1.06sec over Foyt at this time, and was lapping easily at 155 m.p.h.

Foyt dropped out on the 116th lap with a broken transmission, and Tingelstad spun out and hit the wall on the 119th. This mishap brought out the yellow flag for seven minutes – and brought Andretti up into third place, Mickey Rupp to fourth (in a rear-engine Offy), and Don Branson to fifth in a rear-engine Watson-Ford. Everybody was surprised when Clark didn't take advantage of the slow-speed period to come in for fuel. But apparently the Lotus team had their strategy planned so precisely that there was little flexibility in the picture. As it was they pitted for the second time on the 136th lap, with the field running at race speeds. But by now they had such a fat lead over second-place Jones (well over one minute) that they made their second stop without losing their lead – a very rare occurrence at Indy. And then after Jones made his third stop on the 162nd lap the lead went up well over a minute again. It was just about all over bar the shouting.

The European lightweight rear-engine car has definitely taken over the Indy scene, with the Ford d.o.h.c. V8 engine for power. I see nothing on the horizon to change that picture. Certainly our American rear-engine cars will be more competitive next year, as we learn more and more from people like Colin Chapman. But Chapman will probably be back, too!

England beat Germany 4-2 to win the World Cup

The original masters did it! England, the fathers of football, missionaries of the game, played host to the World Cup and won it. The ebb and flow of an emotional final, the tumultuous reception and sheer joy that greeted the conclusion, was captured by **Alan Hoby** *in The Sunday Express*

AROUND 5.15 P.M. THE MOST TRIUMPHANT and tumultuous din I have ever heard rose from the stands and terraces of Wembley Stadium. From every side of what has been described as 'this historic cathedral of football' a blaze of Union Jacks waved as people, unashamedly gripped by emotion and patriotism, danced, wept, and hugged each other.

For as the whistle of Swiss referee Gottfried Dienst sounded the end of this truly manly and magnificent battle, it meant that at last West Germany had conceded defeat. England had won... England, who gave soccer to the rest of the earth, were Football Champions of the World. Never in its long history of sporting spectaculars had Wembley witnessed such scenes or such action on this glorious stretch of turf. For this was the match to end all

matches. This was a titanic struggle which had everything, played for long stretches against a Wagnerian backdrop of dark clouds. For two hours the 93,000 spectators, who had paid a record-breaking £200,000, plus the invisible audience of 400,000,000 television viewers throughout the world, had stood on a tightrope of drama and almost unbearable excitement.

They had seen three dynamic goals by West Ham's Geoffrey Hurst. They had seen Alan Ball, that little, much-criticised red-haired bundle of dynamite, emerge as man of the match. They had seen Bobby Moore never more majestic and assured in a defence which, understandably in the frying tension, had faltered at odd moments. But, above all, what they will tell their grandchildren in the years to come is that it was English nerve and English heart and English stamina which finally overcame the tenacious resistance of Uwe Seeler and his white-shirted men.

They will, in particular, relate that their hearts thudded and raced as, with England leading 2-1, Germany equalised 15 seconds from the end of ordinary time. With only these fractions of moments separating England from winning the World Cup, referee Dienst awarded what I thought was a completely unwarranted free kick against England's noble centre half Jackie Charlton, when he climbed up to head the ball away.

The Swiss referee penalised Charlton for going up over the back of Germany's No. 1 star, Siegfried Held which in German means 'hero'. But I was convinced that Held, a rangy, fluid, fast-dribbling forward, had 'made a back' for Charlton. However, in the resultant blur of action, Emmerich drove a blasting free kick towards the English goal. The ball vanished into a melee of white and red shirts – England were playing in red – and there was the blond Helmut Haller guiding the ball to the right with his hand where, after agonising moments, Germany's stern Wolfgang Weber lashed it into goal.

This was a solar-plexus blow for England with the World Cup apparently in their grasp. As the referee's whistle shrilled the end of 90

Bobby Moore, captain of England, majestic and assured in defence, savours the moment of victory, the Jules Rimet trophy secure in his hand

minutes players collapsed on the grass. For the pace had been electric and the football superb. Ray Wilson had to receive attention on the touch line for cramp, and several of the German players were rubbing their legs.

Now we were into extra time and the tension was almost unendurable. With legs weighted down like lead and breath rasping in the lungs, the tempo had inevitably dropped. Schnellinger, Germany's polished left back from Milan, who had set out to mark Alan Ball but in the end had found himself outspeeded, and out-smarted, came to a halt with cram. Goalkeeper Hanz Tilkowski was limping badly as he turned Bobby Charlton's waspish shot from brother Jackie's downward header on to the post. Then, with Ball leading the charge of the red shirts, flicking and darting into every available open space like a scarlet firefly,

England scored the golden goal which set them on the last short haul to the tip of this football Everest.

With 10 minutes of the extra time showing on our stopwatches, Ball swooped on Nobby Stiles's pass and swung it over. Amid a hulla-baloo of sound, Hurst, that indomitable and heroic figure, twisted on to it and crashed it with his right foot against the underside of the crossbar. There was an awful moment of eternity as the ball ricocheted down and from where I sat hit the turf just inside the white line. But many foreign observers sitting in a line with the German goal thought that the ball

The winning moment in the World Cup and, at last, Alf Ramsey, England's manager, allows himself to smile as he rises to acclaim his team

had not crossed the line. So did the entire German team.

As the goal roar resounded through the stadium the referee ran to the Russian linesman, Tofit Bakhramov. There was another paralysing passage of seconds while the white-haired Russian nodded his head vigorously as referee Dienst interrogated him in a short but decisive dialogue which confirmed that England had scored.

A controversial goal maybe.... A goal which had its doubters, true... But fair compensation, I thought, for the decision 15 seconds from time which had earlier robbed England of victory. In any case England, who created more chances than West Germany, clinched this marvellous match when, in the very last kick, Hurst, pounding on to a long ball, dredged the last shreds of energy from his aching legs, shrugged off the challenge of a desperate German defender and lashed the ball with his left foot heroically into the net (4-2).

England were home, and in the next few seconds the whole arena erupted in joy and gratitude. Below me as the England team ran off, manager Alf Ramsey at last stepped forward into the spotlight he so detests to congratulate each of his Englishmen – the team he has always believed in despite the critics.

It was a heartbreaking moment for left-back Ray Wilson when he made his first mistake of the entire World Cup series in the 12th minute. Held, that tenacious German, out on his favourite left side of the field, had crossed from a corner when Wilson, amid a collective gulp of horror, headed straight to Haller on the right. The quick-thinking German forward shot and the ball seemed to skid past Jackie Charlton into the net and past the best goalkeeper in the 1966 World Cup, Gordon Banks, who was probably unsighted. This was a body blow and the black, orange, and gold banners of West Germany were brandished from side to side of the stadium.

But five minutes later Germany's Wolfgang Overath fouled Moore, and while the referee was still lecturing the German, the English captain pinpointed the most elegant of free kicks into the heart of the German defence. Distracted for a moment, not one of the German 'wall,' not even the relentless sweeper Willi Schultz or their strong-tackling Wolfgang Weber, spotted Hurst starting his run from the angle of the box. It was a brilliant piece of intuitive thinking – first-class anticipation. For before a single German could explode into action Hurst completed his great run with a soaring header which billowed the back of the net with goalkeeper Tilkowski utterly helpless (1-1).

The tactical pattern of play flowed and eddied, with ironically the two marksmen, fluent Bobby Charlton and West Germany's stylish Franz Beckenbauer often cancelling each other out. Even so, as the thunderclouds gathered, our team seemed to run down, both in energy and enterprise. Indeed, in the 36th minute a whole army of butterflies must have swirled in the stomachs of every Englishman as Gordon Banks made an absolutely out-of-this-world save from a scorching Overath drive from inside the box. Banks got his hands to the ball but could not hold it. Yet this great goalkeeper, sliding on to his rump, saved yet again, close in, from another piledriver by Lothar Emmerich.

In the 42nd minute Banks had to leap like a trapeze artist to fingertip over a swerving, dia-

Geoff Hurst scored three goals and arms outstretched, after his last, he is held by Martin Peters, scorer of England's second goal

bolical 40-yard brute of a shot from Uwe Seeler. And so it went on, a game which, as time ate up the second half, resembled a blend of the endurance of an Olympic marathon, the sudden thrills of a film epic and all the starlit drama of great theatre. But towards the end of the second period England got their second wind and fittingly it was Ball dribbling in from the right, who bundled Tilkowski into touch for the corner which was indirectly to produce England's second goal.

But by this time nerves were raw from suspense and one wondered how much more we could take when from the corner there was a wild skirmish of shirts, Hurst shot, and a German defender mis-cued his clearance right into his own box where Martin Peters – yes, another West Ham man! – who has played such an important part in England's midfield set-up, cracked the ball into the net to put England 2-1 up.

The rest is history.

ENGLAND

Banks; Cohen, J. Charlton, Moore (captain), Wilson; Stiles, R. Charlton, Peters; Ball, Hurst, Hunt.

WEST GERMANY

Tilkowski; Hottges, Schultz, Weber, Schnellinger; Beckenbauer, Haller, Overath; Seeler, Held, Emmerich.

Referee: G. Dienst.

1967
25 May

Celtic beat Inter Milan 2-1 to win the European Cup

*While the distinguished football correspondent of The Times, **Geoffrey Green** wrote a most compelling book about great moments in soccer. In it, was a warm, magical account of Celtic's great triumph and the Scottish invasion of Lisbon. Internazionale of Milan were beaten 2-1 and the kilts were swirling*

ALMOST ANYWHERE YOU GO in this world, I suppose, you will find a Scotsman. Maybe not in Katmandu or the Palace of Heaven, in Peking. But most places. I wonder, however, if ever there have been so many of them gathered together at one time in one place on the soil of Europe as there were for a few days towards the end of May 1967.

The occasion was the final of the European Cup, when Celtic faced Internazionale-Milan – the Continental champions of 1964 and 1965 – to become the first British side to reach that exalted position. The climax was fixed for the handsome National Stadium of Portugal, a fine, egg-shaped bowl built between Lisbon and Estoril, with a marble colonnade for the V.I.P.s, and set in groves of eucalyptus trees at the head of a wide valley that sweeps down to the

Atlantic in the distance. It is an enchanting situation. Cars are parked in clusters among the trees, and people picnic in the sylvan setting to lend an air of holiday and unreality not usually associated with a football ground. It is a showplace and the Portuguese are understandably proud of it.

However, little did the local populace realise what they were in for when Celtic reached that final. There must have been some 20,000 Scotsmen let loose on their capital. They virtually took over Lisbon with their high spirits – the whisky almost flowed in the gutters. Flight after flight came in from Glasgow, to deposit a human cargo on the tarmac. It was like an invasion from the skies. They became almost an army of occupation. The 'Ladies from Hell' were abroad again.

That particular year – 1967 – Scotland had won 3-2 at Wembley and, having inflicted defeat on 'the auld enemy', the reigning World Champions at the time, they arrived in Lisbon a few weeks later at the end of May absolutely cock-a-hoop. Never mind the World Cup. England were beaten, the Number One enemy; Scotland were the greatest and Celtic were the greatest...

But more history was about to be made. Celtic beat Inter 2-1 that 25th May.

It was a great triumph for Celtic to become the first British side to lift this prize and when McNeil, the Celtic captain, at last held the trophy aloft in the glinting sunlight of a lovely evening, the 70,000 crowd stood to him as one man, for there was no doubt where the Portuguese hearts lay. They remembered how Inter only two years earlier had, by subtle negotiation, made Benfica, the local heroes, play the European final in Milan.

But that was past and now, at last, the Latin domination of this European competition had been broken. After years of rule by Real Madrid, then by Benfica and the two clubs of Milan, the emphasis of power was switched. So the Scots won a place of honour that can never be taken from them.

The scenes at the end were almost tribal. Thousands of Celtic supporters invaded the pitch waving their banners and uttering wild whoops of joy. Hundreds knelt to kiss the ground and, having cut slices from the turf of Wembley only a few weeks earlier, these Scotsmen now did the same to the Cumberland turf of the stately National Stadium of Portugal.

The size of Celtic's performance can be measured by one fact. This was only Milan's second defeat in Continental competitions in four years. By half-time they looked to be in extremis, and as the second half unfolded under a continuous Celtic bombardment, the Italian trainer was busy dousing his players with water in the hot sunshine that should have been their ally. Long before Celtic equalised half an hour from the end, and finally took the victory with only five minutes left, Inter looked ravaged and unlovely. Not even talented men like Mazzola, Corso, or Facchetti could revive them.

Here was a wonderful team feat by Celtic. To recover from the psychological disadvantage of conceding a penalty kick after only seven minutes when Craig upended Cappellini, and Mazzola stroked home his shot from the spot, was a performance indeed. But the longer the struggle unwound, the surer it was that Celtic would win.

If any one man deserved a crown on his own, it was Gemmell. Working on a long-standing plan deeply laid, and worked out in the hope that Inter would have no counter, he swept time and again into attack down the left flank, overlapping the men in front and supplementing the 4-2-4 formation. Craig also followed suit on the right, helping the darting footwork of Johnstone. This bemused Milan and helped to undermine their packed defence in depth.

Every time Gemmell thrust forward, a big blond cat was set among the Italian pigeons, and when at last Craig, also up in attack, pulled the ball back diagonally from the right, there was Gemmell roaring through the middle to send home a thunderbolt for 1-1.

Celtic took the cue and built on it. They finally got their reward five minutes from the end, when Gemmell again came up the left and pulled the ball back to Murdoch, whose flashing, low shot was diverted home to the corner by Chalmers. Moments later it was over. The field was full of dancing kilts.

The celebration starts as Billy McNeil, captain of Celtic, walks barechested from the stadium in Lisbon

CELTIC

Simpson; Craig, Gemmell; Murdoch, McNeil, Clark; Johnstone, Wallace, Chalmers, Auld, Lennox.

INTERNAZIONALE MILAN

Sarti; Picchi, Burgnich; Guarneri, Facchetti; Bedin, Corso; Bicicli, Mazzola, Cappellini, Domenghini.

Referee
Herr Teschencher.

Mike Hailwood roars to TT immortality

The Isle of Man TT celebrated its Diamond Jubilee in 1967. It was also the fifth year in succession that the Senior TT race was won by Mike Hailwood, a rider who dominated the event like no other. **John Lovesey** *in The Sunday Times portrayed a British hero and the stage on which he strode*

IN THE ISLE OF MAN TT RACES, Mike Hailwood wore an old black leather riding suit, turned almost a shade of brown with long use, and beat the hide off practically every other rider present. He is an English hero, sardonic and endlessly courageous. 'The saying goes,' he remarked at one moment, 'that when you're down among the brown leather boys, you're not doing so well.'

By late Friday afternoon, he had become indisputably the greatest motorcycle rider who has ever lived.

He is 27 years old, and has about him the look of all men who live close to great danger. His fair hair is rapidly thinning on top and his blue eyes flash frequently with impatience. His prominent chin is famous and fondled everywhere from the Sachsenring in East Germany

to Monza in Italy. But it is the TT races that represent for him, as all riders, the Mecca of the sport. During them he loses 7lb, off his normal 11 stones, distributed sparsely about his tall frame.

Before a race Hailwood may share a joke and smile, while inwardly he is tense and nervous. But after he has zipped up that old suit, put on his white, red and gold helmet, pulled on his gloves, he is cool and deadly precise. He pushes his machine to start it firing, sits side-saddle for a moment, and then puts his leg over as it roars. His chest hugs the petrol tank and he disappears, the noise cutting the air ahead like a serrated knife.

Round the 37 mile Isle of Man course, which starts right outside the Douglas cemetery, where a half dozen or so TT riders killed in the races are buried or have been cremated, he last week broke every record it was conceivable for him to smash. Lap records, race records and the record of Dubliner Stanley Woods, who until this year had won more TTs (ten) than any other man.

In all, Hailwood has won 360 races, 60 Grands Prix, holds the world one hour record, 250 lap and race records all over the globe, and has now set a seemingly insurmountable total of 12 TT victories. His nearest rival is the Italian Giacomo Agostini, and the clash between the two provided the focus of the 1967 Diamond Jubilee TT races.

The TT week amounts to a motorcycle festival, the British equivalent of the bulls running the streets of Pamplona, but with more danger and sexuality. Nothing, however, even in Spain, exceeds Black Sunday for lunacy, the day before the first TT race, when visiting motor cyclists try out the course for themselves, apparently as intent on suicide as lemmings. Only the introduction of a one-way system on the mountain section has cut down the work at Noble's Hospital.

Annually, the Manx Government donates £20,000 to the Auto Cycle Union for running the TT races. It works, for during the practice and race period, the population doubles and the visitors spend well over £1,000,000. Hoteliers' overheads are met for the rest of the

Mike Hailwood said 'the motivation is strictly money' but he was the greatest rider of them all

year. 'I reckon if they stop the TT,' said one Manxman, 'the place would just grind to a halt.'

If Hailwood is motorcycling's most dramatic hero, Giacomo Agostini is its pop star. 'The girls are all chasing him now, not me,' jokes Hailwood somewhat untruthfully. None the less Agostini does have a presence that makes young females scream. Before it became fashionable for male film stars to have frankly ugly faces or simply interesting mugs, he would have seemed automatically destined for a Hollywood career. He is devastatingly handsome, 5ft 7in tall with hazel eyes and a lambent grin. On Friday, he became 25, but while Hailwood was winning the Lightweight TT (250 cc) on Monday, in which Agostini did not compete, the Italian was watching and waiting for the Junior (350 cc) and Senior (500 cc) races, a bright red leather cap perched jauntily on his head.

In his hotel, where a lobby telephone booth was assigned exclusively to him with a notice 'Casa chiusa Agostini', he expounded as well as he can in English what it takes to ride the Manx course.

'It is necessary to always look in front,' he said. And added with a touch of disappointment: 'It's impossible to look here, there and say bye-bye.'

He is, compared with Hailwood, remarkably placid. Agostini joined the English rider in the Italian M V Augusta team in 1965. The following year, Hailwood switched to Honda and a battle started in the biggest class that lasted the complete season. In the final championship race, Agostini won and became the first Italian since 1957 to win the 500 cc title.

Honda's motorcycles however are troublesome beasts. They have six cylinder engines and it is difficult to make a frame that can adequately solve the consequent problems, such as weight distribution. The bikes therefore behave, in the sport's special parlance, like camels. With their tendency to whip, and jump about like kangaroos, they are yet another measure of Hailwood's brilliance, as he rides them at speeds up to 160 m.p.h. 'I used to whistle as I went round once,' remarked Hailwood. 'I haven't got time now.'

In the Junior race, his tactic was to demoralise Agostini with a scorching first lap. The riders start off in pairs at 10 second intervals in a TT, and a plan of campaign necessarily depends on whether you are drawn to start ahead or behind a rival. 'If you start behind somebody, you've got the advantage,' explained Hailwood. 'You can see them.' But in the two big races Hailwood had to go first, ahead of Agostini.

On Wednesday, Agostini never got a chance to glimpse Hailwood. On his first lap, from his standing start, Hailwood went round in a record 107.73 m.p.h., establishing an immediate lead of 89 seconds. He finally won by more than three minutes over the six laps of the course.

The race on Friday, the Senior TT, Hailwood knew would never be so easy. If the handling of the Honda 350 leaves much to be desired, the 500 is a writhing handful of bounces, so bad Hailwood hardly dare open it up fully. He hoped it would rain, when his greater familiarity with the course would give him an advantage, but the sun lasted till the end of the week. Sitting under it with two TT victories behind him, the Senior ahead, and Agostini gunning for him, Hailwood surveyed his life and what it means to be ahead:

'When you eventually get to the top, there is so much pressure everybody's always shouting for the underdog, and you don't want the underdog to beat you. You often see people who've been at the top going down. It's pathetic. Here, on the island, there's the greatest pressure of all. You just can't escape it. I still like racing, but everything, the bickering, I'm sick to death of. The main motivation is money, money, strictly money.'

Hailwood almost certainly earns more than any motor cyclist ever before. He makes a reputed £30,000 a year, but none of it is easy. He takes four or five spills annually for a start. According to himself he holds the all-time record of ten spills in one 12-month period. He has got out of bed after influenza to win the Senior TT, and will ride stiff, bruised and bandaged. Oddly enough, the thing he lacks is mechanical aptitude. 'Mike,' explained a friend, 'can't tell you what's going on between his legs.'

The biggest influence on his life has been his father, Stanley, who is retired and lives in Nassau, but was in the Isle of Man. Apart from him, there is also his father's second wife. 'Of all the crumpet he knows,' said an intimate,

'the only one Mike has real respect and affection for is his stepmother.' Aside from these two, he appears a lonely man, though seemingly surrounded. 'He is,' observed somebody else, 'surrounded by hangers-on.'

Before the Senior TT, Hailwood sat astride his bike on the grid, while the crowd, the photographers, the well-wishers and mechanics milled around. He looked down at his petrol tank and at nobody. Then, Mike Hailwood was certainly alone.

The race went very much as he predicted, until the end. He had to wrestle his machine round, and at the end of the first lap, Hailwood was 12 seconds down on Agostini. But with a lighter tank, he began to pull back, and when he came in for refuelling at the end of the third, the Italian was only two seconds in front. Hailwood lost ten seconds during the pit stop, partly because his throttle grip was sliding about and he had to try to fix it. Despite this disadvantage, a handicap which could have settled the result, according to Hailwood, he went one second ahead of Agostini 25 miles round in the fifth lap. It was incredible and miraculous, and motorcycling has now been left to wonder at what might have happened but for Agostini's drive-chain breaking shortly after he had himself once more gone ahead. On the last lap Hailwood was on his own, and in a Senior in which at one point his throttle grip actually came off, he won at an average speed of 105.62 m.p.h. setting on the way a new lap record of 108.77 m.p.h.

In the winner's enclosure, Peter Williams, who became the second man home, after Agostini and another Italian rider, Renso Pasolini, had retired, told Hailwood, 'You're a bleeding genius, mate.' It is hard to say it any other way. Hailwood, reserved, even withdrawn, never would. 'It is a relief that you feel, I suppose, that it is all over,' he said simply.

But if he cannot articulate his immeasurable talent, his feats on the Isle of Man do. Down a small corridor in time the legend will live forever that Mike Hailwood was the man who mastered better than any man the 200 bends through Ballacraine, over Ballaugh Bridge to Creg-ny-Baa and the finish.

Manchester United and George Best win European Cup

In February 1958 a dream died when the Busby Babes, the team created by Matt Busby, was decimated in an air crash at Munich airport. Ten years on, George Best, an errant genius, ensured the European Cup was secured at last when United beat Benfica 4-1. **Desmond Hackett** *reported in the Daily Express*

George Best was the mercurial linchpin of marvellous victory

MAGNIFICENT UNITED brought the European Cup to England last night with football that was not only European class – it was out of this world. United did an England World Cup show.

They were tied to a 1-1 draw at the end of 90 minutes against the Eagles of Benfica. But in extra time United stormed to a 4-1 win. As the 90 minutes ended the men of United collapsed on to the green turf of Wembley. The turf they knew so well and across which this night they had etched deeply their glowing skills and unflinching bravery. It seemed as though this solid old Wembley Stadium could not contain the joy of the faithful of Manchester, whose anthems soared into the black night and whose banners had waved on defiantly.

When the trophy belonged to England,

Manchester United manager Matt Busby, the architect of it all, walked slowly on to the pitch. His arms were outstretched as first he embraced Benfica players, and then he turned to the men who had kept faith with him. His arms were outstretched still as though to take in and hold forever this scene of Manchester United's finest hour.

Their finest hour? Well, certainly their greatest 10 minutes. Eleven tired men suddenly found heart early in extra time. Alex Stepney kicked the ball powerfully into the Benfica area. It was finally taken over by George Best. And this man of magic appeared to mesmerise the Benfica defenders as he threaded the ball through like a skilled weaver. So complete was Best's destruction of the defence that he saucily rounded goalkeeper Henrique and noncha-

MANCHESTER UNITED

Stepney; Brennan, Dunne, Crerand, Foulkes,
Stiles, Best, Kidd, Charlton (capt.), Sadler, Aston.
Subst: Rimmer.

BENFICA

Jose Henrique: Adolfo, Humberto, Jacinto, Cruz,
Graca, Coluna (capt.), Augusto, Torres, Eusebio,
Simoes. Subst: Nascimento.
Referee: Concetto Lo Bello (Italy).

Manchester United and Busby, displaying the European Cup, returned home to cheering crowds and a civic reception

lantly flicked the ball into goal.

The thunder of exultant, rejoicing thousands was pounding out when United scored again. There could never have been a more kindly goal. Brian Kidd, 19 on this unforgettable day, had been having a nightmare match. But, as United again raked relentlessly through a shattered defence, the ball came to him and he headed in. The noise blasted your ears and you welcomed every note. Bobby Charlton turned a back somersault. Kidd walked down the pitch wiping the tears from his eyes. But those eyes were undimmed when, six minutes later, he was striding gracefully down the wing. He centred and Charlton, an athletic immortal in his own golden age, flicked in a shot that was a gem, a jewel of gold – no, a Crown Jewel. Kidd had the biggest birthday party in the world as tens of thousands sang: 'Happy birthday, dear Brian, happy birthday to you.'

I suppose for Matt Busby this was just the happiest day. The golden dream was now a reality after 11 years of tragedy and bitter disappointment. United were the champions of Europe. They were the greatest – and even the subdued and well-thrashed men from Benfica stayed to give tribute.

It had not all been so gallant and knightly. The first-half behaviour of Benfica was a disgrace to a noble competition. Perhaps it would be better to forget the savagery of the tackles, the manner in which Best was lashed down and kicked brutally. Humberto had his name taken, and at least four players were desperately lucky not to have been sent off. But as the red and white cauldron of Wembley bubbled joyously, and you saw the honest joy gleaming on Matt Busby's face, it was possible to forget, if not forgive.

United has not only beaten Benfica, the eagles who were more like vultures, they have endured with dignity the worst refereeing ever to come near to wrecking a game. Referee Concetto Lo Bello, of Italy, was at his worst when Eusebio brought up his knees into Crerand's groin and a foul was given against

Crerand. Stiles leaped at Eusebio and there was an ugly maul until Charlton quelled this near-riot. While both sides faltered nervously, it was John Aston, the lad seldom in the head-lines, who showed how to play football under stress.

The game was much more civilised in the second half when United took command. Three goal chances were missed before Charlton, the man for all great occasions, scored after 53 tension-haunted minutes. David Sadler crossed and Charlton got his head to the ball to flick it beyond the goalkeeper.

The game should have been neatly tied up and the Cup heading for Manchester in the same minute. Best once again beat the entire defence and put the ball into an empty goal. But a typically outrageous decision made him offside. Wait until they see the film. Eleven minutes from the end of normal time the unhappy Kidd fumbled a move in midfield. The ball moved in a zig-zag pattern until Graca, unmarked by the far post, pounded it beyond Stepney. So the agony had to be repeated all over again. But not for too long.

United, in seven minutes of the first 10 min-utes of extra time, magnificently, gloriously, wonderfully, riotously, won the European Cup.

Round the world sailor Alec Rose comes home

He was by no means a traditional hero, which made him all the more heroic. A greengrocer, Alec Rose realised a dream for all seemingly ordinary men and women. He sailed alone round the world and on his return was engulfed in a tidal wave of admiration and goodwill, as **Vincent Mulchrone** *wrote in the Daily Mail*

HE BLEW IN LIKE A BREATH of sea air. Eyelids drooping, voice faltering, rising 60 and half dead on his feet, Alec Rose yet rose to his greatest hour yesterday. He brought Lively Lady safely back to Portsmouth just as he said he would 354 days 'and a circumnavigation of the globe' ago. Not all the pomp that Pompey lavished on him could change the sweet humility of the man, the common touch which has made him a special sort of hero.

It is not the nature of the quiet greengrocer to have rehearsed fine phrases for the occasion. Rather, that he dipped deep into his store of memories and confessed: 'I did a lot of soul searching. I felt very humble and rather selfish at pursuing something which I myself had desired since the days of my boyhood, and I felt I was rather putting on to the people

back home something I should have carried.'

Glimpses of his lonely year around the world came in his slow, halting words as he met the press at Portsmouth Guildhall. He prayed. 'I did say my prayers. Why not? I said my prayers as sincerely and honestly as I could. I felt at times rather a hypocrite saying my prayers when I really felt I needed... asking for help when I needed it, and not asking for help when I didn't need it. However, I felt my prayers were answered at times and we got through.'

He talked to his mascot, Algy, an oversized and rather gormless looking woolly rabbit. 'He's the one who gave the orders, and he's the one who made decisions.' Then he added drily: 'They always coincided with mine. He always gave the right answers. We got on very well together.'

I asked him how he felt. He said: 'I feel very fit, really. But this last couple of nights coming up the Channel I haven't had much rest with the shipping about. I am a little tired, but actually I'm very fit. I feel very well, and there's nothing a good night's sleep won't put right.'

He talked of the time he lay unconscious. He was trying to correct a fault in his small charging engine. 'I passed out. I came to in, I estimated, about two hours, and I was very weak. I realised what had happened. All I could do was lie on my bunk and recuperate. It was several days before I could raise an appetite.'

Had he any regrets? 'It's a thing I've always wanted to do from a small boy. I've always wanted to sail round the Horn, the ultimate test of man and ship. I've no regrets about doing it.' He spoke of his debt to his wife, Dorothy, who has throughout stuck to the belief that the greatest compliment she could pay her man was never to worry. She had been such a good manager, he said, that 'I arrived back in England with foodstuffs almost sufficient to take me back to Australia.'

He came ashore with her, hand in hand, almost rushing her off her high heels along the jetty, the C-in-C, Portsmouth, Admiral Sir John Frewen, following, at a respectful distance.

Portsmouth has seen them come and go. But this was a homecoming whose hallmark

Alec Rose, later knighted, lived a dream for all ordinary folk during his epic sail round the world

was a very special pride and affection. Alec Rose sailed wanting none of what he called the 'Chichester ballyhoo.' He got none. Instead he sailed into an irresistible tidal wave of admiration and goodwill, into a torrent of cheers rolling across Spithead which tried to express what we all feel about him.

When he appeared he was shaggily in need of a haircut. He had changed from his faded brown smock and woollen pompon cap into a navy yachting blazer and crumpled slacks. The scene that met him would have daunted any man, let alone one so obviously fatigued. Around Lively Lady his welcoming armada bobbed and jostled for position – ferry boats and tugs listing under crowded rails, yachts, rowing boats, canoes, kayaks and even rubber dinghies crowded in for a look at him. The crowds which thickened all the way from Southsea Castle to the entrance to Portsmouth Harbour pressed down the shingle, until the front ranks were waist deep in the sea.

Alec Rose said when he got his breath back: 'This makes one feel very humble.' He was back on Southsea Common, one of history's favourite patches, where Richard II sped an army to Spain, where Nelson embarked for Trafalgar, where Queen Victoria presented some of the first of her VCs. The point about Alec Rose is that he doesn't look, or pretend to look, like the stuff of history. He simply landed there because it is the closest point to his greengrocer's shop, 300 yards away. Like the modest man he is, he greeted the Lord Mayor respectfully on the platform on the beach. They handed him a telegram from the Queen. He fumbled for his glasses, but had to let the Lord Mayor read it. It said: 'Warmest congratulations on your magnificent voyage. Welcome home, Elizabeth and Philip.'

1968
15 October

Hemery conquers 400m hurdles at the Mexico Olympics

The 400 metres hurdles is a brutal event. Yet, in 1968, Britain had an abundance of top performers and in the Olympic final arrived two of them, John Sherwood and David Hemery. Sherwood came third while Hemery won. **Neil Allen** *in The Times called Hemery's gold 'the outstanding British athletics performance of all time'*

Hemery's gold in the punishing 400m hurdles was 'the victory of a giant'

DAVID HEMERY WON the Olympic 400 metres hurdles gold medal for Britain in a world record time of 48.1sec. and left all his rivals, including the much feared Americans, in his wake with a demonstration of hurdling fluency and athletic power and judgement.

It was the victory of a giant, for though many Olympic medals are gained by fractions of a second, and more than a share of luck, Hemery thrashed a field which included the current world record holder, Geoff Vanderstock, and left no doubt in anyone's mind that he is the King of the event which a famous American coach once called 'the mankiller of track and field.'

As I knelt to congratulate the other British finalist, John Sherwood, who excelled himself with third place and a bronze medal in 49sec., I inadvertently trod on the hand of the exhausted Vanderstock. He said, when I apologised, 'That's all right. Pain means nothing to me anymore.' That pain had been inflicted on the young American by the blazing pace which Hemery set from the sixth lane on a night of dark clouds and heavy showers. He went off like a rocket, having said the previous evening that he was sure he still had something extra left for the final. And so it proved, as he swallowed up even the redoubtable American Ron Whitney.

I could not believe that Hemery could go off so explosively without paying something of a price when he changed his stride pattern after the seventh hurdle. But there was no noticeable check. He came into the home straight long, lean and hungry for victory, with his fair hair gleaming under the floodlights. He attacked the last two flights of striped three-foot barriers as though he had now forgotten human competition and was only out to stop the watch as soon as possible. He got a double reward of gold and record and I believe this was the outstanding British athletics performance of all time.

Jonah Barrington and Geoff Hunt turn squash into torture

In the British Open squash championship Jonah Barrington beat Geoff Hunt 9-7, 3-9, 3-9, 9-4, 9-4 in the longest such final on record. The match lasted 2 hours 13 minutes, but it was only one of a series of battles. After another such duel the essence of the rivalry was distilled by **Tony Clifton** *in The Sunday Times*

GEOFF HUNT IS THE GREATEST squash player in the world. He was leaning against the mirror in the dressing room at Northwood Squash Club. The only chair was full of Jonah Barrington, who was slumped against the wash basin, suicidally depressed and trying to make a joke with a reporter. 'Why don't you write: Barrington is struggling,' he suggested. Both of them were suffering from the fallout of the match Hunt had just won 9-6 in the fifth game after two hours. Squash played by the world champion and his nearest rival isn't the game played by good old Nigel and Tim at the Lansdowne Club every Tuesday after work. It is cruel and vicious and noisy and subtle and after two hours even the world champion is so weary he can just lean against the mirror and say 'yeah...yeah...yeah' when some fruity-voiced sportsman in an old school cravat is telling him how he really ought to pay more attention to his drop shots.

The game at the Northwood Club last week-end was the third in a 15-match series the two are playing to prove who is the greatest. The games are being played because Barrington is so obsessive about proving he is the best that

Jonah's dedication finally brought reward and a broad smile to his face

he actually paid Hunt's expenses to come to Britain to play him. The matches are jokingly called 'exhibitions,' which seems to mean that Hunt and Barrington stop just short of bursting their hearts to win.

The real thing apparently will be the British Open this week when the two should meet in the final and one will damn near die before the other wins.

Geoff Hunt hits it so fast it would land somewhere near Cumberland if the back wall wasn't there to stop it. He's the typically aggressive Australian, thrashing it back again and again, eventually forcing Barrington into error. Barrington hates every minute of it because he knows he isn't at top form yet and here he is being beaten by this boy who is only 23 and world champion on an English court with a partisan crowd behind him.

Barrington hits a drop shot into the tin. 'Discipline,' he shouts at his right leg and smashes it with his racket. 'You idiot, you fool... come on Jonah, let's have a game of squash...what are you doing here?' Hunt is quieter. 'Silly' he shouts when he hits a drop shot into the tin. Most of the abuse he directs at himself is brief. 'Silly,' 'Stupid,' 'No' are the main cries.

Both men argue with the referee. No one smiles at all and each one gets unhappier as the night goes on and the walls and floor get slippery as the warm air generated by players and spectators condenses on the cold surfaces. At 6-5 in the vital fifth game the nadir is reached when the lights go out because some fool hasn't put enough two-bobs in the meter.

Amazingly neither of these tense men attack the club officials.

Hunt went on to his 9-6 victory. Afterwards he talked about himself and the game, and began by criticising the English ball, which he thinks bounces with all the spring of a ping-pong ball, so that any club tortoise can get a racquet to it before it dies. 'This means that a

Jonah Barrington has beaten Geoff Hunt (behind him) in the British Open and exhaustion becomes the final victor

top level player knows he will never be beaten by power or speed. He knows he will always be able to get it back into play, so he plays this waiting game, playing these enormously long rallies hoping that his opponent will either make a mistake or lose through sheer exhaustion.'

Hunt talks and plays with such authority it is hard to believe he is just 23, nearly five years younger than Barrington. Yet he is a squash veteran and has been playing at championship level for eight years... He won the Victorian senior championship at 15. He got very little formal coaching. One man, Alan McCausland, taught him ball control at 13 ('his strokes were terrible but his length was brilliant') and another, Brian Boys, a former Australian champion, got him for ten weeks when he was about 15 and gave him some unorthodox advice which he says enormously improved his game.

Hunt for example hits his backhands when leading with his left foot. The classical way is to lean forward on the right but Hunt says this leaves you badly balanced to turn back to the centre of the court, whereas you pivot from the left with the minimum of leg and body movement.

'When I train for the world championships, I train for one hour a day, maybe five or six days a week, I do stomach exercises, some sprinting and that's about all. I could never train like Jonah. Weights nearly killed me when I tried them. The reason I don't turn pro is that I think a professional's life is short and uncertain, and I'm not sure I could stand the game if I had to play it all the time. I have nothing but admiration for Jonah's dedication but I reckon I would last two months if I went at it like he does.'

If Hunt admires Barrington, so the feeling is mutual. 'We still persist with this attitude that it is not gentlemanly to appear to work at a game so the Australians come and bury us. Geoff Hunt is now the greatest Australian of them all. I think he will always hold this place, like Nurmi or Elliott or the other great champions, a man who will be remembered as remarkable as long as the game is played.'

1970

Jacklin takes US Open and becomes an all-time great

*When it seemed that the USA had a monopoly of golf's championships, the lad from Scunthorpe upped and matched the might of America, winning the Open in 1969 and the US Open the following year, paving the way for other Europeans. Back from America **Henry Longhurst** paid tribute in The Sunday Times*

CONTRARY TO WHAT all the commentators, including myself, have written and said, our golfing hero of last week is not the third but the first Englishman to win the US Open championship. The other two, Vardon and Ray, as a pained reader from that island points out, were Jerseymen. British, yes!...English, never! Whatever the nationality, however, Jacklin's victory was the most remarkable single episode I have seen in golf and still has an air of unreality about it.

For an outsider to win the US Open is unlikely enough. To win it by seven shots in a field containing every one of the world's best golfers is like the conjurer's final trick – not only extremely difficult, ladies and gentlemen, but actually impossible.

Jacklin's win was set up on the first day when blasts of up to 40 mph swept treacherously through the trees and blew away the rest of the field, great and small, like chaff. He led with a 71, the quality of which may be judged by the fact that no-one managed 72 and only four managed 73. He followed it with a 70, itself beaten by only five players. This meant that he went out last at 2.30 and here the pressure really did begin to build up. But in the end it was Jacklin's putter that did it. In the third round, he holed one after the other from eight feet or less and what might have been 76 became another 70.

You have to have a bit of luck somewhere to win at golf and on the last day Jacklin had it on the ninth. He had missed a short one on the sixth, which at last did seem to unsettle him; he dropped shots on each of the next two holes and the gap between him and America's Dave Hill, playing just in front, narrowed ominously. What saved the day, a turning point if ever there was one, was his putt on the ninth, perhaps 25ft or more. The ball raced towards the hole and one just had time to think, 'Oh, Lord, here comes three putts and the beginning of the end,' when it hit the back of the hole, jumped six inches in the air and disappeared. Thereafter victory was a certainty and I do hope you sat up to watch the triumph.

Jacklin is wiry and tough, both mentally and physically, and he will need to be with what faces him! Flying home on the night plane, you arrive at about 3 a.m. and put the clock on five hours, so that instead of bedtime it is 8 a.m. and the start of a bright new day. Younger men than I find that it takes at least two days to recover.

Jacklin's plane arrived at Heathrow, London, about half an hour before mine and he had had, said the porter, as we threaded our way between the massed Indians and Pakistanis and their worldly goods, a wonderful reception. After all this, he got into a fast car and drove all the way to Scunthorpe. From now on he will be like an election candidate, 'giving' and 'giving' till there is nothing left in the battery, not for three hectic weeks but for months, maybe years, as Palmer has done.

Jacklin said in America that the British Open

had made him financially independent for life. Now money no longer means anything. Indeed, like royalty and the late Lord Castlerosse, Jacklin now need never deign to carry any. If he wants six Aston Martins, let them be sent round – and so it will go on. No taxes to worry about. Everything will have been taken care of by his agent's offices, all over the world. All this at 25 years of age – and only 10 years ago

Life was never going to be the same again, once Jacklin won the US Open

a steam-fitter's apprentice in a steelworks at Scunthorpe! Let me say simply that it could not have happened to a better man, nor to one more likely to take the same size hats in 10 years' time.

1971
17 February

Ray Illingworth and England regain the Ashes

Sir Len Hutton, the previous captain to bring back the Ashes from Australia, demanded a welcome home fit for heroes. He cited one in particular, Illingworth, who was described as having won 'in the face of every stinking, shabby trick that luck could play on him' in a paean of praise composed by **Clive Taylor** *in The Sun*

FOR A MAN who had just injected red blood into the ailing body of English cricket, Ray Illingworth was indecently calm. Only an hour before, he had been carried off the field on the shoulders of John Edrich and Ken Shuttleworth, who must become the most famous substitute in the game's history because pictures of this scene will be shown forever. Yet here was Illy talking in the detached way that diplomats do. He had won The Ashes. In terms of other sports, that is the equivalent of running up Everest with a 40lb pack on your back, or outpointing Cassius Clay with both feet encased in cement.

Since the First World War, only four captains of England have succeeded in Australia. Chapman, of Kent, did it in 1928-29, Jardine, of Surrey, 1932-33, Hutton of Yorkshire, 1954-55, and Illingworth, of Leicestershire, who was so little regarded by Yorkshire that they let him go, 1970-71.

The moment when it happened was emotional. You can never recapture through the glassy eye of the television set the feeling that came when Fletcher pranced about in front of Jenner to take a catch that meant that Australia had lost by 62 runs. The result had been inevitable for some time, but the stomach still lurched with that one catch and this result. All the plans for reviving the game in England – the one-day programmes, the sponsorship schemes, the raffles – were all surpassed. For that Illingworth must be thanked. He got the blame when his party were playing poor cricket in the first half of the tour. Now, in fairness, he must get the credit. His strength has been as a director of operations on the field. He has not been an ideal captain of a touring party off the field, for he has divorced himself from many of the duties which have been accepted by other captains.

Equally he was inclined to become involved in stalemates with Bill Lawry, who seemed to bring out the worst in him. But put him in a match where he had a chance, like the two Tests he won at Sydney, or against an aggressive captain like Ian Chappell, who did his share towards making the Seventh Test the best between the two countries in a decade, and he was incomparable. He is a professional opportunist in the grand tradition and that was why his players chaired him off the field.

He is an open, easy-to-talk-to man, this Illingworth, and his performance in the Seventh Test, which has been unique for its tension, has been amazing in terms of pure cricket. He controlled it with the coolness of a man under a cold shower. In a good, open battle with Chappell, he missed nothing. Having done a ridiculously small amount of bowling on the tour, he took three wickets in Australia's last innings and decided the result by dismissing Greg Chappell.

Surprisingly, he brought on D'Oliveira, and while everybody was trying to work out the meaning of that, Dolly dismissed O'Keeffe and Lillee in two balls. He was so tactically confident that it was impossible to imagine that he was winning The Ashes in the face of every stinking, shabby trick that luck could play on him.

He had lost Ward before the campaign started, he had lost Boycott before the start of this match and Snow before he could have a real bowl in Australia's vital last innings. His difficulties were cameoed in the ceremony before a horseshoe ring of spectators after the match was over when the sponsors were handing out prizes to the best players in the series. There were the two outstanding ones, Snow and Boycott, standing next to each other, each with a different arm in a sling.

The tension of Test matches can be unbearable. When it was over, Illingworth said only: 'Anybody who suggests seven Test matches in future needs shooting. Six is more than enough. Five is the right number.'

Illingworth is not likely to be remembered as a great leader of men, but after today, he will always be known as a successful one. That must be good, for it puts him on a level with that other Yorkshireman, Sir Leonard Hutton.

Illingworth took three wickets in Australia's last innings, including Chappell's

SCOREBOARD

ENGLAND - First Innings 184 (Illingworth 42, Jenner 3-42, O'Keeffe 3-48)
AUSTRALIA - First Innings 264 (G. Chappell 65, Lever 3-43,Willis 3-58)
ENGLAND - Second Innings 302 (Luckhurst 59, Edrich 57, Dell 3-65, O'Keeffe 3-96)

AUSTRALIA - Second Innings

(Overnight 123 for 5)

Batsman	Runs	Fall	Mins	Balls	4'S	6'S	How out
G. CHAPPELL st Knott b Illingworth	30	7-142	135	127	3	-	Beaten by flight
MARSH b Underwood	16	6-131	79	63	-	-	Played offside off break
O'KEEFFE c sub b D'Oliveira	12	8-154	52	46	2	-	Skier to square leg
JENNER c Fletcher b Underwood	4	10-160	46	43	-	-	Bat and pad
LILLEE c Hampshire b D'Oliveira	0	9-154	1	1	-	-	Edge to second slip
DELL not out	3	-	12	14	-	-	-
EXTRAS (b 2, nb 5)	7						
TOTAL	160						

BOWLING: Snow 2-1-7-1, Lever 12-2-23-1, D'Oliveira 5-1-15-2, Willis 9-1-32-1, Underwood 13.6-5-28-2, Illingworth 20-7-39-3,Fletcher 1-0-9-0

FIRST TEST (Brisbane) draw; SECOND (Perth) draw; THIRD (Melbourne) abandoned; FOURTH (Sydney) England won by 299 runs; FIFTH (Melbourne) draw; SIXTH (Adelaide) draw; SEVENTH (Sydney) England won by 62 runs.

1971

8 May

Arsenal clinch the double with a 2-1 victory at Wembley

Tottenham Hotspur had done it but when it came to Arsenal's turn, the excitement was no less with the elusive League and Cup double at stake. Thus the Cup Final, always a high point of excitement, was beset by more tensions than usual. It was reported on by **Brian Glanville** *in The Sunday Times*

THE DOUBLE IS ARSENAL'S. Where Herbert Chapman failed, Bertie Mee has succeeded. Yesterday, at Wembley, the North London club became the second to accomplish the feat this century, the first since Tottenham, 10 years ago.

If this side lacks the aggressive fluency of Blanchflower's team, if it has still to find its considerable peak, its achievement is nonetheless astonishing. It was an almost intolerably dramatic, pulsating Cup Final. The mystery of it was that all the goals should come in extra time when Arsenal had been so markedly superior for most of the first 90 minutes. Yet it was Heighway who gave Liverpool the lead, in the second minute of the extra period; Arsenal who had to call on their vast reserves of morale to come back with an equaliser by

Kelly and a winning goal by George. What, indeed, could be more appropriate than that it should be scored by a youngster born virtually on the club's doorstep. Though every credit must be given to Liverpool for a late revival, inspired by the mercurial Thompson, for an exciting first goal by Heighway, there was no gainsaying Arsenal's superiority over the distance.

They were better in midfield, they were better at the back, they were by and large better at the front. And if Kennedy had taken the two good chances which fell to him, if one of Graham's headers had gone in, there would have been no need for extra time. Arsenal bestrode the field, playing in the sunshine some of their most impressive football of the season. Liverpool's celebrated defence looked, in the wider spaces of Wembley, quite disorientated, like men with a defective sense of spatial relations.

It must be said that Arsenal's beginning hardly suggested their later dominance. In the opening minutes, they gave away four free-kicks, and were almost torn open by Hall. It was precisely then that the ball reached George, who, looking up with that remarkable, panoramic vision of his, saw Kennedy and sent him clear. The big inside left was in his own half, indisputably onside, and the field was set for the kind of goal Milburn got, exactly 20 years ago. But Kennedy, for all his virtues, is a stayer, not a sprinter. Liverpool's defenders forced him left and his eventual shot was no more than a trite gesture.

Yet Liverpool continued to live dangerously and they owed much to Clemence. He had to come off his line very quickly when Hall, with a silly back pass, gave Kennedy another chance. When Graham, receiving from McNab, split Liverpool's statuesque defence again and sent Radford in from the left, Clemence once more was out of goal in a flash. It was high time that Liverpool gave their loyal, melodious fans behind the Arsenal goal a little encouragement; and they did. When a free-kick was given on the edge of the box, Smith leaped over the ball and Callaghan pushed it to Lindsay whose shot was a bullet to the right-hand corner.

Wilson justified the applause with which the Kop had generously greeted him by turning the ball round the post.

After 63 minutes, Arsenal took off the highly-physical Storey and brought on the more creative Kelly, as they could well afford to. Five minutes later, Liverpool produced Thompson, and for a little while came genuinely into the game. Yet 12 minutes from time, Graham twice came within a fraction of heading Arsenal into the lead they deserved. First, he rose superbly to Radford's prodigious throw from the right, to beat Clemence but head on to the bar, Smith's acrobatic scissor-kick clearing for a corner. Armstrong took it, Graham got up once again, but this time Lindsay cleared off the line.

So we had extra-time and after a mere two minutes of it, Heighway's simple, splendid goal put Liverpool ahead. Hughes found Thompson, Thompson set Heighway free on the left, and he, with the sort of burst we'd been waiting for all afternoon, cut in to shoot behind Wilson into the right-hand corner. There could well

---

Arsenal's captain Frank McLintock is chaired by his teammates, the FA Cup held aloft, the double done

---

ARSENAL
Wilson; Rice, McNab; Storey (Kelly), McLintock, Simpson; Armstrong, Graham, Radford, Kennedy, George.

LIVERPOOL
Clemence; Lawler, Lindsay; Smith, Lloyd, Hughes; Callaghan, Evans (Thompson), Heighway, Toshack, Hall.
Referee: N. Burtenshaw (Gt. Yarmouth).

have been a second Liverpool goal when Toshack headed back Thompson's right-wing corner, Hall volleyed, but Wilson made another gallant save.

Thus, in the 11th minute of extra time, Arsenal were able to equalise. Those two strong men, Kennedy and Radford, forced their passes through the thick of the Liverpool defence and Kelly fought sturdily to turn the ball over the line. The pendulum had swung again. Six minutes into the final period, George deftly nodded the ball to Radford on his left, got it back from him again and struck a mighty, right-footed drive past Clemence. It was a goal fully worthy to win the Cup and League double even though it had been an unconscionable time a-coming.

1971
27 June

British Lions achieve a triumph of the spirit

No touring rugby side ever has an easy tour of New Zealand, and the 1971 Lions had been badly buffeted – losing key players – in the run-up to the important first Test. The Lions, however, heroically fought for, and won, an emotional 9-3 victory, reported on by **Vivian Jenkins** *in The Sunday Times*

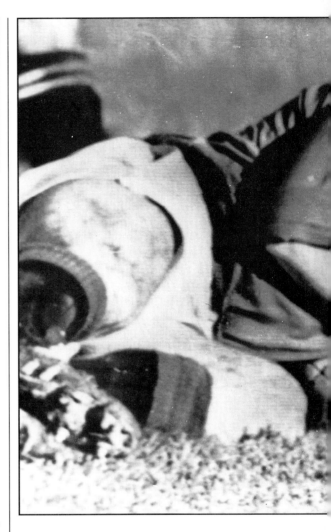

HALLELUJAH! Sound the trumpets, bang the drums, crash the cymbals, make any old noise you like! They did it. The Lions did it, they beat the All Blacks in this all-important first Test at Dunedin by two penalty goals and a try to a penalty goal. If ever there was a wet rag walking it was your correspondent as he tottered out of the grandstand at the end to pay homage to the magnificent winners; and never before have I kissed a rugby manager, let alone a 17st one like Dr Doug Smith.

It was indeed a famous victory, in front of a record crowd for the ground of 48,000 with 10,000 more locked out and forced to watch the match from the 'Scotsmen's Grandstands' on a nearby hill and railway line. The All Blacks began as though they were going to demolish the Lions before the latter had even taken breath, and for the first quarter of an hour it was as though a colossal pounding machine had gone into action, with the Lions on the receiving end.

But the Lions held magnificently while some of us averted our eyes. Then came the first, and vital, counter-thrust. Having won their way to the other end, an amazing little bull of a man from Scotland had a moment of glory that shall aye endure. Ian McLauchlan is only 5ft 9in tall and 14 st in weight – almost a pygmy in the company he was keeping yesterday. But never once did the 'Mighty Mouse' flinch. The Lions won the set-scrummage count 24-9, with the help of most of the put-in, and Pullin took the tight-heads 3-1.

Ian McLauchlan, the 'Mighty Mouse', scored the try that broke the All Blacks' hold

NEW ZEALAND

W. P. McCormick; B. A. Hunter, B. G. Williams, W. D. Cottrell, K. R. Carrington, R. E. Burgess, S. M. Going; **No.8** A. R. Sutherland; **Second Row:** I. A. Kirkpatrick, C. E. Meads (captain), P. J. Whiting, A. M. McNaughton; **Front Row:** B. L. Muller, R. W. Norton, R. A. Guy.

BRITISH ISLES

J. P. R. Williams; T. G. R. Davies, C. M. H. Gibson, S. J. Dawes (captain), J. C. Bevan, B. John, G. O. Edwards; **No.8** T. M. Davies; **Second Row:** P. J. Dixon, W. D. Thomas, W. J. McBride, J. Taylor; **Front Row:** J. F. Lynch, J. V. Pullin, J. McLauchlan; **replacement:** R. Hopkins for Edwards (10 min).
Referee: J. P. G. Pring (Auckland)

line. Sutherland attempted to kick for touch, but there was the 'Mouse' up in a flash to throw up his arms, charge down the kick and race after the rebound, behind the line, to score. He looked back from the ground, almost unbelievingly, as the referee awarded the try, and then raced back to half-way festooned with enraptured Lions.

The touring team's battle was not yet over by a long chalk. McCormick equalised with a penalty just before half-time, but the All Black full-back was to miss further kickable penalties in a disastrous day. He was tantalised all through by some wonderful clearing touch-kicking by John.

But the most wonderful part of the Lions' performance in that endless second half was the heroic tackling by Gibson and Dawes in the centre and the covering work by the three loose forwards, Dixon, Mervyn Davies and Taylor. Then there was John Williams at full-back, playing the game of his life, catching towering up-and-unders, taking fearsome punishment from the All Black forwards and always coming up for more.

As Dr Smith said, with a sidelong smile, at the after-match reception: 'You can say I am reasonably satisfied.' Then, to the Lions: 'Training at nine-thirty in the morning!' The spirit in this side was something to wonder at even before the game started. Now it has soared to the firmament.

This alone would have been a mighty feather in McLauchlan's cap, as it was equally for Sean Lynch on the tight-head side. But McLauchlan's contribution did not end there. In that 16th minute, when the Lions reached the other end he got the try that broke the All Blacks' hold at last. It also gave the Lions hope again and altered the whole psychological tenor of the game.

Fergie McCormick, the All Black full-back, sent back a pass under pressure to his No.8 forward, Sutherland, 10 yards from his own

Edward Heath leads Britain to Admiral's Cup win

As 300 suspected IRA supporters were arrested in raids in Ulster, Prime Minister Edward Heath, in his yacht Morning Cloud, led Britain's team to an Admiral's Cup victory. There were questions on the dockside in Plymouth, adroitly fielded by Heath's press secretary, as **John Windsor** *reported in The Guardian*

THE PRIME MINISTER'S press secretary explained yesterday why Mr Heath went boating while Belfast burned. He had no choice: to have scratched from the Fastnet race would have given away last Thursday's decision to bring in internment, Mr Henry James said.

'He had to sail for the very good reason that, had he delayed embarkation on Saturday, it could have given a clear warning to the 300 suspects who were rounded up on Monday morning.'

Mr James was speaking at Millbank Docks, Plymouth, where he was awaiting the Prime Minister's return. 'All decisions were taken before he embarked in anticipation of events. So far there has been nothing unforeseen in the situation,' he said.

No one could have foreseen the deaths, but the violence had been anticipated. The Prime Minister would have been taken off only if his presence had been essential for decision taking. Mr Heath would fly straight back to London after docking.

'There is no imperative that he should go back to London,' Mr James said. 'There is no deadline to be met. It is just that he wants to see the Home Secretary decide which other

ADMIRAL'S CUP (corrected times)

1. Ragamuffin (S. Fischer, Australia)...76hr 08min 38sec;
2. Cervantes IV (R. Watson, GB) 79hr 00min 33sec;
3. Yankee Girl (D. Steere, US)........... 79hr 37min 25sec;
4. Improbable (D. Allen, NZ) 79hr 52min 30sec;
5. Bay Bea (P. Haggerty, US) 80hr 28min 56sec;
6. Jakaranda (B. Dalling, SA) ....80hr 41min 54sec.

Other British placings:

13. Prospect of Whitby (A. Slater) 82hr 13min 49sec;
14. Morning Cloud (E. Heath) .... 82hr 16min 01sec.

FASTNET RACE Class I

1. Ragamuffin (S.Fischer, Australia)....76hr 08min 38sec;
2. Quailo III (D. Parr, GB) 78hr 31min 10sec;
3. American Eagle (T. Turner, US)...... 79hr 31min 45sec;
4. Yankee Girl (D. Steere, US)............79hr 37min 25sec;
5. Improbable (D. Allen, NZ) 79hr 52min 30sec;
6. Apollo (A. Bond, Australia)............ 80hr 23min 50sec.

Trouble in Ulster for the Prime Minister and an apparent near miss for Edward Heath's Morning Cloud in the Admiral's Cup

Ministers he needs to consult, and decide what points have to be followed up by the Foreign and Commonwealth Office.'

Mr Heath himself breezed into Plymouth at a rate of knots, watched a celebratory ducking, told of his yachting adventure at a press conference, attended a cocktail reception, and then flew to London to discuss Ulster. There was no champagne. And he refused to answer political questions. A crowd of over 1,000 lined the docks to welcome Morning Cloud. Mr Heath – deeply tanned after five days at sea – was at the helm. About 20 craft accompanied him, including two Navy minesweepers, two Navy fleet tenders, and a Navy police barge.

After berthing alongside other competitors' boats, Morning Cloud's navigator, Mr Anthony Churchill, was ducked by jolly members of the American crew. The biggest cheer came when Mr Churchill announced cautiously that Britain's three-yacht team had won the Admiral's Cup series – the first British win since 1965. The Fastnet race is the deciding factor, and a provisional estimate put the team ahead of the Americans.

Morning Cloud has only four berths for eight crew. Traditionally, crews in the Fastnet race get little sleep, and Mr Heath appeared rather tired. He said he had radio calls to keep him abreast of the political situation. 'They came through from time to time. If I was napping that was just too bad.'

Mill Reef dominates the Prix de l'Arc de Triomphe

The partnership of jockey Geoff Lewis and Mill Reef was a perfect blending of skills. Lewis was at his peak and Mill Reef a horse with grace. They won the Derby, the Eclipse, the King George VI and Queen Elizabeth Diamond Stakes and the Arc at Longchamp. From there **Richard Baerlein** *reported for The Guardian*

DERBY WINNER MILL REEF fully earned the title of champion of champions, when he set the seal on his three-year-old career by winning the Prix de l'Arc de Triomphe at Longchamp today by three lengths from the top French bay, Pistol Packer, in the record time of 2 minutes 28.30 secs. Another filly Cambrazzia was a length and a half away third.

Another neck away fourth came Caro with Lester Piggott's mount Hallez three quarters of a length further away fifth and Royalty half a length away behind in sixth place. Then came the French St. Leger winner, Bourbon, Arlequino and the American horse One for All.

It was the first English trained winner since 1948 when Charlie Smirke won on Migoh. It is not often at this time of the year that a fast time is possible but Mill Reef took full advan-tage of the prevailing conditions to put up the most spectacular display ever seen in this magnificent race since See Bird.

Geoff Lewis had planned his tactics before-hand and had never intended to be out of the first six. He found his mount running more freely than in any previous race but Geoff said this did not worry him. He held his intended position about fifth for most of the way and was on the rails. As he came round the final bend Geoff realised that the two horses on the rails at that stage, including Ortis, were going to tire. He did not want any interference so he

Mill Reef, partnered by Geoff Lewis, surged clear of his rivals to become the first English trained winner of the Arc since 1948

switched his mount towards the inner. Then, when they tired, he came inside Lester Piggott on Hallez, who had taken the lead entering the straight.

From that point Mill Reef gradually went away from his field. Pistol Packer came with a determined run to take a second place but she could make no impression on Mill Reef, who, driven out, went on to extend his lead. Pistol Packer had run a magnificent race but she was up against the best horse we have seen in Europe since the war.

Both first and second were American bred. The fourth, Caro, ran a fine race for a mile and a quarter but he did not stay. He finished about the same distance behind Mill Reef as he had done in the Eclipse Stakes at Sandown in July. Caro will probably come over for the champion Stakes at Newmarket where he can take on Brigadier Gerard and give us a line to the present relative merits of Mill Reef and Brigadier Gerard. Lester Piggott had given Hallez a magnificent ride and the horse was always going well until Mill Reef swept past him.

Royalty, unbeaten in England so far this year, had never tackled this company before but he ran a good race and was far from disgraced. The American colt, One for All, by Northern Dancer, the sire of Nijinsky, was always travelling on the wrong leg because all American tracks are left-handed. In the circumstances he did well but as there are no further races for him in Europe he will go back to America. Miss Dan, third last year, made no show and the champion stayer of Europe, Ramsin, third in the early stages, dropped out as soon as the pace was increased.

After the race, Geoff Lewis was presented to the President of the French Republic, M. Pompidou. He has now been presented to the Head of State of England and France in the same season, for he went before the Queen after winning the Derby. Mill Reef has now won more stake money than any other European colt. He will not run again this season but is to be kept in training next year and all being well should continue to confirm the impression that the modern generation of racegoers has never seen such a good horse.

His trainer, Ian Balding, thinks that the reason the horse had not been working brilliantly in the last few days was that he is beginning to settle down with age. Certainly no horse has been more impressive in top-class company in my lifetime and it was a particularly satisfactory race with no hard-luck stories.

Alex Higgins takes world snooker title at first attempt

Once the world professional snooker championship was not the glittery event it is today. One man, Alex Higgins, changed all that when he won the title at his first attempt, gripping the public's imagination and prodding the entreprenurial spirits. From the eye of the hurricane, **David Hunn** *reported for The Observer*

SOMETHING LIKE A MIRACLE received its final polish last night in a gloomy British Legion hall south-west of the Birmingham Bull Ring. A phenomenal little Irishman, younger than George Best, and twice as cocky, became professional snooker champion of the world. The world had hardly given him a chance, but he won the final frame 140-0.

It was unbelievable even when you sat there in the smoke and watched it; a sporting achievement you could match only if Taylor won Wimbledon without conceding a set, or Leeds lost 10-0 to Spurs. The Belfast Telegraph sent a man to sit there all week and watch him. For wasn't this Higgie, the little lad from the Belfast YMCA, the fellow who went to Berkshire as an apprentice jockey and had to come back home when he grew too much?

Then at 18 he was amateur champion of Northern Ireland and there wasn't a man there to give him a game, so pretty soon he packs his cue and takes the boat over the water again and turns up in a Lancashire snooker hall and says: 'Look, I play for money. Who'll give me a game?' And they find him a professional with more frames under his belt than Higgie has hot dinners and they put up £100 and our lad has it in his pocket before the other fellow has his cue chalked. Something like that, anyway, and between whiles he was cutting cloth for a tailor in Limehouse.

Here he is now just 22 and will you look what he's done. The first man to reach the final the first time he enters, the first to reach the final from the qualifying rounds, and the youngest ever there. That's our man, that's Higgie, Alex Higgins to you. They don't like him too much, the older pros, his manager says, because he hasn't done it right. He was never amateur champion, said he was too good to bother with that. He has cut corners, taken short cuts and there he is at the top.

You know Joe Davis, he took 27 years to get 500 century breaks in public matches. And here's this kid already made 580: that's in private too, of course, but you can see what I mean. He's done it all too quick. 'I wanted to be billed as Alexander the Great,' said Higgins demurely. The idea, one gathers, did not find favour. 'Anyway, he wasn't as fast as me. Now I'm Hurricane Higgins.'

He's a quiet, neat lad, the sort a mother would be glad to own. Short hair, clean face, strong jaw, and eyes that seem to have suffered a shade from squinting down a cue seven nights a week. A sharp dresser - shawl collar to his vest as well as his jacket - he moves quickly and lightly, like a good bantamweight, or a snooker player in a hurry. 'I've always been a great crowd-puller, he said, 'but I'm not sure why.'

For the world championship that ended at Selly Park last night, there was a £480-£320 split of the purse. A hard week's work, two three-hour sessions a day for six days, 73 frames, some of it in dim, car-battery lighting. 'I don't care about the power cuts,' said

Alex Higgins took on a hard week's work, two three-hour sessions a day for six days, some of it in dim, car-battery lighting

Higgins. 'I can see better than the other fellow.'

Through the black Birmingham streets stumbled the snooker fans to pack the hall, chairs banked on beer crates. Loud applause for John Spencer, the defending champion, louder applause for the lad. Already you know it's he they want to see. On Thursday the wind rose and Higgins blew Spencer off the table with snooker that should exist only in dreams.

Higgie takes a whisky-and-water with his spaghetti bolognaise, follows with a purifying slice of steamed halibut and a glass of milk. 'I think it's this way,' he says, very gently. 'I shall be world champion, and I shall maybe stay champion five or six years. When I'm 30 I shall retire. You see, Mr Hunn, I'm very good at this game, and I'm going to make a lot of money playing it.' 'Bloody big-head,' laughs his manager. 'No,' says Higgie, 'it's a fact.'

1972
24 May

The European Cup-winners' Cup falls to Rangers

*In Barcelona a European football final created a mixture of joy and anguish for Glasgow. Rangers beat Moscow Dynamo 3-2, but its fanatical supporters invaded the field and fought a pitched battle later with the Guardia Civil. In the Glasgow Herald the match was reported by **Jim Parkinson***

RANGERS FOUND THEIR RAINBOW'S END at the Camp Nou Stadium here tonight when they beat Russia's football masters, Moscow Dynamo, and won the European Cup-winners' Cup for the first time.

Rangers' future in Europe, however, may have been jeopardised by hostility that marred a night that should have rated as their finest hour. Intermittent invasions of the field had earlier threatened to have the game abandoned. Then only a minute from time the most highly excited contingent among the 20,000-plus Rangers supporters impatiently anticipated the end and rushed on to the field. They just could not wait for their moment of glory and thus endangered the efforts of a team who had played magnificently in the first 50 minutes to build a three-goal lead and then spent the rest of the match trying desperately to hold it.

After the match Konstantin Beskov, Dynamo's senior coach, appealed to the European Football Union to have the game replayed. He claimed that his players were intimidated by the Rangers supporters who spilled on to the pitch before play had ended. As he complained angrily and bitterly, he said: 'Some of our players had to dive for their lives and were injured. It robbed us of a possible equalising goal.'

Rangers succeeded nervously, but those earlier invasions must have done a lot to break the players' concentration. It should never have happened when everything was going so well. The players, highly tense, and Willie Waddell, their manager, did not deserve to have it all marred by the pitched battle between police and spectators after the last break-in. The Ibrox players were not even accorded the honour of having the trophy presented to them with the medals on the field. This was done somewhat shamefully in an underground dressing-room.

The ugly scenes overshadowed the real merit of the triumph. Rangers had conditioned themselves for the match, and it was proved in the first half that they intended to wrap it up early. It appeared as though they had done so until after the third goal the Russians brought on a substitute, Eschtrekov for Jakubik. It transformed the Russians as the replacement scored a goal almost immediately, and that sparked off a Dynamo revival. When the game swung Rangers had a giant in defence in Peter McCloy. The 6ft 4in goalkeeper was brilliant in defying the methodical Dynamo players when they reproduced the football expected of such a world-class club.

Rangers were just that shade better over the game. When they were attacking they had Dave Smith conducting the play in remarkably stylish fashion from deep in defence. It was his precise passes that led to the first two goals. Rangers at that time had plenty of front runners. McLean trickily threaded his way past big Russian defenders bemused by his acceleration and footwork. He had a willing partner in

Colin Stein, and William Johnston on the other wing kept his rivals well occupied.

It was McLean who threatened to scheme the first goal, but when it did come, in 24 minutes, it was from that uncanny man, Smith. From the middle of his own half he prodded the ball forward for Colin Stein to run on to just at the edge of the penalty box, and the centre forward hit a fierce drive past Pilgul.

Smith ventured much farther downfield five minutes before the interval to set up the second goal. With the Russians retreating before

John Greig, the captain of Rangers, receives the European Cup-winners' Cup on a night marred by the team's fans

him and funnelling desperately into the penalty area, Smith chipped the ball over on to the head of Willie Johnston, who flicked it into the net. Rangers' confidence increased three minutes after the interval when Stein took the brunt of a challenge from two Russians to get to a high ball. It spun off to Willie Johnston, who stroked it in.

Then the Russians made the switch that almost swung the match their way. Rangers had to pull more and more men back after Eschtrekov had reduced the deficit in 59 minutes, but they were magnificently encouraged by the supporters who paradoxically have put the club's European future at risk. In the cliff-hanging finish Smith kicked off the line, Jardine almost scored an own goal, and with five minutes to go Mahovikov scored Dynamo's second goal.

RANGERS
McCloy; Jardine, Mathieson; Greig, D. Johnstone, Smith; McLean, Conn, Stein, MacDonald, W. Johnston.

MOSCOW DYNAMO
Pilgul; Basalacev, Dolmatov, Zsykov, Dolbonossov; Jukov; Baldachnyi,Jakubik; Sabo, Mahovikov, Evrizhikin.
Referee: O. de Mendibil (Spain).

1972
3 September

Mary Peters wins Olympic gold in Munich

There was never a more popular British victory than that of Mary Peters in the pentathlon competition in Munich. At 32, she became only the third British woman to win an Olympic gold medal. Her triumph was carefully documented by **James Coote** *and* **John Goodbody** *in their book on the 1972 Olympics*

Jumping for glory in the pentathlon long jump in Munich, Mary Peters devoted a year to her build-up

THE SUCCESS OF MARY PETERS, at the age of 32, should stand as an example to all athletes: that no matter how bad or good you may think you are there is always time for improvement and that it is never too late to change techniques or even to take a year off to train. Mary is only the third British girl to win a gold medal in an Olympic Games, the other two being Mary Rand-Toomey, who was on hand in Munich to watch her old friend win, and Ann Packer-Brightwell, both in 1964 when Mary herself finished fourth in the Olympic pentathlon.

Mary and her coach decided that to build up for the Olympics they would have to take off the whole of 1971, even to the extent of missing the European Championships in Helsinki. In the winter of 1971-72, Mary re-appeared in indoor competition, looking lighter and sharper than she had ever done and showed in her shot-putting and hurdling that she was indeed becoming a first class performer. But it was in the high jump where her change was the most drastic. In her former conventional way of high jumping, she was a competent competitor, counting on around 5ft 5in (1.65m), but then she decided to change to the Fosbury flop. She adapted to it better than any other British girl with the exception of Barbara Inkpen, and established herself as No. 2 woman at high jumping in Britain.

Statistically, Mary's British record total of 4,630 points ranked her fifth behind Burglinde Pollak, the world record holder, Valentina Tikhomirova, 1966 European champion, Heidi Rosendahl, the reigning European champion and the improving young East German, Christine Bodner. The first event was the 100m hurdles. Miss Rosendahl won her heat in 13.34sec with Miss Pollak 13.53sec. Miss Bodner won her heat of 13.25sec with Mary pushing her all the way with 13.29sec, two-tenths of a second faster than she had ever run before without the assistance of a following wind. Already she had a seven point lead on Miss Rosendahl, for whom the crowd were rooting, without ever forgetting the British girl. Pollak was 33 points down – thus there was an unexpected bonus when she might well have been expected only to hold her own.

The next event was the shot put in which Mary Peters already held the British record of 53ft 6 in (16.31m). But that was set back in 1966 and since concentrating on the pentathlon, Mary had necessarily lost the bulk needed to make a good shot putter. Nevertheless, she had a superb second round toss of 53ft 1in (16.20m) which was her best ever in a pentathlon. It was just as well, for Pollak came very near her own personal best with 52ft 7 in (16.04m). Thus after two events Mary Peters totalled 1,920 points, Pollak 1,879, and Rosendahl 1,783. The final event of the first day, the high jump, was the one where the crowd really warmed to Mary. When she became the only girl to clear 5ft 10in (1.78m) she stood up in the pit and blew kisses to a delighted crowd who never had seen such a cheerful competitor. Then urged on by 80,000 she set a personal record of 5ft 10 3/4in (1.80m) on her first attempt, up went the bar and unbelievably again she cleared the first time 5ft 11 in (1.82m). Then the bar was moved up to 6ft 0in (1.83m). She almost cleared it on her second attempt but all good things come to an end and she earned 1,049 points.

Thus at the end of the first day, Mary with 2,969, led Pollak by 97 points, Tikhomirova by 125, Bodner by 260. More important, Rosendahl, whose forte was the long jump and pentathlon, was 301 adrift which meant she would have to break the world record in the long jump and run one of the fastest 200m ever seen to beat Mary. In fact Heidi missed her world record of 22ft 5 in (6.84m) by one cen-

timetre which gave her 1,082 points and moved her up to third place after four events. Mary, in the meantime, started off the long jump with a foul which was not far short of 20ft. Pollak seemed to sprain her ankle when landing after an opening 19ft 6 in (5.95m). Mary had a reasonable second jump of 19ft 4 in (5.90m), while the East German girl leaped to 20ft 4 in (6.21m). Heidi then had a huge leap, well beyond the world record, but fortunately for Britain it was a no jump. The judges deliberated for many minutes before they accepted Mary's final jump which was measured at 19ft 7 in (5.98m). In the final reckoning these extra inches proved essential.

With the 200m to go, Mary led Pollak by 47 points with Rosendahl, already winner of the long jump gold medal, 121 points behind. If all these girls ran up to their best form ever Mary, with 24.2sec, would win the competition with 4,790 points from Pollak (23.8sec) on 4,781 and Rosendahl (23.1sec) on 4,776.

The essential was that the Irish girl had to finish no more than 1.2sec behind Miss Rosendahl or 2/5th sec behind Miss Pollak to win the gold medal. With British throats going dry and the stadium hushed, the 200m heat prepared itself for battle. Mary, in lane three, Pollak in lane two and Rosendahl in lane six. Mary had a good start and held off Pollak until the runners entered the straight. Heading for the tape, Rosendahl was about three metres clear of Pollak and continued to pull steadily away while Mary held desperately on to the fleeing heels of the East German. As they sprinted across the line one thing was certain: that she was well within two-fifths of a second of the East German and certain of a silver medal, but how great a winning margin was Rosendahl's time? First to flash on the electronic board was the winner's time – 22.9sec – but there seemed a too long delay before the rest of the girls' times flashed up. This gave us the opportunity to work out that to win, Mary needed to have run no slower than 24.18sec. Her time flashed up on the board...24.08sec, thus by one-tenth of a second, 10 points, Mary had won the Olympic title with a world record total of 4,801 points.

1975
26 July

Grundy beats Bustino in a battle of true grit

At the end of the King George VI and Queen Elizabeth Diamond Stakes at Ascot in 1975 the spectators knew they had seen a rare and courageous race that transcended the sport itself. The drama of it all was captured by **Brough Scott** *in his report for The Sunday Times*

GRUNDY'S HALF-LENGTH DEFEAT of Bustino in the King George VI and Queen Elizabeth Diamond Stakes at Ascot was much more than a seal to his greatness. It was the hardest, most implacable, most moving flat race that I have ever seen.

Bustino's tactics were predictable, but his courage and strength were almost unfathomable. Led by his two pacemakers, first Highest and then Kinglet, Bustino was never further back than fourth and went to the front four furlongs out. The pace was so strong that the field was stretched at this stage and Grundy had already been pushed up close to last year's St Leger winner and Lester Piggott, on Dahlia, was also moving through to be a danger. Sweeping into the straight, Bustino and Joe Mercer set for home with a furious

determination, and very soon it was obvious that only Grundy, still two lengths adrift, could prevent them taking the £81,910 first prize.

Going to the two furlong post it was also obvious that this was to be no twinkle toed, flaxen-tailed acceleration that would take Grundy past the outstretched leader, but only grit, power and sheer slogging guts.

Behind them Dahlia was running her best race of the season, but the only question that mattered to the huge crowd was whether the Derby winner could close and beat his year older opponent. With the whips out, they came to the final furlong just about level, and from high in the stand one had the feeling that the older horse's slogging stamina might be too much. But then well inside the final furlong it was Bustino who began to weaken, rolling as tired horses do away from the fence and actually, for a moment, touching Grundy. It wasn't much, but it was the chink in the armour and, with Pat Eddery pressing Grundy like a man possessed, the bonny chestnut battled home to the line amid a crescendo of sound topped, of course, by trainer Peter Walwyn's frantically bellowed, 'Come on my son.'

Dahlia ran on to be five lengths away third, with the two other French challengers, On My Way and Card King, fourth and fifth. All these covered themselves in glory but they were only supporting cast compared to the two stars. The mile and a half was covered in a quite astonishing time. Grundy finally clocked 2min 26.98sec, which is no less than 2.46sec within the course record and 3.45sec faster than Dahlia's 2min 30.43sec which is the fastest, electrically-recorded time for this race.

Grundy's winnings now pass Mill Reef's previous record total of £312,122. Coming down in the lift to the unsaddling enclosure, trainer Walwyn mopped his brow and said simply, 'They can't take it away from him now.' As he loped past the crush of well wishers, he understandably didn't want to be drawn on future plans. 'Who cares about the future after that?' he said.

Grundy's Milanese owner, Dr Carlo Vittadini, looked similarly blissful and merely said that he favoured his colt bowing out in the

'Come on my son' and Grundy is beating Bustino in one of the greatest flat races of all time

Champion Stakes in October. Dr Vittadini added: 'This was a bigger thrill than when Grundy won the Epsom Derby or the Irish Derby. He was meeting the best horses in Europe and did it splendidly. There has been common talk that my colt had not beaten much in the classics, but he's proved that wrong today.'

Among the crush in the unsaddling enclosure, no pair looked more pleased than Sir Desmond Plummer, chairman of the Levy Board, and Douglas Gray, retiring director of the National Stud, who, of course, were party to Grundy's purchase by the National Stud at a value of only £1m. The word 'only' is used advisedly as Grundy would now be conservatively assessed at £2m.

Walwyn and Eddery pocketed their exotic trophies from the De Beers Corporation, who put up £44,000 towards this race, and continued their incredible form by winning the next race with Inchmarlo. This completed the most unbelievable fairy story of the day for Walwyn, for he had also taken the first race with Hard Day, ridden by no less a 'cavalier' than Dr Vittadini's lovely daughter, Franca.

As the horses were led away after the big race to be washed down, the buzz was as much of wonderment as of congratulation. Wonder at the way Grundy's record-breaking speed was so flawlessly complemented by his own and his rider's determination. And, perhaps, almost equally, at the magnificence of Bustino in defeat.

British racing has many problems, but the riding and the courage and the ability shown by the two heroes in yesterday's race will be something that it can be proud of forever.

1976

11 February

Curry captivates the Olympic world with sheer artistry

John Curry's performance (picture opposite) was a perfect blend of athletic skating and musical interpretation

At the Winter Olympics in Innsbruck, John Curry made history with a series of jumps blended into a programme of balletic daring and grace. A change in the rules, which weighted the marks more in favour of the free skating, helped him to win the gold medal. **Dennis Bird** *reported the British triumph in The Times*

JOHN CURRY HAS ACHIEVED the greatest British triumph in the history of men's figure skating. For almost 70 years successive Britons have striven to win an Olympic title. John Kieller Greig, of Scotland, was fourth in 1908, and since then no one until now has come within hailing distance of even a bronze medal.

Curry's victory was the climax of a season in which he has paced himself precisely. He won a hard fight against Robin Cousins for the British championship in December; he beat the holder of the European title in January; and now he has gained the most important victory of all. He is the successor of Ulrich Salchow, Gillis Grafstrom, Richard Button, the Jenkins brothers – men who have made a permanent name for themselves in the sport. Curry adds his name to that roll of honour. The judges, in

giving him their almost unanimous votes (seven to two) have recognised the validity of his particular brand of artistry. This has also been a good day for his trainer, Carlo Fassi, who in the afternoon watched his other star pupil, Dorothy Hamill, take the lead at the halfway stage of the women's championship.

Curry was drawn to skate 13th out of 17 men, but owing to the retirement of the excellent Canadian free skater, Ronald Shaver, who had pulled a muscle in yesterday's practice, the British champion did not have to take the supposedly unlucky spot. Instead he went on 12th, after the 1974 world champion, Jan Hoffmann, and the American Terry Kubicka.

Hoffmann skated a technically fine programme, but it was marred by a faulty triple salchow. Kubicka gave a magnificent display, including the best triple lutz jump of the evening. He ended with a back somersault, a jump sit-spin, and six successive butterfly jumps. The somersault was an amazing feat; it has occasionally been seen in ice shows, but never before attempted in a championship.

Curry's performance was masterly in its cool beauty of movement. There were three immaculate triple jumps – fewer than one or two of his rivals, but no matter – and the whole programme was a perfect blend of athletic skating and musical interpretation. The crowd were with him from the start, and the English speaking section roared 'We want six'. The judges did not oblige, for Toller Cranston, of Canada, still had to skate and might have out-done Curry today as he did in Monday's short programme; but they were generous with 5.9s – 15 out of the 18 marks awarded.

Vladimir Kovalyov, of the Soviet Union, did well enough to take the silver medal at the end, although he was no higher than fourth in this evening's event, behind Kubicka. The world champion, Sergei Volkov, fell on his triple loop jump and dropped to fifth overall. Cranston landed his triple toe loop jump on both feet, and although he gave a fine perfor-mance he was unable to catch Curry. He was second in the free skating, and took the bronze medal on combined results. It was good to see this grand skater on the victory stand with Curry as the Union Jack and the Maple Leaf were hoisted side by side.

Curry was obviously happy at this triumph but remained cool and calm as he said: 'I shall go to the world championships and perhaps then I shall retire from amateur skating. Perhaps I might form a theatre of amateur skating.' He described his win as 'the perfect end to my amateur career'. He said: 'I plan to present skating as a performing art in a theatri-cal setting. Being an amateur, I haven't been able to make any definite commitments because if I had done so I would have endan-gered my amateur status, which is something I didn't want to do this year. Forming a skating theatre is something I have wanted to do since I was seven.'

Of his Olympic campaign, Curry said: 'I've enjoyed it very much. I didn't think I would to be honest. I thought I was going to have to hide in my room all day. But it's been very exciting – the perfect end to my amateur career and the perfect start to my professional career – I hope.'

1976

6 March

Wales battle to seventh Grand Slam triumph

It was a match to set pulses racing when Wales beat France 19-13 at Cardiff Arms Park. There were those who would argue that the 1971 Welsh Grand Slam team was better. Moreover, Wales went on to win the Grand Slam again in 1978. But this match was a herculean struggle, as **J. B. G. Thomas** *wrote in the Western Mail*

THE GRAND SLAM FOR WALES – but only just. In a nail-biting, cliff-hanging climax to a hard, start-stop, exciting match Wales survived intense French pressure to carry off their seventh Grand Slam. Some may argue that France deserved to draw because they scored two tries to one, but there was doubt about their second try, while the third was correctly disallowed. Yet above all, the attitude of the French in the first 30 minutes did not justify their winning.

Their unnecessary rough play at rucks and mauls, culminating in Graham Price leaving the field with a badly-injured eye and a gashed ear, did not reflect very kindly upon the French approach in the tight play. Because of this I do not feel they deserved victory – or a chance of the Grand Slam. To go for players' heads and

eyes, intentionally as they did to Graham Price, and to stamp and kick as they did Mervyn Davies, is not in keeping with the spirit or standard of representative rugby. The French may approach their club rugby like that if they wish, but we in the British Isles want no part of it.

In recent years the Welsh team have set a standard of clean play in their approach unless constantly provoked, and looking at the Welsh 'scars' of battle and the incident of Price's eye, I am not at all happy. One would not attempt to offer this as the reason for a close match, but I feel such incidents must be highlighted because rugby football is no place for eye-gouging. Yet this pulsating match, which kept one on the edge of one's seat or swaying on tip-toes in the enclosures, had moments of high skill and drama and brought a host of new records to Wales.

The Grand Slam was Wales's seventh and equalled England's total; Wales became the first country to win all five matches in a season since 1928; they scored a record number of points in the four championship matches with 102 against 37; a new individual points record for a season was achieved by Phil Bennett with 38; and a new appearance record of 45 by Gareth Edwards. Thus it was good value for money and even if the critics were left wonder-

---

WALES

J. P. R. Williams (London Welsh); T. G. R. Davies (Cardiff), R. W. R. Gravell (Llanelli), S. P. Fenwick (Bridgend), J. J. Williams (Llanelli); P. Bennett (Llanelli), G. O. Edwards (Cardiff); A. G. Faulkner (Pontypool), R. W. Windsor (Pontypool), G. Price (Pontypool), A. J. Martin (Aberavon); G.A.D. Wheel (Swansea), T. David (Pontypridd), T. M. Davies (Swansea, captain), T.P. Evans (Swansea).

FRANCE

M. Droitecourt (Montferrand); J. V. F. Gourdon (Racing Club; R. Bertranne (Vangeres), J. Pecune (Tarbes); J. L. Averous (La Voulte); J-P Romeu (Montferrand), J. Fouroux (La Voulte, captain); G. Cholley (Castres), A. Paco (Beziers), R. Paparemborde (Pau), J. F. Imbernon (Perpignan), M. Palmie (Beziers), J-P Rives (Toulouse). J-P Bastiat (Dax), J-C Skrela (Toulouse).

Referee: J.R. West (Ireland).

ing whether the 1976 Grand Slam side were better than the 1971 side, there was satisfaction in having lived and observed through such a season – indeed, the last 12 months.

The French hurdle was the hardest. It was France who rushed into a six-point lead to shock all present and surprise themselves. Gerald Davies ran the ball out of his '25' diagonally, but as he passed to Steve Fenwick the centre was tackled and his attempt to feed back was gathered by Romeu, who raced on. When challenged he put Gourdon over on the right and then converted the try splendidly. Five minutes later Bennett kicked his first penalty from 30 yards before Wales got their try, the best of the match, when they first went right but were checked before moving to the left. Bennett threw a high pass to Fenwick who sent J. J. Williams in at the corner. The Bennett conversion attempt sailed just under the bar.

J. J. Williams (extreme right) scores Wales's solitary try in a match of emotion and drama

Bennett kicked his second penalty after 28 minutes and a beauty followed from Allan Martin, two minutes later, from 48 yards. Romeu replied with a 27 yard penalty for France and at the interval it was 13-9 to Wales and still anyone's match.

For the first 20 minutes of the second half Wales hammered away in the French '25'. They could not turn their pressure into points except for two lovely penalties by Fenwick, who took over from Bennett as kicker-in-chief because the outside half suffered a badly-bruised leg in a Bastiat late tackle which conceded Fenwick's first penalty. The French back row of Skrela, Bastiat and Rives were vigorous and active and ready to risk the penalty despite the sharp eye of referee West.

Aguirre gathered a clearing kick from Fenwick, booted up field and France won the ruck for Aguirre to grub kick over the line where J. P. R. just beat Averous for the touch down, but the try was given and Romeu kicked wide.

David Wilkie breaststrokes to Olympic gold

*Not since 1908 had a British man finished first in an Olympic swimming event. When David Wilkie won the 200 metres breaststroke in Montreal it was a victory truly to celebrate. In The Daily Telegraph, **Pat Besford**, the most respected of swimming writers, reported on a Scot who came good*

DAVID WILKIE'S FOUR YEARS OF DREAMING, toiling and hoping, which culminated in his gold medal for the 200 metres breaststroke in Montreal, earned Britain her first swimming victory by a man since 1908, and the first individual gold in these Games. Now, with every major title – World, European, Commonwealth and Olympic – in his possession, the Scot quits big-time swimming to a more leisurely life and, perhaps, a job in promotions and public relations.

The way Wilkie, 22, beat his great rival, John Hencken, in the apparently impossible time he had forecast two weeks earlier, a world record of 2 minutes 15.11 seconds, 3.10sec inside the two-year-old figures by the American, earned him lavish compliments from experts here. Top American coach Pete Daland said: 'That must be one of the greatest swims of modern times.'

The Briton's majestic, surging, last 50-metre effort left Hencken, already a metre in arrears, trailing home in second place four metres behind. And though the American was also inside his old record, with 2:17.26, it was a performance of little consequence in the wake of the flying Scot.

The whole American men's team, with an unbroken run of 10 wins out of 10 before Wilkie stepped on the block, united before the race to boost Hencken's morale for what they all knew was a losing battle. Hencken, who beat the inexperienced Wilkie into second place over 200 metres in Munich four years ago, admitted: 'I knew I had lost at the last turn.'

Wilkie, who had tested himself in the morning heats by going out fast (1:6.88) and found it didn't 'hurt', told me: 'I felt strong and very fit in the morning race. And in the final, though I took the first 100 metres a bit harder (1:6.49), I still seemed to have a lot left over the last lap. I wanted to win very badly and I wasn't worried at all about the run of American successes here. I just swam for myself and for Britain and it was the most touching moment of my life as I stood on the rostrum and saw the Union Jack raised.'

Before Munich, where Wilkie, a surprise silver medal winner, clocked 2:23.67 behind the American (2:21.55), the Scot had trained seriously for only three months and had gone into the Games as only the 15th fastest. For Montreal, Wilkie, by now the favourite, trained

At Montreal, David Wilkie (left and above) swum to fame. Ever after he could put in autograph books, 'David Wilkie, Olympic gold medallist, G.B.'

for at least four hours a day for over a year. And he spent many wakeful nights just thinking about the race.

Wilkie credits Scotland for giving him his start in swimming, the United States and particularly the University of Miami, where he has been since January, 1973, for providing the polish, and British team coach Dave Haller for his final perfect preparation for the race. The signature in the autograph books now is 'David Wilkie, Olympic gold medallist, G.B.' No British male swimmer has been able to do that since Frederick Holman and Henry Taylor each won their golds at the London Games of 1908.

1977
2 April

Red Rum wins his third Grand National

*On the occasion that the world's greatest steeplechase was won for the third time by Red Rum it was said strong men wept. The horse was already a favourite but with this victory he became a legend. In the Sunday Express, **Tom Forrest** recorded a moment truly to be cherished*

NEVER HAS HEROISM EARNED a tribute as thunderous as the wave upon crashing wave of cheering for immortal Red Rum, as he galloped gloriously to an incredible third victory – by 25 lengths over Churchtown Boy and Eyecatcher – in the Grand National.

Never in history had any horse won more than twice...and Rummy's triumph, backed by two seconds on his only other attempts, adds up to a record so sublime that it never will, never can be approached. So sublime that a tearful Tommy Stack slipped from the saddle to declare: 'Nothing can do justice to this horse, nothing I can say, and nothing you can write. He is just beyond belief!'

So emotional was the ecstatic 50,000-plus crowd's reception for its own special Aintree idol that even the irrepressible effervescence of trainer Ginger McCain dissolved from time to time into the happiest tears I have ever seen.

'Bloody marvellous,' said Ginger again and again. 'Bloody marvellous on Tommy's part and on the horse's. I thought he was a week short of peak fitness – but nothing stops him.'

And nothing could stop Red Rum's owner, Noel Le Mare – 90 in December – from being there to see his champion's historic surge to glory. Told of the tempest-force winds ripping over the Aintree track on the morning of the race, he burst out: 'I was putting up with gales on deep-sea trawlers when I was thirteen years old. Why should the winds worry me now?'

The greatest moment steeplechasing ever knew could only have happened to a phenomenon like Red Rum, who just does not know how to fail, who battles his heart out whatever the odds. But even a Red Rum could never have made it without the fast, favourable turf which strong sun and stronger winds had produced. Liverpool time records were smashed in both races before the National, and those are the conditions the great horse revels in.

And even Red Rum might never have made it but for a dramatic chain of fateful accidents which cleared the opposition right off the track. Only nine of 42 starters finished without mishap. Cheltenham Gold Cup winner Davy Lad, thrown into the handicap with only 10st 13lb, crashed at the third fence. Sebastian V was 10 lengths clear when he nose-dived at Becher's on the first circuit. Boom Docker, even further ahead at the 17th fence, dug in his toes and refused to jump. Then it was the 15-2 favourite Andy Pandy who left the field trailing far behind, until he took his spectacular tumble at Becher's second time round.

All the while Red Rum was making up ground relentlessly, nearer and nearer, until Andy Pandy's fall left him in command. With just three of the 30 mighty fences left to cross, jockey Stack was bothered only about two loose horses, telling himself: 'God, I'm going to get brought down at the second-last, with it all at my mercy.' What Stack did not know was that by this time Martin Blackshaw was right on his heels with Churchtown Boy... his mount

Red Rum jumping his way to victory in the 1977 Grand National. 'He is just beyond belief,' said Tommy Stack, his jockey

cantering and Martin looking backwards for danger, totally confident he could take the leader.

But the loose horses switched from Red Rum, perhaps distracted Churchtown Boy, and brought a sloppy, hind-leg-dragging jump which left that horse struggling. And Rummy racing on alone and uncatchable.

After Eyecatcher – third, six lengths behind Churchtown Boy – The Pilgarlic took fourth prize ahead of Forest King, What a Buck, Happy Ranger, Carroll Street and Collingwood.

1977 GRAND NATIONAL

1. Red Rum (Quorum-Mared) 12, 11-8 (9-1) T. Stack
2. Churchtown Boy 10, 10-0 (20-1)......M. Blackshaw
3. Eyecatcher 11, 10-1 (18-1) ....C. Read
4. The Pilgarlic 9, 10-4 (40-1) ....R. R. Evans

Hidden Value and Saucy Belle were remounted to finish 10th and 11th. Winter Rain broke his neck at Becher's first time round, and Zeta's Son was put down after breaking a leg at Valentine's on the second circuit.

Charlotte Brew's dream of being the first woman to ride the big winner ended, after dogged persistence at the tail end of the field, when Barony Fort refused at the 27th.

Top bookmaking firms reported 'the worst result possible' at starting prices of 9-1 Red Rum, 20-1 Churchtown Boy, 18-1 Eyecatcher, and 40-1 the Pilgarlic. But betting was of no importance whatever on an occasion like this. It was the wonder of Red Rum, not the winnings, which left the race crowds delirious.

1977
1 July

Virginia is final touch to Centenary Wimbledon

In the year that Wimbledon celebrated its centenary, and before the Queen, celebrating her Jubilee, Virginia Wade delivered what she had promised for so long. She beat Betty Stove 4-6, 6-3, 6-1 in the women's final and the Centre Court crowd went wild. **Lance Tingay** *captured it all in The Daily Telegraph*

THE CENTENARY CHAMPIONSHIPS and the Queen's Jubilee Year could not have combined better in the women's singles at Wimbledon yesterday, when Virginia Wade celebrated Her Majesty's presence by winning the crown for Britain. At just about two o'clock, immediately before the Queen sat down, they played 'Land of Hope and Glory' and there was the atmosphere of a festive occasion, rather like the last night at the Proms. An hour and three quarters later, the cheer that went up could have been heard in Putney High Street – so loud, prolonged and frenzied was it. Miss Wade had beaten Betty Stove, of Holland, 4-6, 6-3, 6-1, to ensure that a British player was Queen of Wimbledon again.

Miss Wade was expected by many to beat Miss Stove easily. She did not do that. The fact

is made evident by the score, and when she lost the opening set after 38 minutes the earlier euphoria of the crowd was dimmed. I say she lost the opening set because that is what she did. Equally, Miss Stove lost the second set. And then the Dutch girl lost the third set. It was that sort of match. The result was memorable. The manner in which it came about was to be remembered only by those who have a taste for the grotesque.

It would be absurd to say that Miss Wade did not do her talents justice, since, after all, she won the match and title. But her display in this match compared ill with her brilliance in the semi-final against Chris Evert. Nor, for that matter, did Miss Stove play half as well as she might have done. Curiously enough, there were rallies in which the Dutch player, who took everything that happened so well and sportingly, produced a quality attack well in excess of anything that Miss Wade offered. Some of Miss Stove's volleys, especially from the backhand, made her look the copybook aggressive player to the last inch. Equally, she produced an awful lot of rubbish, when simple forehand returns were such that the captain of a club side would have wondered if she were good enough to be selected.

The tension that pervaded the match came more from the ineptitude of the players on the day than from their real capacity. It happened that for first point of the match, with Miss Wade serving, Miss Stove projected a positive winning lob. It took Miss Wade five minutes and four deuces before she managed to win that first game. Then, when Miss Stove served in game No.2, she began with a double fault. She was destined to serve nine in all during the course of this chequered contest. She fell to 0-40 in that second game but pulled it round nonetheless.

Game No.5 was one of British foreboding. Somehow, Miss Wade seemed to have lost the confidence she exuded during the last few days, and was falling more and more into uneasy, fidgety, fumbling errors which have characterised some of her Wimbledon performances in the past. A bad Wade game was followed by one from Miss Stove that was even

worse, to make the score three games all. Then Miss Wade hauled back a game from 0-40 to lead 4-3, and the temperature of British patriotism rose high again. But Miss Stove drew level. Miss Wade contributed two losers in the next game, Miss Stove two winners, and that was a love game against the serve with Holland in the lead 5-4.

Despite a double fault in the next game and a point for five games all, Miss Stove won the set. In the last game, there were two good rallies – they were scarce enough to deserve a note – and on the last Miss Wade made a volley error from the backhand to lose it. Then British hearts were able to sing again. Miss Wade cut down her proportion of errors and Miss Stove accentuated hers. At any rate, Miss Wade went to 3-0. She had a point to lead 4-0 and another to be 4-1, but Miss Stove climbed back to 3-3 – and all was tense once more.

Miss Wade must have sensed her responsibilities then. Miss Stove seemed to assume that the task was beyond her, winning only three points in the next three games, all of

Virginia Wade, Wimbledon Centre Court queen at last, enjoying a rare moment of British triumph

which left Miss Wade in possession of the set 6-3. She went on to lead 4-0 in the decider as the quality of the play became more reasonable. The crowd warmed to the situation, and every winning shot by Miss Wade, and every losing one by Miss Stove, was greeted with acclamation. The Dutch girl contrived to win the fifth game, but by then Miss Wade was too close to the title to be deterred. She lost one match point, but took the second with a forehand return of service that forced Miss Stove to volley to the net.

Thus came about Wimbledon's rare moment of British triumph. And how sportingly Miss Stove took the enthusiasm that even caused her double faults to be applauded. Miss Wade has now collected her finest lawn tennis crown. Her other major triumphs were the US Open in 1968, the Italian in 1971, the Australian in 1972.

1977
12 August

Boycott's century sets seal on historic return

In 1977 Geoff Boycott returned to Test cricket after a self-imposed exile and spectacularly helped England win the series against Australia 3-0 and regain the Ashes. His return was made glorious by his 100th century in first-class cricket. **Michael Melford** *reported in The Daily Telegraph*

Boycott's 100 and the ball was not half way to the boundary when the hero's bat was raised

ONLY THE MOST MACABRE imagination could have pictured Geoff Boycott failing to make his 100th hundred on his return to Test cricket at Headingley, and at 10 minutes to six yesterday evening the feat for which one and all were waiting was duly accomplished. The day's play thus ended amid tremendous scenes of jubilation, and the fact that England's score stood promisingly at 252 for four did nothing to detract from them.

The churlish might say that 67 runs after tea was a poor haul against tiring bowling lacking variety on a splendid batting pitch. For once, however, England have time on their side and do not need to take risks; moreover, only 87 overs were bowled. In this context, of course, they had the ideal batsman in charge in Boycott, with his massive concentration and unflagging technique. It seemed a wonderful toss for England to win, not least in their strange and felicitous position of being two up; but in three balls Brearley was out, caught at the wicket off a good one from Thomson which he had to play.

Until lunch Boycott and Woolmer put things in perspective, batting with care, restrained confidence and just a little luck. Boycott gave a hard low chance off Walker in front of first slip which Marsh reached and would have held in more prosperous times; but not here.

When Boycott was 26 Pascoe bowled him one of the morning's few bumpers which lobbed up into the slips, apparently off

Boycott's forearm, but otherwise they played some tidy bowling strictly on its merits – Boycott producing one fine square cut.

The bowling still gave little away after lunch and nothing was attempted unless the length erred a lot. Only six runs had been added in 15 minutes after lunch when Woolmer pushed out to Thomson and was picked up, low down at first slip, by Chappell. Randall breezed in and out again making 20 runs in 25 minutes, with some quick, wristy cutting before he played round a ball from Pascoe and was lbw.

Boycott made three runs in nearly 50 minutes after lunch, but, at about the same time as at Trent Bridge, he had completed the reconnaissance and was prepared to advance on all fronts. His 50 received a rapturous ovation, which was a merciful restoration to normality after the hostility which had greeted Greig a few minutes before.

However, there are problems in differentiating between the goodies and the baddies when the alleged baddies are on your side and Greig, on his luckier days, is undeniably a useful batsman to have in when the tempo needs raising. When the ball was pitched up or nearly so he unfolded his long reach and played some good strokes through the covers. Though the ball was not always in the middle of the bat he hooked Chappell for six and England had only one bad moment before tea.

The Australians appealed at full throttle for a catch at the wicket on the leg side when Boycott was 75. When it was refused they expressed such disappointment, some of it presumably verbal, that umpire Alley spoke severely to the bowler, Bright. After tea, when the fourth wicket had added 96 in 105 minutes, Greig was out in a not unfamiliar way, bowled driving outside a ball from Thomson which came back to hit his off stump.

Roope in his early stages would be recommended watching for those of a nervous disposition, but nothing seemed likely to dislodge Boycott as he made five in 45 minutes after tea and moved on towards the inevitable moment of glory.

A hook off Pascoe produced another four, but Walker, in a fine spell of 10 overs for 14

ENGLAND
1st Innings

*J. M. Brearley	c Marsh b Thomson	0
G. Boycott	not out	110
R. A. Woolmer	c Chappell b Thomson	37
D. W. Randall	lbw b Pascoe	20
A. W. Greig	b Thomson	43
G. R. J. Roope	not out	19
Extras	(b 1 lb 3 nb 17 w 2)	23
Total	(4 wkts)	**252**

To bat:
I. T. Botham, *A. P. E. Knott, D. L. Underwood, M. Hendrick, R. G. D. Willis

Fall of wickets: 1-0, 2-82, 3-105, 4-201.
Bowling: Thomson 21-4-78-3, Walker 27-12-59-0, Pascoe 20-7-48-1, Walters 3-0-5-0, Bright 6-3-14-0, Chappell 10-2-25-0

AUSTRALIA
R.B. McCosker, J.C. Davies, *G.S. Chappell, D.W. Hookes, K.D. Walters, R.D. Robinson, †R.W. March, R.J. Bright, M.H.N. Walker, J.R. Thomson, L.S. Pascoe.

Umpires: W.L. Budd and W.E. Alley.

* *Captain*
† *Wicketkeeper*

runs, made him work hard and it was a straight drive to the football stand off Chappell which eventually brought about the historic event. The ball was not half way to the boundary when the hero's bat was raised on high and amid a rare hubbub small boys were converging on him from all over Yorkshire. When he re-appeared from the melee five minutes later he was without his cap, but it was returned by a repentant souvenir-hunter before he resumed operations, looking understandably weary.

There was another, almost equally unusual interruption when Thomson had to be stopped from taking the new ball because only 81 overs had been bowled and not 85, as shown on the scoreboard. It was eventually taken for the last two overs, wherein Thomson was driven by Boycott and Walker cut by Roope, who by now was looking safe without finding the gaps.

And so they came in, followed to the pavilion by a large proportion of the 22,000 who sang and waved and cheered until the genial hero made his last balcony appearance and

1980

1 August

In Moscow, Seb Coe rises from the ashes of defeat

The rivalry between Sebastian Coe and Steve Ovett was one of athletics' greatest. When Ovett won the 800 metres in the 1980 Moscow Olympics, Coe seemed buried. But six days later Coe reversed the form in the 1,500 metres. **Christopher Brasher** *described in The Observer how the resurrection came about*

SEBASTIAN COE IS ALIVE AND WELL again a week after talking of being in the grave and I needed to know how the resurrection had come about. For it was indeed a resurrection, and Sebastian Coe, normally a man of undramatic words, knows that it was. Six days after the crushing disappointment of his 800 metres defeat he had woken up with the feeling inside of him that: 'Yes, this is my day.'

So we talked, in a car hurtling through Moscow from the Lenin Stadium to the TV centre, of how he and his father, Peter, had put aside disaster and had emerged with triumph in the 1,500 metres. First, his father Peter: 'When you have done with all the training, done with all the talk, all the instructions, you realise that there is more to the sport than putting one foot in front of the other. It is about character. The Yanks have a lovely saying: "When the going gets tough, it's the tough who get going." There is no better way of saying it, and for once, I cannot distinguish between my feelings as his coach and my feelings as his parent, because there is only one feeling – pride in his character.

'This has got nothing to do with how well you train: of course he was well trained. Of

course he has got all the bloody equipment, but that equipment was thrown out of the window on the night he lost the 800 metres, and from then on it was Sebastian Coe – all the way – on his own.'

Seb said that he knew only too well what the attitude of his fellow competitors was and, indeed, that of the world: 'I had blown it in the 800, and there was no way back. A lot of peo-

Turning the tables, nothing was going to stop Coe beat Ovett in the Moscow 1,500 metres final

ple have come up to me in these past few days and wished me well – good luck... get in there. They were very well-meaning but you know that they had buried you and that they were patting the earth.

'I'll tell you what kept me going – two things. The first may have sounded a bit glib when I said it on TV but it's true. I just knew that I could not possibly run as badly as I did last Saturday again because that just wasn't me. And the second is that I also knew that if I had lost this one as well, I would have to ask a lot of questions – of myself. Questions about my own character and my own abilities, unpleasant questions.'

I asked whether he had thought that if he failed a second time, he might as well pack it in – that he was dead, for life, as an athlete. That is a strange way of phrasing a question, but there is a certain dramatic shorthand in sport which speaks of the dead athlete who, to others, looks like a normal, live human being. Peter Coe was quick to answer with an insistent 'I don't think that. We've got a big one planned for the Zurich meeting.'

'Now wait a minute,' said Seb. 'Let's be fair about it. I'm 23 and I have another four or five years – hopefully – of good-class running in me. But the Olympics only come around once every four years. I still don't consider them to be the peak of athletic achievement. I think there are so many more factors involved. But... let's put it this way: If I had lost the gold in the 1,500 metres then there is only one guy in Britain.'

He meant, of course, Steve Ovett and that would wound Seb's pride because it would mean that he had had to give way and a great athlete never, ever, gives way. Seb said that Brendan Foster had helped him by 'nibbling away at me for three or four days. He told me that if I lost this one, "there will be only one guy. But pull this one out and you can go on. If you don't you've got four years to sit around and think: am I going to be another Ron Clarke, another David Bedford?"'

Brendan was referring to the two athletes of recent history whom other athletes love best: two men who could set startling world records but who never won gold medals in major events like the Olympic and Commonwealth Games. The same thought had occurred to me during the week: was Coe a phenomenal runner who could reach out to new world records but who just did not have the tactical brain and the aggression to win a major title?

I talked it over with Ron Clarke himself, who is here in Moscow as a commentator for Australian television. One evening we sat long over dinner and concocted a plan for Seb because we wanted to keep alive this duel between the two greatest middle-distance runners we have ever seen – a duel which fascinates the world and which does so much good for our sport. We knew that Seb was the hunter – that nobody could set a pace fast enough to drop him. And we knew also that he was the fastest finisher in the field. That made him favourite. We wrote him a letter telling him this and outlining the tactics that we suggested, relax on the pace, move into position, and strike – remembering that he who strikes first is generally the victor. We said that 'the only person who can beat you is yourself.'

We also urged him to unleash his kick in the semi-final in order to let his opponents, and the world, see what he could do. This was necessary also to prove to himself that the acceleration which he has worked on so hard throughout the year was still there. And finally we said – and here Ron was thinking back to his first Olympic Games in 1964 – that Seb must take his chance because life does not give you many chances. And he was privileged to have another chance just six days – instead of four years – after his disastrous mistakes in the 800 metres.

But when we watched the semi-final and saw Seb make another tactical blunder in the last lap, we said to each other: 'He's had it. He hasn't got a tactical brain.' Earlier in the week Seb had had much the same thought as Peter Coe recalled. 'He said to me: "Dad, this is not a criticism, but I think we have missed a significant amount of those competitive races where there is a lot of stuffing about." It was a natural thought, but what he was really doubting was whether he had the kind of mental make-up that can deal with this type of race. But I knew that he had, because I've been with him in those races in Malmo and Turin, and the Golden Mile in Oslo. Now he knows that he has it, and he'll never look back.'

1981
4 April

Bob Champion triumphs over cancer and Aintree

The story of Bob Champion winning the Grand National on Aldaniti was so moving they eventually made a film of it, Champions, with John Hurt in the jockey's role. Champion had had cancer and Aldaniti had been crippled but they won in stirring fashion, as **Brough Scott** *related in The Sunday Times*

A mountain is climbed as Bob Champion and Aldaniti power their way to victory

IN WHAT MUST BE THE MOST inspiring Grand National result of all, Bob Champion came back from the cancer ward, Aldaniti returned from the cripples' stall, and together they held off by four lengths the challenge of the favourite Spartan Missile and his 54-year-old owner-trainer-breeder-rider John Thorne.

Eighteen months ago I drove home from seeing the thirty-year-old Bob in his Surrey hospital and cried miserably in the car. No amount of gallant 'I'll be back next year' talk could hide the feeling that in his balding, emaciated state the only ride he was going to take was in a long black car.

Yesterday the tears were running again, more tears than even Red Rum brought to the Grand National winner's circle, and they were tears of the purest joy.

No one could exaggerate the mountain Champion had to climb and no jockey could ever have ridden a better race, or indeed a stronger one than he did yesterday. Aldaniti is a big heavy horse and there were doubts even among his supporters that his impetuosity would be too much for him, particularly over the early fences.

Indeed, at the very first, pulling hard, he clouted the fence and pitched dangerously on landing. For watching friends it was not a promising start and yet as Bob said later, 'It turned out the very best thing. It made him think and even though he was going quite free he was having a look at them and after that he really jumped super.'

So well was Aldaniti going that he joined the early leader Carrow Boy and Zongalero at the Canal Turn and actually pulled his way to the front as the great cavalry charge swept towards the stands at the end of the first circuit. There were loose horses around but no dramas at the Chair fence like last year, and going out away from the stands the pattern was set, with Aldaniti in front and Royal Mail coming through to be the biggest threat, with Spartan Missile getting into the race although still some lengths off the leaders.

Becher's, so often a graveyard of the leaders in the Grand National, was navigated with hardly a nod from Aldaniti, as was the Canal Turn, and turning back towards the stands it was clear that the unthinkable was clearly possible, for Royal Mail was hardly going and Spartan Missile still had some running to do.

Aldaniti gave the third last a clout and although he still looked in command it was then that the ultimate test of the rider's strength and horse's endurance was to come, for Aldaniti had suffered such bad leg problems over the years that he has only run twice in two seasons and such a preparation seemed sure to be too light for those final endless 494 yards of the run-in.

By the last fence Aldaniti still had a length advantage over Royal Mail, and if he seemed marginally less weary than his rival, Spartan Missile and John Thorne were working their way back at them and up that long stretch, so that supporters of sporting dreams hardly knew whom to cheer for, the cancer victim and his former invalid mount or the 54-year-old grandfather who shed two stone in weight to ride the horse he bred and trained himself in Warwickshire.

Royal Mail had kept on to be three lengths away third after a brilliant ride from Philip Blacker. Three to One was fourth and Senator Maclacury fifth of twelve finishers, who sadly did not include the only woman, Linda Sheedy, whose mare Deiopea refused at the 19th, the 44-year-old Manchester solicitor John Carden, who went at the fourth, or the oil rig worker Peter Duggan, who refused at the 12th and remounted only to refuse again at the 15th.

Yet in truth the Grand National was only a good luck story. No praise can be too high for the way in which trainer Josh Gifford has kept faith with both his horse and rider. Aldaniti has broken down twice and also broken a bone in his hock. Josh admitted yesterday that he thought owner Nick Embiricos 'was crackers to even try and run the horse again after his last breakdown.' And although he was unwavering in his promises at Champion's sickbed, privately he admitted that he never considered Bob likely to ride again, or even leave hospital with any reasonable prospect of life ahead.

Bob Champion had his cancer first diagnosed in July of 1979; he had one testicle and a rib removed by surgery and had to undergo intensive chemotherapy, leaving hospital for the last time on 1 January last year.

The road back has been steady but has had at least two major crises, the continuing battle with his weight (Bob has had to keep to a drastic regime of spartan rationing and lengthy sauna sessions to keep his weight at 11 stone), and when he began to ride races again this season the winners were slow to come.

Indeed, the mind goes back to one afternoon at Fontwell last December when the game almost seemed gone beyond recall. Horses had been falling, other jockeys had begun to take his rides and then Bob took a heavy crash on the flat in one race and was too shaken to ride the winner of the last.

We had a drink in the little open bar beside the track, he grimaced as he moved an injured shoulder and muttered wistfully, 'It's very hard at the moment, but I am determined to go on.'

Two big winners at Ascot a week later suddenly changed the wheel and since then all the old flair has come back with Aldaniti his 35th winner. Yesterday's triumph was the greatest sporting tribute to the principle that the battle is never over while the mind is strong.

Aintree's right to claim to be the centre of the world for just one Saturday each spring has never been better demonstrated than this time round, when the sun came out and Bob Champion won the Grand National on Aldaniti.

Ian Botham proves to be one in a million

In the 1981 Test series, Ian Botham gave up the captaincy when England were 1-0 down. After Mike Brearley took over Botham hit two centuries, took 18 wickets, held seven catches to ensure England a 3-1 victory. The Sun's **Ian Jarrett** *recorded the Aussie captain's words after the decisive match at Old Trafford*

BEATEN AUSSIE TEST SKIPPER Kim Hughes last night advised England: 'Never try to change Ian Botham. He's one in a million.' Hughes was speaking after England had clinched a 103-run victory in the Fifth Test at Old Trafford to retain the Ashes and Botham had scooped his third consecutive Man of the Match award.

The Australian skipper added: 'The difference between the sides in this series has been one man – Ian Botham. Look at his effort in this match. A brilliant century, five wickets, and a blinder of a catch to get rid of Dennis Lillee at a crucial time today. You don't have to look too hard to discover the reason why England have retained the Ashes.

'Ian Botham as captain wouldn't have played as well. When he was captain I felt he didn't have the support of every member of the team. But once Mike Brearley came into the side, they gathered round and allowed Botham to produce his brilliant best. England will continue to win games as long as they've got a Botham like this. No-one else has the ability to get them into that position. The same

At Headingley Botham, here congratulated by Taylor, Brearley and Gatting, took six wickets for 95 in Australia's first innings

people who praise him are just as likely to rubbish him when he gets out cheaply. But if people try to change Botham, England will have lost their chance of winning Test matches.'

Brearley, victorious in three matches since returning to lead the side, also backed Botham. He said: 'England without Botham would be like the West Indies without Sobers. There's a boyishness about him and he needs a father figure around him to encourage and advise.

'There are odd times when you have to say "come off it" or "go easy". I don't know what Ian honestly thinks, but if anyone else was going to captain England I think he was glad it was me. Since the Headingley Test, we have been expecting to win matches. And that is

In the third Test at Headingley, Botham (picture, left) scored 149 not out in England's second innings. At Edgbaston, when Alderman was bowled by Botham (above) England had the fourth Test in its pocket; Botham had taken no fewer than five of Australia's second innings wickets. In the fifth Test at Old Trafford, Botham played another legendary role, scoring 118 in England's second innings. As if this was not enough he was a tower of strength in the field; witness one example (right) when Yallop is out, bowled Willis, caught Botham

largely due to Botham – and Bob Willis, who now plays like a fast bowler and not an ageing medium-pacer.'

TEST SCOREBOOK

By Bill Frindall, the BBC facts and figures man.

ENGLAND - 1st Inns 231 (Tavare 69, Lillee 4-55, Alderman 4-88)
AUSTRALIA - 1st Inns 130 (Willis 4-63)
ENGLAND - 2nd Inns 404 (Botham 118, Tavare 78, Knott 59, Emburey 57, Alderman 5-109)

AUSTRALIA
Second Innings
(Overnight - 210-5)

Border not out...123
(420mins, 356 balls, 17 fours)
Marsh c Knott b Willis...47
(296-6, 110mins, 101 balls, 6 fours, 1 six, Edged drive)
Bright c Knott b Willis 5
(32-7, 39mins, 29 balls, Gloved leg-glance)
Lillee c Botham b Allott...28
(378-3, 83mins, 65 balls, 3 fours, Edged cut to slip)
Alderman lbw b Botham 0
(378-b, 14mins, 10 balls, Missed straight ball)
Whitney c Gatting b Willis 0
(402-10, 38 mins, 32 balls. Edged via pad to short leg)
Extras (lb 3, w 2, nb 18) 20
TOTAL..**402**
Bowling: Willis 30.5-2-96-3; Allott 17-3-712; Botham 36-16-86-2; Emburey 49-9-107-2; Gatting 3-1-13-0

UMPIRES: D. Constant and K. Palmer.

FIRST TEST (Trent Bridge): Australia won by four wkts. **SECOND (Lord's):** Drawn. **THIRD (Headingley):** England won by 18 runs. **FOURTH (Edgbaston):** England won by 29 runs. **SIXTH (The Oval):** Aug 27-Sept 1.

Torvill and Dean reach pinnacle of perfection

It was the perfect moment, Valentine's Day. To the rhythm of Ravel's Bolero, Jayne Torvill and Christopher Dean skated away with the Olympic gold medal for ice dancing. Their romantic performance earned maximum points for artistic impression. **John Hennessy** *reported from Sarajevo for The Times*

WHAT BETTER WAY for the two sweethearts of British sport to spend St Valentine's Day than to hypnotise a capacity crowd at the Zetra Stadium, among them Princess Anne, as they played out their tragic love story to the music of Ravel's 'Bolero'.

Jayne Torvill and Christopher Dean not only held the crowd, but also the nine judges so completely in their thrall that this time they accumulated 12 maximum marks of 6.0 to surpass their record of 11 in Lyons two years ago and Budapest one month ago, and received a full set of sixes for artistic impression.

Thus, Britain thrillingly acquired their third skating gold medal in successive Olympics in the wake of John Curry in 1976 and Robin Cousins in 1980. With respect to both, this was a greater triumph. Whereas Torvill and Dean came to Sarajevo with three gold medals and the burden of overwhelming favourites, Curry won his one world title after the Olympics and Cousins never did win one.

It was a superlative demonstration of classical skating, interpreted to such perfect pitch that the heart alternately sang and froze as the couple themselves swung between the emotions, a smile here, a haunting gesture of despair there, before their suicide pact cast them into the volcano. Dean said afterwards, to no one's surprise: 'This was the pinnacle of our amateur career.' His partner 'simply couldn't believe it really, couldn't believe it was all over. Everything seemed to click into place.'

How they shamed those of us of little faith who began to see errors in training when none existed – apart from two much publicised falls – and sought out imaginary signs of nerves. When the crunch came they proved themselves stronger even than they had done with the 'Barnum' routine in Helsinki last year. There was character too, not only in the way they faced up to this supreme test, but in the way they had the courage of their convictions to stay with the 'Bolero' when some who should have known better were picking unnecessary holes in it.

The changes they had made since the European championships in Budapest included two stunning highlights early in the programme: a full split by Dean with body twists, and a lift where he took his partner off the ice with his free leg, and which came as such a surprise to the audience that they broke into prolonged applause. From that moment on they were home. The audience, so cold towards their original set pattern Paso Doble, developed a thread of empathy that must have encouraged the British couple still further. It was a beautiful performance, on a different plane from any that had gone before.

There were not many Britons in the audience, in spite of a plane load of reinforcements during the day, so it must be seen as a universal accolade that the stadium rose to them at the end. Americans who had vociferously supported their compatriots, and Russians who

had chanted encouragement to theirs, were one with everybody in saluting a display of interpretive skating that, dare one suggest, has no precedent.

They have done magic things, with 'Mac and Mabel', for instance, and 'Barnum', and a variety of stunning original set patterns, but this surpassed them all. They were perfectly placed in the draw for generous marking, at the tail of the field, but they still had to do their stuff on the ice. If they could turn it on, there was room for the judges to go as high as they wished. In the end three judges gave them two marks of 6.0, those from Hungary, Japan and Britain.

Jayne Torvill and Christopher Dean's performance was on a different plane from any that had gone before

Courtney Jones, then, the 'hanging judge' of old, had dismantled all his defences. A 6.0 in the compulsory dances, his first ever in any form of competition, had now been trebled. Natalya Bestemianova, who finished runner-up with Andrei Bukin, yet again had put on her superb fire cracker act but, as she herself said during the European championships in Budapest: 'It seems impossible to beat Torvill and Dean.'

1984
30 May

Marathon men of Liverpool have their finest hour

The team from Anfield had won the European Cup three times before, but their match against Roma, in Rome's Olympic Stadium, was debatably the most dramatic of all. Still 1-1 after extra time, Liverpool won 4-2 in a penalty shoot-out. **Ian Hargraves** *reported the match for the Liverpool Echo*

TWO MONTHS BEFORE the Olympic Games are due to start in Los Angeles, Liverpool last night completed the greatest marathon in modern times. Their fourth European Cup victory, achieved after the most dramatic of penalty shoot-outs, proved a fitting climax to what has been a quite astonishing season. They now hold the European Cup, the league championship, the Milk Cup and the Central League title, all achieved by the sterling British qualities of guts and sheer hard labour.

No team has ever won so much in one season, or is ever likely to again. No team has ever earned its success in such a hard way. And it is fitting that last night's victory, the greatest triumph of them all, was achieved not so much by individual brilliance as by unflagging teamwork and the refusal to give in. As in the previ-

ous rounds, when they won away four times in a row, Liverpool had to battle all the way. They had to beat Roma on their own ground, where the Italians had not lost all season, in front of a violently partisan crowd and a small army of police. And what's more, they had to do it after surrendering an early lead and in the most unlikely manner conceivable. Nobody who has watched Liverpool over the last few years can have given much for their chances when extra time ended with the scores still level. And when Steve Nicol, unexpectedly asked to shoot first, put his kick high over the crossbar the Liverpool cause seemed hopeless.

Fortunately, those two European veterans, full backs Phil Neal and Alan Kennedy, again rose to the occasion in the grand manner. It was Neal, hero of three previous finals, who put Liverpool in front after 15 minutes – and it was the same player who got them back into the penalty race by netting confidently after Nicol's failure. Then after Souness and Rush had netted their kicks and Roma's two Italian World Cup stars Conti and Graziani had both failed it was Barney Rubble who sent Tancredi the wrong way to put the issue beyond doubt.

The match itself never quite lived up to expectations in terms of sheer entertainment, though that was hardly surprising in view of all that was at stake. However, it lacked nothing in incident or excitement, fluctuating first one way then the other, with neither team able to establish any clear advantage.

ROMA (5-2-3)
Tancredi; Nappi, Bonetti, Righetti, Di Bartolomei, Neia; Cerezo, Falcao; Conti, Pruzzo, Graziani. Subs: Chierice (on for Pruzzo after 63 minutes); Strukelj (on for Cerezo after 115 minutes); Malgioglio; Oddi; Vincenzi (not used).

LIVERPOOL (4-3-3)
Grobbelaar; Neal, Lawrenson, Hansea, Kennedy; Lee, Souness, Whelan; Dalglish, Rush, Johnston. Subs: Nicol (on for Johnston after 72 minutes); Robinson (on for Dalglish after 93 minutes); Bolder; Hodgson; Gillespie (not used).

Goals: Neal (Liverpool) 15 minutes 0-1; Pruzzo (Roma) 44 minutes 1-1; Neal, Souness, Rush, Kennedy scored penalties for Liverpool after extra time; Di Bartolomei and Righetti scored for Roma.
Referee: Mr. Erik Frederikason (Sweden).

The cup is Liverpool's and the team, weary but triumphant, can celebrate at last

In the early stages it was Liverpool who looked the more impressive, and when they took the lead after 15 minutes it seemed the Italians were doomed to defeat. It was a very good goal, created by Johnston's accurate cross which was never cleared, the ball rebounding off the hapless goalkeeper to Neal who banged the ball into the net in the manner born. Liverpool could have increased their lead when a Johnston header was helped into the net by Souness only for the apparent 'score' to be disallowed for offside and Rush might well have scored on two other occasions but for Tancredi's agility, as might Nicol in the closing minutes.

However, towards the end of the first half and again early in the second Roma more than held their own. Though neither of their Brazilians were able to shake off the shackles imposed by Liverpool's tight mid-field marking, their captain, Di Bartolomei, exploited Conti's speed and skill with some lovely diagonal passes. Roma had twice created havoc down Liverpool's right flank, and Graziani had forced Grobbelaar to a fine near post save, when Roma got their equaliser almost immediately before the interval. Neal and Lee seemed to have blocked Conti's way to goal out on the left but Conti collected a rebound and hit a perfect centre which found Pruzzo unmarked and perfectly placed to head past Grobbelaar.

In the second half, and again in extra time, there were plenty of half chances at both ends but somehow one rarely felt there would be further goals. Liverpool seemed over-dependent on Rush to do their scoring while Roma seemed to lack confidence in their own ability to finish off the game.

Both sides were clearly exhausted going into extra time and it was no surprise when the match became the first European Cup final to be settled by penalties. Even Liverpudlians must have felt sympathy for Roma on being beaten in such an unsatisfactory manner but for all that it was a marvellous performance by Liverpool.

1984
10 August

Irrepressible Daley Thompson wins decathlon gold

*To say there has been no other British athlete like Daley Thompson is an understatement. When he won his second Olympic decathlon gold medal, at the Los Angeles Olympics, his off-beat humour brought immediate criticism but not from Princess Anne, as **Neil Wilson** reported in the Daily Mail*

DALEY THOMPSON TWICE took the Olympics by storm yesterday – first by winning his decathlon gold, then with his off-beat sense of humour. Britain's 26-year-old champion was congratulated by Princess Anne at the trackside after his victory-clinching performance in the 1,500 metres and whistled his way through the national anthem during the medal presentation.

And at an international Press conference later, he was obviously still feeling on top of the world. Asked what the Princess had said to him, he replied: 'She said I was a damned good-looking guy.' After a pause he added: 'That's a joke.'

The athlete, who won a decathlon gold in the 1980 Moscow Olympics, is already talking of the next Games, Seoul in 1988. But he said:

'Maybe, it's time I settled down a bit. Maybe I should have some kids.' He was asked whom he intended to settle down with and replied: 'You've just mentioned the lady.' And referring to the children he'd like to have, he said: 'I hope they'll be white.'

His remarks provoked some criticism – but certainly not from Princess Anne, who spoke up for him later. Mr Michael Shea, the Queen's press secretary, said: 'The Princess wants to make it quite clear that she finds it totally and absolutely absurd that anyone should think anything said by Daley Thompson after his outstandingly brilliant achievement was offensive in any way.'

Thompson had appeared at the Press conference wearing a T-shirt posing the question: Is the world's second greatest athlete gay? American reporters took it as a reference to their own golden boy, Carl Lewis, who had denied in a magazine article that he was a homosexual. Thompson teased the Americans, saying 'It could be Carl Lewis, it could be Jurgen Hingsen (Thompson's closest rival in the decathlon) or it could be Daley Thompson.' Then he added: 'Anyway, "gay" in England just means happy.'

Later, he was still wise-cracking. Asked in a U.S. television interview about how he felt when he realised he had won his gold, he said: 'It's the best moment since Granny got her tit caught in the mangle.' But there were moments when his enthusiasm and understandable pride charmed onlookers.

'Two Olympics are nice. Three would be better,' he had said earlier. 'Nobody's done that. You couldn't argue with that, could you? I'd feel happy then to pass it on to others.'

The achievement of Thompson, the boy from Notting Hill, was a truly great one. Faced with a man who had three times set the world record, he produced the highest-ever first-day total and came within one point of the German's world record to beat him. In the end, Thompson totalled 8,797 points and Hingsen 8,673. Hingsen holds the world record with 8,798, Thompson's previous best was 8,743. All he needed finally to break Hingsen's record was a time in the 1,500 metres of 4 min 34.8

sec. He has trained to run comfortably under 4min 20sec but yesterday he managed only 4min 35sec. Canadian coach Andy Higgens, who is a friend, said: 'He should have known that you don't have the true spirit left in you after two days of a decathlon.'

Thompson put it differently. 'I wanted to win with no more effort than was necessary,' he said. 'I can get a world record another time at any other meeting.' He did, however, concede:

In Los Angeles, Daley Thompson won the decathlon gold and got 'the biggest buzz' of his life

'I need the Olympics. My motivation rose here to what it used to be.' And in a remark that possibly explained all his other more exuberant ones yesterday, he said: 'I got the biggest buzz of my life.'

Barry McGuigan becomes king of the featherweights

*It is a Celtic tradition to spawn brilliant boxers among the lighter weights. None was more magnificent than the Irishman Barry McGuigan the night he took the World Boxing Association's featherweight title away from Eusebio Pedroza in London. In The Observer **Hugh McIlvanney** was on a territory he commands best of all*

Barry McGuigan won the world featherweight championship and became the focus of mass euphoria

BARRY MCGUIGAN became surely the most rapturously acclaimed winner in the history of European boxing when the irresistible intensity of his aggression wore down the magnificent resistance of Eusebio Pedroza and battered the great Panamanian's World Boxing Association featherweight championship away from him over 15 rounds at the Queen's Park Rangers Football Ground in West London last night.

The predictable announcement that the referee and two ringside judges had made the 24-year-old from Clones, Co. Monaghan, a unanimous points winner produced the most euphoric scenes witnessed at a sports event in this country in decades. McGuigan had lived up to all the promise of an astonishing career which had seen only one insignificant stumble in the 26 fights that led to last night's challenge. He had refused to be frustrated or diminished by the wonderful talents and unbreakable spirit of one of the finest champions the featherweight division has ever seen.

That Barry McGuigan at last made him bow out of his championship is a triumph which can hardly be exaggerated and no one now is entitled to oppose very strenuously the claims some of us have made that this young man is the most dramatic fighter to emerge from these islands in half a century.

The first three rounds had to be scored for Pedroza as the Panamanian boxed with a cool brilliance on the retreat while McGuigan sought to find his range. In the first Pedroza backed away with a swiftness that betrayed respect for McGuigan's power, but was never flustered as he thrust out his long jab and occasionally crossed the right. It was not a punishing round but the Panamanian did most of the scoring and the same applied to the second round. His was the sharper, more accurate work but there was evidence that the advantage he had at the end of that round might be academic because McGuigan was continuing to press forward with a confidence that encouraged his supporters to be optimistic.

It was impossible even for a prejudiced observer to fail to admire the excellence of Pedroza's boxing in the third. But although he took that round, one thudding left hook by McGuigan as they broke after a clinch suggested exciting happenings were imminent. The Panamanian's extraordinary height for a featherweight (5ft 10ins) made him hard to reach and the length of his arms created extreme awkwardness when the two men closed. However, McGuigan was not in the least discouraged and was out in the middle of the ring waiting to go to war at the start of the fourth as Pedroza came slowly from his corner. That round was much more even in terms of scoring than its predecessors and no less rugged. The world champion had already been warned by the South African referee, Stanley Christodoulou, for holding and for letting his punches drift low.

McGuigan, for his part, was not inclined to be gentle and his head had a tendency to wander towards his opponent's thick moustache. The fifth provided three more minutes of often unscrupulous violence, with Pedroza earning a further reprimand for swinging out. McGuigan was getting stronger rather than weaker at this point and the Panamanian, for all his impassive expression, must have felt concerned.

There was even more pronounced roughness in the sixth round of what was shaping to become a memorably unrelenting struggle. McGuigan had three warnings for minor misconduct, notably his old habit of forgetting where the waistline is, but self-belief was growing in him with every minute and his expression as he went back towards his manager Barney Eastwood in the corner was one to cheer every Irish heart in the stadium. What

occurred in the seventh was sufficient to make his vast following ecstatic. He kept boring in through the champion's virtuosity right through the round and near the end of it the dark sky above the football ground was almost split by a massive roar as McGuigan caught the champion with a brutal right hand to the head near Pedroza's own corner.

Those marvellous legs that have carried the older man through 19 defences of his title suddenly wilted and when a left hand crashed against his head he keeled over onto his side. He climbed bravely to his feet to take a mandatory eight count but at the end of the round the signs were that his championship might be heading across the Irish Sea. Of course, this dark, serious-faced man is the truest of champions and he came back in the eighth to box superbly and fight ferociously.

But that hardly seemed to matter in the ninth as McGuigan enveloped him again. The climax of the challenger's aggression once more came near Pedroza's corner and this time, too, it was not the famous left hook but another thunderous right that started the bad troubles for his victim. That blow was followed by a calculated flurry of hooks and the champion's long legs looked like going completely. There were several heavy punches landed by McGuigan after the bell and as Pedroza teetered back to his stool he showed particularly the effects of three numbing right hands.

The tenth round was quieter but in the eleventh McGuigan, whose face shone with an eagerness for the fray, was crowding in cruelly again on a struggling veteran. Now his body punches were clearly telling and twice Pedroza dropped on one knee to claim the rest he sorely needed. In the twelfth McGuigan maintained the pressure and the Irishman was the controlling influence.

All of the assessments of what had gone before now appeared scarcely relevant. They meant no more than the wonderful techniques Pedroza had exhibited to take his early, deceptive and by this time almost forgotten lead. McGuigan was punishingly in command and his progression to the title one of exhilarating inevitability.

Britain win the men's Olympic hockey tournament

For decades the hockey players of the Indian subcontinent dominated the sport. Then the force ebbed away to other nations. But it was not until the 1988 Seoul Olympics that a fairy tale came true. Great Britain beat Germany 3-1 to strike gold. **Rob Hughes** *reported for The Sunday Times*

OF ALL 237 GOLD MEDALS at these Olympics, none has been more honourably come by than that won yesterday by Great Britain's men's hockey team. They beat West Germany by three goals to one, but the performance is hardly the point. The essence of our hockey players is that they are Olympians. They are amateurs. They made personal sacrifices – of time, money and business opportunities – to take part in the Games.

Take part be damned! The one un-Olympian facet of these 11 men and their coach and their reserves was that they came for nothing but the gold. They had struck bronze in the last Olympics, silver at the 1986 World Cup. Gold was the only way to go up and out. Four of the team retired from international hockey while on yesterday's high. The goalkeeper, Ian

Taylor, a schoolteacher from Bromsgrove, has retired at 33 to give time to his family. We were reminded from start to finish of his qualities. He has an eye so rapid, an inner sense of danger and a willingness to spread his hugely padded 6ft frame in front of a ball travelling at 90mph. It quite devastated the opposition. West Germany, with their usual great determination, thrust Britain back to force eight penalty corners, but did not score from a single one.

It seemed an age since Taylor had carried the British flag into the arena for the opening ceremony. 'It is a different feeling, the pride for one's country, compared to this, a sporting achievement won with the rest of the team,' said Taylor. 'I get a lot of the credit but what I'm trying to say is that we are, we always have been, very much a team.'

Always is a long time. With this particular side it goes back eight years to when a former player, David Whitaker, became coach. Whitaker knew there were talents to exploit, but his most demanding job was to cut down the unnecessary running, the hell-bent aggressiveness which was part of Britain's hockey as it so often is of our football. 'I feel that the greatest thing in any sport is effectiveness,' said Whitaker. 'Every person has only so much energy, though Kerly has more than most.'

Sean Kerly inevitably penetrated the conversation. He penetrates virtually every defence he comes up against. Like Taylor, he has that incredible gift of an eye that sees the play before it develops, and reflexes and pace to deliver the shot from all manner of angles, almost before defenders are aware. Naturally, Kerly scored again yesterday, his eighth goal of the Olympic tournament. But it was his hat-trick in the semi-final against the world champions Australia which really broke the back of the tournament, during a contest in which England went two up, surrendered the lead, and then won it in the dying moments.

But yesterday Kerly's ultimate value was as decoy. The German defence surrounded him with dogged minders. His personal bodyguard, Volker Fried, like most of the Germans, is officially listed as a 27-year-old student. In other words, a state athlete. Fried, and other defend-

A golden moment as Britain's Stephen Batchelor leads the celebration of an historic victory

ers, were pulled out of the goal-mouth in the 21st minute yesterday when Britain struck. Stephen Batchelor, so often the goal-maker with his eel-like dribbles, had run the ball straight into the opposing rear lines. He flicked it to his right, and there, finding space, was Kerly. And after that? Kerly passed and we were treated to the dexterity of Imran Sherwani.

A Stoke-on-Trent newsagent Sherwani may be in real life, but in front of goal he dreams exotic dreams. And he makes them happen. Taking the pass from Kerly on the edge of his stick he seemed to stun it, his whole body-weight moved to the right. One defender and

the goalkeeper instinctively went that way, and somehow Sherwani deflected the ball the other. 'What happened,' he said, 'is that Sean was looking to pass to my ankle stick, the ball went in front of me and I had to reverse it. Then I just noticed a glaring gap and so I hit it.'

Later in the game, again from Batchelor's wing play, Kerly had distracted the defenders and Sherwani came in from wide out on the left to strike his second goal. But unity and honesty is what has kept this side together from the moment it was fortunate enough to go to the Los Angeles Olympics as a reserve when the Soviet Union pulled out. Such honesty was evident when I congratulated Whitaker on his tactics of deploying Kerly as a decoy.

A smile spread across the coach's face. 'I'd love to say we planned it,' he remarked. 'But we had only one tactical discussion. It was that the team should play as often as possible to Richard Dodds in the midfield, and he would release it. After that, the only orders were to "do everything you do normally, guys, only do it better."'

Dodds, the captain, is a surgeon who has organised his time so that he works on contracts fitted around his love for hockey. He finished the last one in June, has been on the road with Britain and will resume his next contract later this month. And as with Taylor, quantity surveyor Paul Barber and computer consultant Richard Leman, Dodds is finishing his career with Olympic gold. He was told, as he left the field, that this had been Britain's first victory against West Germany in 20 years. Succinctly, Dodds replied: 'They can keep them all. We have what we came for.'

Desert Orchid's courageous Gold Cup victory

*Up to the last moment it was not certain that Desert Orchid would run in the 1989 Gold Cup at Cheltenham. But despite atrocious conditions he did run and history was made. Desert Orchid held a nation in thrall and now a dream came true. In The Daily Telegraph **Peter Scott** recorded the peak of the great horse's career*

DESERT ORCHID SUMMONED EVERY OUNCE of courage for his finest hour. He wore down the equally gallant Yahoo in a Tote Cheltenham Gold Cup battle that was made gruelling by the heavy ground, but enabled the massive crowd to briefly forget the miserable weather.

Mr Richard Burridge, Desert Orchid's principal owner, had considered withdrawing him, but left the final say to trainer David Elsworth, who decided to go ahead. Neither Elsworth nor jockey Simon Sherwood had feared dead ground, but hours of rain turned it heavy. Snow started falling at breakfast time in neighbouring areas, so Cheltenham were lucky to race. The stewards made a precautionary inspection at noon.

Ten Plus's death marred what was other-wise a great occasion. Leading Desert Orchid three fences from home, he fell and broke a hind fetlock. Desert Orchid was in front to halfway, but then Sherwood allowed Ten Plus to go ahead. Sherwood was still biding his time when Ten Plus fell, and reckons the favourite would have won anyway.

Ten Plus's departure still did not leave matters easy because the almost unconsidered Yahoo then took command, and had a slight lead over the final two fences. Desert Orchid refused to give best and tackling the uphill run-in he inched ahead.

The lead steadily increased to one and a half lengths. Desert Orchid edged left towards Yahoo in his fatigue, but Sherwood straightened him in time to prevent any interference.

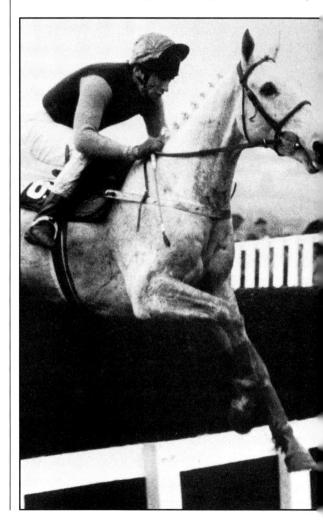

'Desert Orchid gave every ounce and I am honoured to be associated with such a horse,' said the winning jockey.

Charter Party, successful in last year's Gold Cup, finished eight lengths behind Yahoo in third place. Bonanza Boy was a distant fourth, with West Tip the only other finisher. The Irish-trained second favourite, Carvill's Hill, was a seventh-fence faller. 'He went straight through it like a novice,' said jockey Ken Morgan, who dislocated a shoulder. Carvill's Hill appeared none the worse and may run again at the Fairyhouse Easter meeting.

The Thinker, Golden Freeze and Slalom were other fallers on the first circuit. Cavvies Clown, second-string for the Desert Orchid stable, ran well for a long way, but then became very tired and was pulled up at the last. Ballyhane was brought down by Ten Plus's fall. Pegwell Bay's stamina proved unequal to the conditions. He dropped out in the last mile and was pulled up.

The grey was mobbed by his admirers when returning to unsaddle. 'He took it all in good part and knew he had accomplished something special,' said Sherwood. Tom Morgan, who rode Yahoo, was hopeful of scoring an upset until his mount began to 'tie-up' towards the finish. 'They were two tired horses,' said Morgan.

Over the final fence Yahoo (far side) led, but in the uphill run-in Desert Orchid inched ahead, finally to be mobbed by admirers

Scudamore's 200 winners create a compelling tale

*When Peter Scudamore became the first jump jockey in history to notch up 200 winners in a season he carved his place forever in the pantheon of great riders. The day he did it, **Dudley Doust**, who wrote the book 221, an account of the record season, was with him every moment of the way*

IT WAS THE MORNING of April 27, 1989, Peter Scudamore was on 197 wins and he seemed certain to reach his double-century sometime during the day: after all, he had four rides at Hereford and three more at Towcester in the evening. 'Four more at Towcester,' corrected Peter, meeting the TV boys as he arrived at Hereford. He'd only just got word of a fourth evening ride over his car phone: Jimmy Duggan called to say he was 'struggling'. He couldn't do the weight in the 7:45 at Towcester. Would Scu ride the horse, a gelding called Gay Moore? Likes heavy going. He'll go close. Trained by Michael Robinson.

That lifted Scu's rides to eight for the day. He'd need three winners and, if the world took this for granted, he didn't: three of eight was pitching it a bit high since only two of his mounts were fancied. 'I was confident at the beginning of the week,' he told the press. 'But now I'm getting cold feet. The races are much hotter than I reckoned.'

At Hereford, Scudamore drew a bust. No winners. And by late afternoon, buckled into his seat as the helicopter tilted towards Towcester, Scudamore had more reason to feel sick than the motion of the aircraft. A treble wasn't on. If he could pick up just one winner in Northamptonshire, perhaps on the hurdler Old Kilpatrick in the 5:45 there was tomorrow at Taunton, maybe Saturday at Worcester for the other two.

The helicopter landed in good time for the opening Towcester race, the Tiffield Claiming Hurdle, and Scudamore hurried from the infield, saddle under his arm, bag over his shoulder and made his way to the weighing-room. His opening mount, Old Kilpatrick, had liked the heavy at Chepstow a month earlier and he was soon to like the heavy at Towcester. The dark, glistening gelding slopped to a 12-length victory as, incongruously, a calypso band rattled away to keep warm in the stands. Scu now had 198 winners. Two away from the target. Three rides to go. Hope flickered. Press photographers, in an agony of frustration, held up their light meters in the gathering gloom.

His next race was the 6:15, the Wood Burcote Novices' Chase, and astride Canford Palm Scudamore rode his 199th winner, his 26th for Charlie Brooks for the season. The horse made the 2m 5f novices' chase look easy, running out the twenty lengths winner. One to go. Two chances to do it. First came the 7:45, a 3-mile race that bore the forgettable name of the City Trucks Handicap Chase.

In the weighing-room Duggan, who'd earlier in the season taken Gay Moore to his first victory over fences, gave Peter a last run-down on the horse. His verbal shorthand was brief and immaculate. 'He jumps like a buck,' said Duggan, 'but he's fairly one-paced. He won't be afraid of going in front. Keep him handy.'

As he cantered down towards the three-mile start at the far side of the track, Gay Moore was nicely balanced. He spooked once at a

The moment, 200 winners in a single season, and Scudamore can at last afford to grin

hedge, but Peter was not disconcerted: at least, he thought, the fellow's going to be careful. What the jockey liked most about Gay Moore was the low head carriage. The horse took a nice amount of rein. Scudamore could ride him with his hands on the withers. He could get his legs behind, which was all the better for his own balance and for pushing the horse, driving him on. It's good, concluded Peter, I'll be able to attack.

In the mud, the first fence had been dolled off. Scudamore guided Gay Moore round it and went downhill and into a plain fence, upsides in front but came out of it slowly with most of the ten-horse field now ahead of him. 'I don't know why,' he later recalled, 'but I was very confident. It was the feel of the horse.'

Dropping through Towcester's signature deep bottom land on the back straight, the going was sucking and Scudamore dropped away to second last but not hopelessly far off the pace. He was comfortable. He was having a good run on the inside. He stayed there, sensing the field was travelling too fast, and he remained happy, despite blundering in the greasy going over the second last first time round.

'That was my low point,' he recalled, 'things improved from then on.' Indeed they did and, slogging relentlessly on, Scudamore took up the challenge coming up the hill off the back straight. Good boy, he said, turning for home. The horse responded and, churning through the mud, Scu knew he'd win two fences from home. He took no chances, drove him on. 'Peter Scudamore...' screamed the commentator, and not for the first time this season, he was drowned out shouting. Peter kicked past the post, twelve lengths in front. The calypso band struck up.

Lester Piggott returns with the old magic

*A miracle of sorts occurred in racing when Lester Piggott, at 54, made a sensational return as a professional jockey. He went on to prove that little, even none, of his former skill had gone. His first outing was at Leicester and **Tim Richards** witnessed the resurrection for Racing Post*

GREAT TO BE BACK. And great to have him back. Lester Piggott was mobbed on his return to the saddle at Leicester yesterday when the old magic only just failed to make it a winning comeback.

Racegoers, fans and autograph-hunters followed their legendary pale-faced idol's every stride on every occasion he stepped out of the weighing room. He was swamped in a sea of photographers the moment he set foot on the racecourse. To Lester, who retired five years ago and will be 55 in three weeks' time, it was like a homecoming. He loved it all. After failing by a short head on Lupescu, his comeback ride in the first, Piggott stood surrounded by a mass of media men in the winner's enclosure. He summed up his feelings when he said: 'It's great to see you all.'

He had come back a winner even though his three mounts failed to produce the goods. Lupescu went under a short head to the Gary Carter-ridden Sumonda in the first. Balasani was seventh to Gilt Preference, and Patricia beat only four home. Now Piggott and his legion of followers head for Chepstow today, where his four mounts are Ruddy Cheek, Nicholas, Shining Jewel and Lost City.

He admitted of his narrow defeat in the first: 'I'd love to have won and I thought for a second I was going to. Gary came to beat me and then I nearly got back at him. It was great to get so close; I was frightened I might be last.'

Piggott, his hair slightly greyer than when he hung up his saddle at Nottingham in 1985, looked drawn and it was hardly surprising when he admitted: 'I can do 8st 5lb. I just missed my lunch yesterday. I'm pretty fit, though I'm bound to need a race or two to get race-fit.' When asked if his technique had changed due to his five-year absence Piggott, who has ridden more than 5,200 winners world-wide, said: 'I haven't changed it. It's always there.'

Piggott's mount Lupescu bumped Sumonda and wandered about due to greenness and Piggott had to make an early visit to the stewards' room to explain what happened. Before the inquiry Lord Gainsborough, senior steward at the meeting, shook Piggott's hand and welcomed him back on such an historic occasion. Piggott was back on his patch and no-one enjoyed it more than the man himself.

As he walked into the course in dark glasses, tweed jacket, grey trousers, a mackintosh on his arm and carrying a white plastic bag he became centre stage again. Photographers surrounded him all the way to the weighing room, only to find to their surprise they were barred from entry.

Leicester's racecourse manager David Henson, who reckons Piggott put 1,000 on the gate, making the attendance around 3,000, said: 'From where Lester was sitting on the scales they looked like a bunch of monkeys outside as they scrambled to get their cameras against the glass to snap Lester.'

Piggott arrived on the course at 1.15 and at

Lester returns and one punter roars: 'You're still the champion of the world. You're back'

1.50 the police were called to the weighing room. When Piggott emerged he was flanked by a policeman and policewoman. But still racegoers reached out to slap him on the back and cheer him to the parade ring. Piggott smiled all the way.

Even when they knew he had just been beaten as he returned on Lupescu, they refused to believe it. One punter roared: 'You're still the champion of the world. You're back.' Another said: 'I just wanted Lester to go out there and prove he could do it. I knew he wouldn't let us down. He's come back to prove his point, and done just that. It was great. He's the main man.'

Piggott received a bigger cheer than Gary Carter on Geoff Wragg-trained Sumonda, the odds-on winner. Carter, 29 years Piggott's junior, spoiled the Long Fellow's 'homecoming' and said: 'When you're in a photo it doesn't matter who you're against. You just want to win. If Lester thinks he can come back and step out of the shadows, good luck to him. It's great that he's back.'

Britain's rugby league heroes beat Australia 19-12

Never before had Great Britain so shaken the mighty men of Australian rugby league, but shake them the home team did at Wembley in the first Test. **Paul Fitzpatrick** *in The Guardian reported on a triumph he described as 'one of the unlikeliest victories since the sides first locked horns in 1908'*

AFTER THE UNEQUAL ASHES SERIES of 1982, 1984 and 1986 there appeared no overwhelming reason why Great Britain should ever be able to beat the Australians. The only thing likely to overcome them, it seemed, was boredom. Sydney in July 1988 brought the first significant shift in power. Great Britain, stricken by injury, fashioned one of the unlikeliest victories since the sides first locked horns in 1908. But glorious though the win was, it would have been unwise to invest it with too much importance.

Australia had, after all, won the series by then and not everyone was convinced that they had chosen their best side. What was significant was that the British players learned that day the importance of adhering to a game plan. The Australians were never going to be beaten by brute force alone, but they were not going to be beaten if physical commitment was anything less than absolute. Nor would they lose to opponents devoid of imagination. These lessons have been gradually absorbed by the sometimes maligned British players and on Saturday, before a record Test crowd of 52,274 at Wembley, they got it all superlatively together. Their victory by 19-12 was as near perfection as we have a right to expect.

For the time being, though, and for the first time in well over a decade, the sense of bewilderment is confined exclusively to the Australian camp. Their coach, Bobby Fulton, is under pressure if not yet under siege. As for Britain, those crazy days of 1982, when the international side changed more rapidly than Italian governments, should now have gone for good.

Malcolm Reilly, the coach, will certainly find it difficult to omit any of the 15 men who served him so nobly on Saturday. From fullback, where Steve Hampson made some spectacular catches under pressure as well as a string of superb, clearing runs, to the loose forward and inspirational captain Ellery Hanley it was impossible to find serious fault. Some British followers were concerned at the choice of the centres, Daryl Powell and Carl Gibson, who were conceding massive weight advantage to their opposites, Mal Meninga and Mark McGaw. But that concern was possibly an ignorance of the progress they made on the summer tour of Papua New Guinea and New Zealand. Gibson, making powerful claims to the Man of the Match award by half-time but shaded in the second half by Schofield and Hanley, deserves particular praise. It is hard to believe that this is the same player who toured Australia so anonymously in 1988.

Phil Larder, the assistant coach, encapsulated one of the essential ingredients of the afternoon when he said that what mattered was not so much size as size of heart. Powell and Gibson illustrated the truth of that. A case can still be made for the inclusion of Jonathan Davies, on the substitutes' bench at least, but Paul Eastwood fully justified his selection on the right wing. His place kicking was nervous and wayward and four of his seven kicks failed, two of them from the most inviting positions, but he is a strong man and he scored two muscular tries, defended impeccably and claimed 14 of the side's 19 points. The last two came from a fine, wide kick three minutes from time.

Gratifyingly, Britain's other try came from the opposite wing. Martin Offiah showed his alertness when Gary Belcher's nerve and technique failed under a testing kick hoisted with mathematical precision by Hanley in the 56th minute. Offiah has already earned a big chunk of remission for his blunder in Christchurch in July when he failed to ground the ball under pressure as Britain lost to New Zealand.

Eastwood's contribution and the excellent form of Karl Harrison, on his debut, and the young hooker Lee Jackson made this a day for the re-emerging Hull club to celebrate; Dixon showed again what an underrated and resilient character he is; Gregory was as persistent and irritating as a hornet, and his colleague, Denis Betts, found the stirring form that has been eluding him for Wigan.

But above all were Hanley and Schofield. In his development from a centre of instinctive finishing skills into a brilliant stand-off half, Schofield has perhaps lost a yard of pace. But he has gained so much, an astute kicking game included, and looks the finished article. Hanley was astonishing. His strength defies belief and his stamina and determination have no limits. Sheer persistence, of the kind he showed in

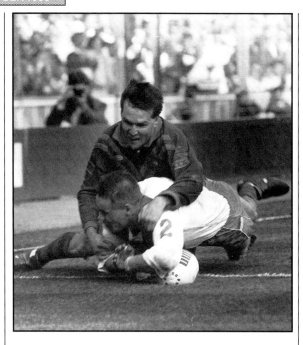

Great Britain's Paul Eastwood scores his second muscular try. He claimed 14 of his team's 19 points

the build-up to Eastwood's try in the 44th minute, will create opportunities when none exists. Lindner was impressive, but the Australians had no one as remotely inspiring.

Against opponents showing such security in defence, enterprise in attack and such a clear grasp of their objectives, Australia were fortunate to be on terms at 2-2 at half-time. But they were gradually forced out of the contest throughout a pulsating second half. Britain's only vulnerable moments came in the 51st minute, when Meninga exploited some ragged defence on the left, and 13 minutes later when the dangerous McGaw did the same on the right. Meninga improved that try to bring the score to 13-12, but Britain were not to be denied their first win here over the Kangaroos since 1978. Schofield, who had dropped a valuable goal in the 62nd minute, was the architect of Eastwood's second try in the 70th minute and a five-point lead looked enough. Eastwood's late, splendid goal was the last twist of the knife.

GREAT BRITAIN

Hampson (Wigan); Eastwood (Hull), D. Powell (Sheffield Eagles), Gibson (Leeds), Offiah (Widnes); Schofield (Leeds), Gregory (Wigan); Harrison (Hull); Fairbank (Bradford N 71min), Jackson (Hull), Dixon (Leeds), Betts (Wigan), R. Powell (Leeds), Hanley (Wigan).

AUSTRALIA

Belcher; Hancock (Shearer, 79), Meninga, McGaw, Ettingshausen; Stuart, Langer (Alexander, 77); Roach, Kerrod Walters, Bella (Lazarus, 71), Sironen, Cartwright (Hasler, 71), Lindner.

Referee: A. Sablayrolles (France).

1991
16 March

England stem French flair to win rugby's Grand Slam

*Twickenham had never witnessed anything like the renaissance of English rugby. Particularly when England, captained by Will Carling, beat France 21-19. Exaltation was unrestrained. In The Sunday Times, **Stephen Jones** wrote a classic account of a moving victory*

IT WAS FABULOUS. It was Twickenham's loudest and most tumultuous day and a game to rank with any in the history of the Five Nations tournament. France scored three tries to one, the first of them the most wonderful score the old-new stadium has ever seen, and England won the most deeply coveted and, in a way, the most concrete of mythical trophies ever awarded in sport, the Grand Slam and the championship title itself to add to the Triple Crown.

They did it with leonine hearts and the most ferocious commitment and application. They also did it with real skill and wit. They were marshalled expertly by Hill and Andrew at half-back, and some of the kicking of this pair was inch-perfect as the ball rained down on Blanco and the French wing and the screw kept turn-ing and turning. Both England flankers contributed herculean efforts, and there was yet another dazzling demonstration of the finishing arts of Underwood on the wing.

Yet if England did not have to sweat quite as profusely as the final score might suggest, and if they always just had their noses ahead, they were given a titanic battle by a team at least 18 months away from any sort of peak. There was hardly anything in the French performance of which they could not be proud, bar one or two isolated outbursts of temper and five handling errors brought about by the sheer ambition and energy they brought to the occasion.

They scored two brilliant, brilliant tries, their attitude was on the heroic side of wholesome, and Blanco, that stupendous man, that wonderful attacker and ambassador, marked what everyone felt would be his final appearance at Twickenham with a Blanco-like performance. On the other hand, if France improve in the next few months and at the same rate, they could quite easily be back at Twickenham, Blanco and all, in the final of the World Cup in November. In the last analysis they did not quite have the forward platform, and they did not quite have the technical discipline needed so sorely when up against a kicker like Hodgkinson and a team so determined to cash in on errors. They lacked a hard core, so that when England drove at them they often scattered to the fringes, where they were either ineffective or offside.

Blond in the back row was one of the chief culprits, but on the other hand there was a mighty effort in the lineout from Roumat and Benazzi, and the tall Moroccan had a game of world class all over the field. Certainly he sent a shiver through the stadium when he hurled back the mighty Richards at a scrum near the French line in the second half. Nor did the French scrum lack anything by comparison.

There is equally good news about the one neutral on the field, because Mr Peard contributed exactly the right measure of control and sympathy the world of international rugby has been seeking from its referees for some time. There was a consistency about him, and he even appeared to be having a little fun. It threw into sharp relief the mistake of the organisers in spreading the World Cup refereeing jobs around many countries.

The opening stages were a powerful statement on the course of the match, as England immediately began to thunder at the heart of France behind the pounding Teague and his mates, and Hodgkinson kicked England ahead after Blond duly gave away a penalty. England and the high-decibel crowd began to dream of a platform and of dictating the day and lots of points. They dreamt even more fervently of these things after 13 minutes, when Hodgkinson had another kick at goal. But he pulled it to the right. England turned half-away, but France were conjuring. Blanco brought the ball back behind his own posts, and Lafond and Camberabero picked up the move just as the first stirrings of English anxiety rose. Sella launched Camberabero over halfway with a return pass, and Camberabero chipped ahead, regained the ball and cross-kicked perfectly. Saint-Andre came scorching down the middle of the field, had a moment to wait for the bounce and collected to go over for a fine score between the posts.

Do not bother telling how some old codger scored a better try in some half-forgotten game years ago. The ball that Blanco brought back towards England was dead and buried, and the

Under pressure here, Will Carling led a team with leonine hearts and ferocious commitment

ENGLAND
Hodgkinson (Nottingham); N. Heslop (Orrell), W. Carling (Harlequins, capt), J. Guscott (Bath), R. Underwood (Leicester); R. Andrew (Wasps), R. Hill (Bath); J. Leonard (Harlequins), B. Moore (Harlequins), J. Probyn (Wasps), P. Ackford (Harlequins), W. Dooley (Preston Grasshoppers), M. Teague (Gloucester), D. Richards (Leicester), P. Winterbottom (Harlequins).

FRANCE
Blanco (Biarritz, capt); J-B Lafond (Racing Club), P. Sella (Agen), F. Mesnel (Racing Club), P. Saint-Andre (Montferrand); D. Camberabero (Beziers), P. Berbizier (Agen); G. Lascube (Agen), P. Marocco (Montferrand), P. Ondarts (Biarritz), M. Tachdjian (Racing Club; rep. M. Cecillon, Bourgoin, 54min), O. Roumat (Dax), X. Blond (Racing Club), A. Benazzi (Agen), L. Cabannes (Racing Club).

Referee: L. Peard (Wales).

match was still in its formative and nerve-jangling stages. It was one of rugby's wondrous moments; and it served sharp notice on England. To their credit, England were alive to all attempted repetitions bar one, and by half-time they had reasserted themselves powerfully, with a drop goal from Andrew, Hodgkinson's second penalty and Underwood's cutting-edge try. That came when Teague picked up a dreadfully slow ball from behind an England scrum when all that seemed on was a shallow burial under the studs of the onrushing French. Yet Teague hurled himself towards and over the advantage line, Carling, Andrew and Hodgkinson were able to take the ball running at pace, and Underwood fixed Lafond like a rabbit in the headlights and ran past him to score. Lafond himself is one of Racing Club's aristocratic backs who delight in such micro-seconds of skill; and no doubt deep inside him there was a pair of mental hands applauding in appreciation.

England were away at 18-9 into the second half, but even though the superiority was always there and the territorial advantage massive, they could not for a second savour the prospect of a Grand Slam. Camberabero scored after chasing his own chip and France had a try to compare even with their first when Berbizier launched a sweeping movement down the left and Sella and Blanco put Mesnel clear. He knifed past Hill with all the brilliance shown by Underwood earlier, and with a glorious conversion it was suddenly 21-19. The last two minutes were agonising for England, but the whistle was sweet.

England lost a Grand Slam at this very same stage in Scotland last season. It hurt them sav-

agely, more than they have ever admitted. It could have shattered them mentally, and one of the great feats of the season is that they have unscrambled the inner man and remotivated themselves so fiercely. And all the time, at every match, there was always the chance that a defeat would lead to the break-up of the team and a most bitter sense of unfulfilment. And, contrary to what you may have heard, most of them are still true-blue amateurs, still negotiating their way through the problems of home and work, and yet still prepared to shoulder the tremendous workload needed to take part in top-class rugby. These are regular guys. They are men of stature, and at least six of them arrived back in the dressing-room tunnel borne on the shoulders of supporters. They now have something tangible to savour in old age and, with the French, they gave a lot of people a delightful day.

The match over, the Grand Slam won, Twickenham celebrates and Carling is only one of several England players who have to struggle to the dressing room

Graham Gooch towers over West Indies

In the second innings of the Headingley Test Graham Gooch batted for seven and a half hours against four of the best fast bowlers in the world. He made 154 and won the match for England, the first home win against the West Indies for two decades. **Christopher Martin-Jenkins** *reported in The Daily Telegraph*

ALMOST FROM THE MOMENT that he became captain of England, amid some scepticism, Graham Gooch has been a Gulliver amongst Lilliputians. His 154 not out, 61 per cent of England's 252, will rank among the most famous of Test innings, whether or not it proves today to have been the prelude to England's first home victory over the West Indies for 22 years.

Weather permitting, that seems more than likely, because when a day of showers and staccato drama ended at 7pm, West Indies were 11 for one, needing another 267 runs and the highest total of the match to win.

Showers are forecast for Leeds today, but nothing worse. With free entry for those who saw only 48 overs yesterday, plus a maximum entrance fee of £8, there should be an atmos-

phere worthy of the climax of a typical Headingley thriller. The West Indies, however, will not meekly submit. The theory that they are weak under pressure has been exploded umpteen times since the Packer years hardened and enriched them. And the sight of Richards and Haynes having an impromptu net in twilight gloom after close of play underlined their resolve.

Gooch, unruffled by three interruptions for rain and batting for the most part in grim light on a pitch of gentle pace but continuing deviations both vertical and lateral, played with quite remarkable poise, certainty and judgement. He was seldom hurried, gave not a single chance and with his high-handed technique proved himself again a masterful player of fast bowling. Gooch's percentage of the total has been exceeded only five times in Test history. Bannerman, curiously enough, made 67 per cent of the first Test innings of all. Only four other Englishmen have carried their bat through a Test innings and only Len Hutton, whose records Gooch seems fond of chasing, has managed it before in England, against the West Indies also, at the Oval in 1950.

This was Gooch's sixth Test hundred in a year, not to mention four 80s: extraordinary in itself, even more so when he has been carrying the burdens of captaincy – to which players like Sobers, Lloyd and Richards reacted by dropping down the order. He has scored five centuries in his last five home Tests. Few cricketers have so deceptively hidden their light under their bushel as Gooch. Both as a player and as a character, he has been misunderstood. Apparently a flat, even boring man, he in fact has great reserves of determination and strong convictions, leavened by a very British sense of dry wry humour. Naturally undemonstrative and shy, he once on this ground lightened the later stages of a moribund Test by going through a repertoire of his impressions of famous bowling actions.

He has scored nearly 6,500 runs at an average of 42. A failure when first taking over the captaincy of Essex, he has become an increasingly respected Test captain. Once described to me by an England selector as being 'as soft as putty' – long before Ted Dexter compared his charisma to a wet fish – he has now made five Test hundreds against the fastest and nastiest attack in world cricket. Gooch actually scored 72 of the 109 added by England's last four wickets on the fourth day, his only substantial assistance coming from Derek Pringle in a seventh-wicket stand of 98, much the best of the match.

This is, incredibly enough, Pringle's 12th incarnation as a Test cricketer and if he is perhaps half a class below the best, he is still a cricketer of character, a shrewd selection for Headingley with a further part to play today, perhaps. The odd thing is that they like to bait him up here, mistaking his amiability for softness and his heavy movements for lack of talent. There was real warmth and a new respect about the crowd's applause, however, when having played with little trouble and the occasional well-timed shot off his legs, he finally fell after lunch in the third over with the new ball to an outside edge. It was the first of three wickets for Marshall, underlining the mistaken decision to open the day with Patterson.

Ambrose could not find his inspiration of Saturday, largely because Pringle used his reach to get well forward and Gooch mastered him with such simple, massive authority. His timing was more certain than it had been when holding the fort so stoically on Saturday. Despite four men on the boundary much of the time and a far slower outfield than is normal here, he hit 18 fours in all.

It was only a matter of time, of course, before Gooch ran out of partners. DeFreitas walked in front of a straight one and Marshall, having enabled Hooper to take his fourth catch of the innings at second slip, soon put paid to Malcolm. With grey clouds scudding over Headingley as they had all day, the West Indies were obliged in the end to bat only for eight overs, in two short, tense sessions. The experience of Greenidge was sorely missed when Simmons, cutting at the first bail of the innings from DeFreitas, dragged it on.

England will be even more determined to take their chance today, because Angus Fraser will not be bowling again this season. His prob-

Graham Gooch, a Gulliver amongst Lilliputians, has scored 100 and raises his bat to acknowledge the Yorkshire crowd's applause

lem has finally been diagnosed as 'AVN', a lack of blood circulation to the hip. This is rare if not unique to cricketers, but common in deep-sea divers. Complete rest for three months has been ordered by Johnny Johnson, the London bone specialist, and Middlesex are considering an American treatment which involves the patient wearing a pair of special shorts at night which transmit a curative magnetic field round the hip joint.

Robin Smith was yesterday given a guaranteed winter contract (but not selection) by England. He joins a list including Gooch, Lamb, Atherton, Fraser, Malcolm and Russell.

THE SCOREBOARD
at Headingley

ENGLAND - First Innings

*G A Gooch c Dujon b Marshall (61 min, 49balls, 6x4, 0x6..... 34
M A Atherton b Patterson (22-16-0-0) 2
G A Hick c Dujon b Walsh (51-31-1-0) 6
A J Lamb c Hooper b Marshall (55-37-1-0) 11
M R Ramprakash c Hooper b Marshall (142-103-4-0) 27
R A Smith run out (Ambrose/Dujon)(135-88-7-1x5) 54
†R C Russell lbw Patterson (45-29-1-0) 5
D R Pringle c Logie b Patterson (111-73-0-0).....................16
P A J DeFreitas c Simmons b Ambrose (43-34-2-0)................ 15
S L Watkin b Ambrose (14-9-0-0) 2
D E Malcolm not out (41-31-1-0).. 5
Extras (lb 5, w 2, nb 14)...2
Total   (79.2 overs, 366 mins) **198**

Fall of wickets: 1-13 (Atherton); 2-45 (Gooch), 3-45 (Hick), 4-64 (Lamb), 5-129 (Ramprakash), 6-149 (Smith), 7-154 (Russell), 8-177 (DeFreitas), 9-181 (Watkin).

Bowling: Ambrose 26-8-49-2 (nb8), Patterson 26-2-8-67-3 (nb9), Walsh 14-7-31-1 (nb3, w1), Marshall 13-4-46-3 (nb4, w1).

Second Innings

*G A Gooch not out (452-331-18-0) 154
M A Atherton c Dujon b Ambrose (38-33-0-0) 6
(Edged low, diving catch to 'keeper)
G A Hick b Ambrose (25-20-1-0) 6
(Slow yorker rolls off bat and pad)
A J Lamb c Hooper b Ambrose (1-1-0-0) 0
(Surprised by extra bounce)
M R Ramprakash c Dujon b Ambrose (142-109-2-0) 27
(Edge taken by 'keeper on his knees)
R A Smith lbw Ambrose (1-1-0-0)...0
(Playing back to ball that kept low)
R C Russell c Dujon b Ambrose (14-12-1-0)............................4
(Faint edge to 'keeper)
D R Pringle c Dujon b Marshall (144-94-2-0)..........................27
(Edged outswinger to 'keeper)
P A J DeFreitas lbw Walsh (41-27-0-0) 3
(Played across line)
S L Watkin c Hooper b Marshall (6-5-0-0) 0
(Edge to second slip)
D E Malcolm b Marshall (29-11-1-0) 4
(Played around straight ball)
Extras (b 4, lb 9, w 1, nb 7 21
Total (106 overs, 452 mins)........................... **252**

Fall of wickets: 1-22 (Atherton), 2-38 (Hick), 3-38 (Lamb), 4-116 (Ramprakash), 5-116 (Smith), 6-124 (Russell), 7-222 (Pringle), 8-236 (DeFreitas), 9-238 (Watkin).

Bowling: Ambrose 28-6-52-6; Patterson 15-1-52-0 (nb5); Marshall 25-4-58-3 (nb3 w1); Walsh 30-5-61-1; Hooper 4-1-11-0; Richards 4-1-5-0.

WEST INDIES - First Innings

P V Simmons c Ramprakash b DeFreitas (77-62-6-0) 38
(Square cut taken by diving cover point)
D L Haynes c Russell b Watkin (55-38-1-0)............................ 7
(Edged lifting ball to 'keeper – juggling catch)
R B Richardson run out (Gooch/Malcolm/Russell) (97-62-2-0) ..29
(Stranded in mid-pitch attempting third run)
C L Hooper run out (Ramprakash) (8-5-0-0) 0
(Direct hit, running in from cover point)
*I V A Richards c Lamb b Pringle (129-98-7-2).......................73
(Edged outswinger to first slip)
A L Logie c Lamb b DeFreitas (25-15-1-0) 6
(Cutting to first slip)
†P J L Dujon c Ramprakash b Watkin (14-13-1-0) 6
(Mis-hit to extra cover)
M D Marshall c Hick b Pringle (8-5-0-0) 0
(Low edge top second slip)
C E L Ambrose c Hick b DeFreitas (4-3-0-0) 0
(Ankle-high to second slip)
C A Walsh c Gooch b DeFreitas (23-16-0-0) 3
(Swirling skyer to extra cover)
B P Patterson not out (18-14-1-0) 5
Extras (lb 1, nb 5) 6
Total (54.1 overs, 236 mins) **173**

Fall of wickets: 1-36 (Haynes), 2-54 (Simmons), 3-58 (Hooper), 4-102 (Richardson), 5-139 (Logie), 6-156 (Dujon), 7-160 (Marshall), 8-165 (Ambrose), 9-167 (Richards).

Bowling: Malcolm 14-0-69-0 (nb6); DeFreitas 17.1-5-34-4; Watkin 14-2-55-2; Pringle 9-3-14-2.

Second Innings

P V Simmons b DeFreitas (2-1-0-0) 0
(Edged ball on to leg stump)
D L Haynes not out (35-20-0-0) 3
R B Richardson not out (31-27-1-0).......................................8
Total (8 overs, 35 mins) **11**

Fall of wicket: 1-0 (Simmons).

Bowling: DeFreitas 4-2-6-1, Malcolm 1-0-1-0, Pringle 3-1-4-0

Umpires: H D Bird & D R Shepherd

West Indies won the toss

1991
30 August

The world's best bow to Liz McColgan

Britain only won two events at the third World championships, the men's 4x400m relay and the women's 10,000 metres race. Liz McColgan won from the front, vanquishing the finest field of women athletes ever gathered together for the event. **David Powell** *of The Times reported the triumph*

The smile of victory adorning her face, Liz McColgan has just destroyed the other competitors in the women's 10,000 metres

LIKE FATIMA WHITBREAD in the javelin four years ago, Liz McColgan ensured yesterday that Britain does not go home from the world championships without a gold medal by obliterating the finest women's 10,000 metres field ever assembled.

Twice Commonwealth champion, and Olympic runner-up in 1988, McColgan has taken the greatest prize outside the Olympics. Leading from the start, she forced a relentless pace. Only Derartu Tulu, 19, of Ethiopia, remained as she and McColgan passed 5,000 metres in 15min 34.15sec. In 78 per cent humidity too.

No bursts, no chopping of stride to bring Tulu forward to take on the work. Just McColgan doing what she does best: grinding it out from the front. Suddenly, Tulu snapped

and McColgan had five laps to do on her own. Among those who have followed her, there was no doubt that now she would win.

Aged 27, she has learned how to judge pace. Without being blessed with a sprint, she knows she always has to get away. With three laps to go, McColgan's lead was 26 seconds, but by the finish it had narrowed to 21. 'I knew I had it won from 600 metres out,' she said. There was a stumble on to the inside of the track with 380 metres to go, but anxiety among British supporters in the stadium was temporary.

In the finishing straight there was no need for a burst. 'I just relaxed and enjoyed it,' said McColgan, who crossed the line in 31min 14.31sec. 'My victory was more for Britain than myself.'

Nigel Mansell sends his fans into Grand Prix orbit

British motor racing followers had waited long for the moment when Nigel Mansell would prove invincible. In 1992 he did and when he won the British Grand Prix at Silverstone, well on the way to his world championship, their joy burst like water through a broken dam. **Norman Howell** *in The Times was swept along with the flood*

NIGEL MANSELL WON the B.itish Grand Prix amid scenes of rejoicing the like of which Silverstone has never seen. It was his seventh victory in nine Formula One races this season, and with it Mansell overtook Jackie Stewart's 19-year-old British record of 27 wins. The celebrations began as Mansell took the chequered flag, 39 seconds ahead of his Williams-Renault team-mate, Riccardo Patrese.

Thousands of supporters broke through inadequate security on to the track and tried to stop Mansell's car at the end of the pit straight while a number of drivers were still racing for position. Fortunately nobody was hurt but FISA, the sport's governing body, may investigate.

Mansell, manhandled out of his car and rescued by police and marshals, did not mind.

'This is the best crowd in the world,' he said. 'And if some people got overexcited, that is OK as this is a great day for British motor racing.' Indeed it was, as the 38-year-old took another step towards his first world championship and so becoming the first British driver to win the title since James Hunt in 1976. Mansell is now 36 points ahead of Patrese, while the Williams team leads by a country mile in the constructors' table. They are followed by Benetton, who also enjoyed a good day at Silverstone, with Martin Brundle taking third place for the second week running.

Lotus had their moments with Mika Hakkinen in the points behind Michael Schumacher, in the second Benetton, and Gerhard Berger, in the McLaren. Johnny Herbert retired on the 32nd lap when he was comfortably in sixth position.

Mansell led practically from start to finish, except for the rush into the first bend, when Patrese once more beat him off the start line. But the race was a spectacular affair, with Union Jacks waving each time Mansell went past, and two extraordinary battles going on behind him. It was one of the best days of Grand Prix racing for a long time and, of course, Mansell was at the centre of it. On the grid he was the focus of attention from Prince Michael of Kent, who wished him the best of luck, to gushing young women who had somehow eluded security.

Despite the tension that must grip him before a race as important as this, or any Formula One race, he took it all in his stride, smiling and polite. Mansell waved continually to the adoring crowds in the grandstand and his warm-up lap 'was quite extraordinary'.

'I thought I had won the race already, such was the cheering and the flag waving,' Mansell said. He felt the passion of the crowd, a passion that moved members of the Italian press to comment that this was like Monza, where the *tifosi* first started calling Mansell Il Leone during his time at Ferrari. 'On the straight I felt as if I had another 300 revs, as people were willing me along, while I suspect that my rivals were instead going 300 revs slower,' he said.

Mansell was clearly much faster than every-

body. At the end of the first lap, after he had retaken the lead from Patrese, he was already more than three seconds ahead of his team-mate. By the time the two cars had completed five laps, his lead had stretched to nearly 12 seconds. It was a magnificent display in a sport where time differences are usually measured in tenths and hundredths of a second. On it went, 22 seconds ahead by lap 20, and as a race it was all over.

There was a brief frisson when Mansell came in for tyres after 29 laps, as minds went back to Estoril last year and to the other occasions when his tyre changes have been less than adequate. He rolled slowly in and, sure enough, the rear left tyre did give some trou-

Driving a Williams-Renault (above), Nigel Mansell led practically from start to finish. By the time Mansell (right) took the plaudits of the crowd, the British Grand Prix had become a very British celebration of a very special hero

ble to the mechanic. He got away, though 11.7 seconds was a slow time for a tyre change, and he motored on to victory.

After Mansell had recovered from excessive wheelspin at the start and gone past him, Patrese settled for second place. It gave Williams their sixth one-two finish of the season, and with Brundle's third place, it was a repeat of the result in France last week.

Ayrton Senna and the two Benettons had a classic confrontation, with Schumacher eventually dropping off and leaving Brundle to fight off Senna, a man nobody wants to see looming in the rearview mirrors. Brundle admitted it was difficult having Senna so close. He told himself not to watch Senna and not to make any mistakes.

Brundle remained in front of the Brazilian until the 52nd lap, when Senna surged past, only to be sidelined immediately with a broken transmission. Senna was full of praise. 'I was pushing like hell for the whole race, knowing that I might pass him at the end of the race,' he said. 'I did, but I broke down and he really deserves his third place.'

For Brundle it evoked memories of battles with Senna for the 1983 British Formula 3000 championship, a title the Brazilian won. 'It was like old times, scrapping round Silverstone with Senna. I really enjoyed it and the car was fantastic,' Brundle said, having moved into sixth place in the championship.

Schumacher also became involved in an exciting duel with Berger and Hakkinen. They, too, drove nose to tail, machines on the limit and drivers giving their all. But it was Mansell's day and, despite his comfortable lead, he broke the lap record again two laps from the finish of the 59-lap race. 'I did it for the fans, it was my way of saying thank you,' he said.

Linford Christie strikes in the gold rush

*In the Olympic stadium of Barcelona, when Linford Christie won the 100 metres sprint at the age of 32 he became that comparative rarity, a Briton who could claim to be the fastest man in the world. **Cliff Temple** wrote with rare insight about the victory in The Sunday Times*

NEARLY 25 YEARS AGO, in the echoingly cavernous White City stadium, a small boy in floppy shorts and plimsolls ran in the Hammersmith schools' sports. Then he knew nothing of the Olympic ghosts from the third Games of 1908 which inhabited the stones around him; as a recently-arrived immigrant from Jamaica, running was a natural activity, a way of earning respect from his schoolmates, and something at which he could excel.

That same boy, now a grown man of 32, once again ran in an Olympic stadium. This time, the arena was full: every step, every aisle, was packed on a hot, sticky Barcelona evening to see Linford Christie transformed into an Olympic champion and take his place in sporting history. His name now follows Olympic champions like Reginald Walker, the South African who won the same title in 1908, and two other Britons: Harold Abrahams, in 1924, and Allan Wells, in 1980. He also succeeds Wells in another respect: Christie became the oldest athlete, by four years, ever to win this blue riband event of the Games.

If it had not been an easy week for British sprinting, and for Christie himself, the entire path to the gold medal had not been an easy one. Only in his mid-20s, as a talented but somewhat wayward club sprinter with Thames Valley Harriers, was he finally convinced that perhaps there really was a more rewarding path on offer to him than all-night parties on rum and blackcurrant. And he developed with the ever-growing confidence in his coach, Ron Roddan, and in his own ability to become an Olympic champion. He had greater faith, perhaps, than some of us who watched his successes and near misses since then.

There can be no question he was already Europe's fastest sprinter. But it seemed there would always be at least one unbeatable American at the most important occasions. His international career, which began in 1986, fell into a parallel course with that of his predecessor as an Olympic champion, Carl Lewis. The absence of Lewis last night was due to the inflexible American system, rather than fading muscles. Lewis finished only sixth in the US Olympic trials and is in Barcelona merely as a relay reserve and long jumper. That is not to say that Lewis would have beaten Christie, but he should at least have been in the field, which was the strongest since last year's world championship final in Tokyo.

On that day, on a similarly humid night, Lewis won the world title in 9.86sec, still the world record. Christie was fourth. He left Tokyo irritated and frustrated, not simply at missing a medal but at what he considered the subsequent dismissal of his performance, a European record of 9.92sec, as some sort of failure. Retirement was briefly threatened, and then he became determined to make amends in Barcelona. 'I am glad I didn't retire after Tokyo,' he said. 'It was the best decision of my life.'

At that time, it had seemed a worthy, sensible plan, if rather unlikely to succeed. Three Americans, Lewis, Leroy Burrell and Dennis Mitchell, had all finished in front of him in Tokyo, and one, at least, would surely bar his way in the Olympic final. With Lewis reduced to spectating, Burrell in less than sparkling form, and with Mitchell not showing the form of his American trials victory, Christie's moment had arrived. As the finalists went to the start line, each with just a lonely lane stretching in front of them, a one-metre-wide path to immortality, Christie was clearly the most in control. Burrell twitched and shook, trying to induce relaxation; the Namibian, Frankie Fredericks, a major threat from the preliminaries, caused a false start. 'It didn't worry me,' Christie said. 'I was totally focused. Nothing would have distracted me.'

It takes perhaps 10 metres of running to be convinced the race has really begun. The erratic starting in the heats had prepared us for the worst. But at the third attempt, it really was history in the making. Bruny Surin, the Canadian, briefly enjoyed an unexpected lead. But then the spearhead developed: the men in the middle lanes, the real contenders, emerged, with Christie's hugely developed arms pumping furiously. If you can move your arms quickly enough, your legs have no choice but to keep up. The gap opened ever so slightly, and as that white line across the track the other side of which was a sea into which very few ever dipped a toe drew closer, we had to remind ourselves that this was not just another televised spectacular meeting, another crowd-pleaser with a bouquet to throw to the spectators. This was the Olympic Games.

As the runners finished, only Christie knew for certain. He was able to enjoy the moment, both arms aloft, and set off on a lap of honour draped in a Union Jack. The rest, who for years had been waiting for these 10 explosive seconds, were spent cartridges, drawn down on knees, hands and backs across the track. Not exhaustion, just the anti-climax that they had come so close and even without knowing exactly their position, they had failed at the crucial moment. Christie's time of 9.96sec gave him a winning margin of 0.06sec, three times

Linford Christie, from small boy to grown man, a dream at last realised

greater than the women's race, a few minutes earlier, when just 0.02sec had covered all three medallists, led by the surprise new champion, Gail Devers, of the United States.

They say that when you achieve a goal you have long sought, the immediate feeling is also one of anti-climax. Certainly, Christie looked relaxed and calm as he faced the press afterwards. It was a day, perhaps, for the small boy in the floppy shorts and plimsolls who began his Olympic career in that old stadium. The stadium has gone now, victim of the demolition pick and shovel, but Christie's name has been cast in gold forever.

1992
2 August

Boys' Own victory for the Searle brothers

No victory in rowing was ever more stirring than that of the Searle brothers in the coxed pairs at the 1992 Olympics. They achieved what had begun to be deemed impossible: the Searles beat Italy's legendary Abbagnale brothers. In The Guardian **Frank Keating** *reported in his own inimitable fashion*

THE SEARLE BROTHERS' palpitating victory put a glistening gilt lid on the most illustrious weekend for British men's rowing in modern times. It truly was Boys' Own stuff. The two Surrey students were still considered novices at the event in the spring. Yesterday they gave 10 years in age, as well as a handsome start, to Italy's hitherto invincible legends and overtook them right on the line with one final, almost mischievous, heave. It was youthful bravado; it was also utterly heroic.

The previous day Redgrave and Pinsent had overwhelmed their rivals in the coxless pairs by the relentless power of their oars as well as their massive reputation. Each of the other boats carried an inferiority complex in its hold. At the finish a man from each of the silver and bronze medal boats was hauled out, collapsed and in distress, by crews of the ambulance launch, such was the intensity of the British pair's domination. Redgrave and Pinsent displayed awesomely cruel rowing.

What the Searles did was not so much rowing as racing. This was hats-in-the-air stuff. This was Piggott getting up on The Minstrel, Desert Orchid at Cheltenham, or Chataway v Kuts at White City. And what made it the grander was that it was Boys v Men.

The Abbagnale brothers have been world champions seven times. Yesterday they set a serene and severe course for an unprecedented hat-trick of Olympic titles. Horny-handed, unsmiling assassins, they train in the choppy dawn sea each morning in the dark shadow of Vesuvius, after running the five miles to their boat from their home in Pompeii. They started this Olympic final even hotter favourites than Redgrave's boat had been the day before. Who were these kids to challenge them?

The trusted tactics, as sadistically followed down the years, would destroy the upstarts – jump out of the traps at a lick, burn off the other boats by halfway, or three-quarters at the latest, then relax, savour the cheers and collect the gold medals. But even stony-faced granite, we discovered, can be dynamited by youthful will, daring and stomach-wrenching guts. The two part-time oarsmen and full-time British students – one at law school, the other in estate management – knew it would be terminal if 'the Abbers' led by more than three lengths at halfway. And they were duly three lengths down – but only three and not desperately hanging on by a thread.

'Did you see our bang at 1,250 metres?' said Jonny. 'We poured on the power just when they weren't expecting it, and it must have given them a psychological shock to think what we might have left. Garry [the cox] told us he could see their faces and he said, 'C'mon, boys, they really know we're coming to get them now.' And so they did.

Greg, who returns to his books at South Bank University next week, said at the finish he had been momentarily overwhelmed by 'a sort of dead silence of ecstasy – while Jonny and Garry just leapt about out of control.' The

It is the stuff of dreams as (left to right) Greg and Jonny Searle and cox Garry Herbert celebrate victory

younger boy said he looked across at the two Italians, vanquished at last, all-in and 'suddenly very old, and I felt a sudden pang of guilt for having done what we had, for they have been very, very great champions, and I could tell how devastated they were and utterly gutted. And they rowed over and said "well done" and "bravo". There was really nothing else they could say but I was very touched by their graciousness and chivalry.'

Greg said he didn't think he could row in a pair with anyone but his brother. 'There is no one I trust more. We'll go on, I suppose, mixing sport with our studies. If I became a full-time rower, I think I'd become a very boring person.' Jonny, who passed his first law exams six weeks ago, added: 'I may yap a lot but out on the water Greg is stronger than I am. And yes, it does hurt out there.'

The Abbagnale brothers have not been talkative through their illustrious career. But at Seoul four years ago, before they went out to demolish the Redgrave boat, they agreed that their racing secret was 'to start and finish every time as if it is the very last big race of our lives.' And yesterday it was.

Essex girl Sally Gunnell leaves them in her wake

*It was the first time since Ann Packer won the Olympic 800 metres that a British woman had triumphed in a pure track event. In Today, a report by **Roy Collins** of Sally Gunnell's victory in the 400 metres hurdles at Barcelona, encapsulated the sheer joy of the occasion.*

SALLY GUNNELL'S SECOND LAP of the Olympic track was considerably slower than the 53.23 seconds in which she sprinted to gold. If Gunnell set a record for the slowest Olympic lap of honour, around 10 minutes and counting, never in the history of British athletics had it been more deserved. Gunnell's performance in the 400 metre hurdles, one lap of absolute torture in which she literally rose to the occasion, ranks among the greatest feats of any British woman at any Olympics. So it was only right that she should celebrate a run of absolute perfection by milking every last drop of the victory lap, which she took at a deliberate, savouring dawdle.

Gunnell, a simple Essex girl, destroyed the painted glamour girls from the United States, Sandra Farmer-Patrick and Janeene Vickers, with sheer technical ability. The physical contrast between them couldn't have been more stark. Farmer-Patrick, in an outfit slashed to display a bare midriff, strawberry lipstick and nail polish and long hair teased into a lace bob, looked dressed for a night on La Rambla, where Barcelona's poseurs parade and party through the night. Gunnell, free of make-up and with her hair scraped back off her face and secured with a simple red bow, was dressed for business. Farmer-Patrick, America's new Flo-Jo who often runs with a tutu flowing out behind her, had an eye for the camera, for the multi-million dollar endorsements that an Olympic gold would have brought. Gunnell had eyes only for the job in hand.

Drawn in lane three, inside Farmer-Patrick, her only strategy, she said, was to get herself thereabouts at the eighth hurdle and kick for home. Plans are one thing. Carrying them out another matter. Gunnell ran from the gun like someone who had never even contemplated the idea of defeat.

The temptation in any staggered lane event is to try to close the gap on those outside you too quickly, to burn up energy too fast. Gunnell put all such temptation behind her. She ran like a girl who had the Montjuic Stadium to herself which, to all intents and purposes, she had, maintaining the exact pace she'd decided would bring her victory. She didn't so much jump the hurdles as slip over them, a performance of such mastery that it brought ungrudging admiration from Farmer-Patrick: 'Sally and I are about equal when it comes to strength. What separated us tonight was the technical aspect of her race.'

Not since Ann Packer grabbed a 800m gold in 1964 has Britain celebrated a gold medal for women in a pure track event. If she runs for another 10 years, she can't hope to be as foot perfect again. 'I was confident,' she said, 'so it was a case of me telling myself, you know you can do it, so go and enjoy it.'

Sally Gunnell has won, beaten the painted glamour girls, and now she can enjoy her moment

1993
26 April

Brian Clough signals the end of his reign

It was only on the retirement of Brian Clough that English football fully acknowledged the force he had been, possibly the best manager England never had. **Rob Hughes**, *the football correspondent of The Times, reported on the departure of a man who had brought colour and credit to the game*

THE RACE BETWEEN BRIAN CLOUGH and catastrophe has broken down, two hurdles from the end of his eighteenth full season managing Nottingham Forest. The manner of his going, a retirement forced from within the boardroom, reveals a football club of betrayal, turmoil and decay.

If these are the men of power that Clough leaves behind, not even the admirers of the style of his teams would care if his final side should now plummet out of the Premier League. It was clear from the faltering voice of Fred Reacher, when he announced yesterday morning that Clough would see out the last two matches and go, where the chairman stood and that he had been unable to carry his board. 'Brian and I have spent one-third of our lives together,' he said.

It is incredible that he lost to a minor member of that board, Chris Wootton, after Wootton had had a meeting with a Sunday newspaper. Wootton, alleged The People, had demanded £15,000 for his allegations of Clough's incapacity to manage and for a video-tape showing him incapable of fulfilling a television commercial.

Wootton denied yesterday that he had asked for or received money for his information. Nevertheless, it was the final straw for Clough who, one month ago, received the Freedom of Nottingham and, before that, a vote of 126-41 against a motion at an extraordinary meeting of Forest's shareholders to declare a loss of faith in the manager.

From within the team, Neil Webb, who returned this season from Manchester United but had spent, in all, five years under Clough, came this wish: 'Hopefully, the emotion at our final two games will help us to gain the results that keep Forest in the Premier League and give the gaffer a good send-off. Brian Clough has ruled the roost at Forest for so long, it will be weird starting again under a new manager.'

That was the kindest of the informed observations of the longest serving post-war manager. Some, including journalists who have lived for years off the crumbs of Clough quotes, have spent this season throwing jibes at him as if the apparent physical deterioration of his face were a dartboard made for their revenge. For most of yesterday, it seemed that Clough himself would be confined on his retirement day to the single, characteristic rebuff to a press photographer encroaching on his home ground in the village of Quarndon: 'Get off my grass, young man!'

However, Clough, 58, did later show himself to say: 'Retirement is something I have been thinking about for nine months but, like a woman, I might use my prerogative to change my mind. I have been in the game for 41 years and maybe the time has come to sit back and enjoy my pension.'

Some pension. He had recently negotiated a year's extension on his contract, which defied yesterday's claim that retirement was a long-considered prospect and all those who thought sickness was affecting his ability to manage clubs as he had done with astonishing distinction at Derby County and Forest. With them, he won two European Cups, two League championships and four League Cups. But he had his failures, too. The FA Cup eluded him, two semi-finals being the closest he came, and he had doleful and short spells at Leeds United and Brighton.

His forte used to be that he could inspire players to get every ounce of energy and effort out of their bodies. It was galvanised from the memory of having his own career stunted by a knee injury in his prime. Clough once admitted that his refuge from his own broken career had been the bottle and that admission has come back to haunt him in last weekend's allegations. Now, while some of his enemies within the game have given voice to sycophantic tributes, there have been some telling words, too.

Jack Charlton, rebuffed by the Football Association for the England manager's position in the same way that Clough was, said: 'It looks as though he has been hounded out of the game. It's a damn shame. Who will replace him over the next ten years? Plastic people no doubt.' And Graham Taylor, the England manager, said: 'It will bring the close to a glorious managerial career, one that has lifted football in many respects. People will always say that Brian should have been the international manager but the job usually goes to only one man of each generation. But Brian was a man of many parts, very opinionated, unpredictable and yet his achievements speak for themselves.'

Giancarlo Galavotti, of Italy's Gazzetta Dello Sport, commented: 'Like all the great dictators, from de Gaulle to Thatcher, he stayed on a little too long.'

Over and out, and a gesture, characteristic of Brian Clough, to the Nottingham Forest fans

Credits

PICTURE CREDITS

2-3	William Gordon Davis, Hulton-Deutsch, Patrick Eagar, Gerry Cranham, Press Association	**53**	Times Newspapers	**99**	Times Newspapers	**144**	Patrick Eagar
7	Times Newspapers	**55**	Times Newspapers	**100**	Gerry Cranham	**147**	Gerry Cranham
9	Hulton-Deutsch	**56**	Hulton-Deutsch	**101**	Times Newspapers	**148-9**	Times Newspapers
11	Hulton-Deutsch	**58**	Hulton-Deutsch	**103**	Associated Press	**151**	Gerry Cranham
12	Hulton-Deutsch	**60**	Times Newspapers	**105**	Gerry Cranham	**153**	Patrick Eagar
14	Hulton-Deutsch	**62**	Times Newspapers	**107**	Press Association	**154**	Patrick Eagar
15	Hulton-Deutsch	**63**	Hulton-Deutsch	**108-9**	Press Association	**154-5**	Patrick Eagar
17	William Gordon Davis	**64**	Hulton-Deutsch	**111**	Times Newspapers	**155**	Patrick Eagar
19	Press Association	**67**	Hulton-Deutsch	**112**	Gerry Cranham	**157**	Times Newspapers
21	Hulton-Deutsch	**68-9**	Times Newspapers	**113**	Times Newspapers	**159**	Associated Press
23	Hulton-Deutsch	**71**	Times Newspapers	**114**	Ken Kelly	**161**	Allsport
25	Hulton-Deutsch	**73**	Hulton-Deutsch	**117**	Associated Press	**162**	Press Association
27	Hulton-Deutsch	**75**	Hulton-Deutsch	**119**	Patrick Eagar	**165**	Associated Press
29	Hulton-Deutsch	**77**	Hulton-Deutsch	**121**	Times Newspapers	**166-7**	Gerry Cranham
30	Press Association	**79**	Times Newspapers	**122-3**	Associated Press	**169**	Edward Whitaker
33	Hulton-Deutsch	**81**	Associated Press	**124-5**	Gerry Cranham	**171**	Gerry Cranham
35	Hulton-Deutsch	**83**	Times Newspapers	**126-7**	P. Bertrand & Fils	**173**	Press Association
37	Hulton-Deutsch	**84-5**	Times Newspapers	**129**	David Muscroft	**175**	Press Association
39	Hulton-Deutsch	**86**	Gerry Cranham	**131**	Associated Press	**176**	Press Association
41	Hulton-Deutsch	**87**	Hulton-Deutsch	**132**	Gerry Cranham	**178**	Press Association
43	Hulton-Deutsch	**88**	Times Newspapers	**135**	Gerry Cranham	**180**	Press Association
45	Associated Press	**90**	Times Newspapers	**136**	Gerry Cranham	**182**	Neil Randon
47	Hulton-Deutsch	**91**	Associated Press	**137**	Gerry Cranham	**183**	Press Association
48-9	Times Newspapers	**92**	Gerry Cranham	**139**	Press Association	**185**	Press Association
51	Hulton-Deutsch	**94-5**	AssociatedPress	**140**	Gerry Cranham	**187**	Press Association
		96	AssociatedPress	**141**	Gerry Cranham	**189**	Press Association
		97	AssociatedPress	**143**	Times Newspapers	**191**	Allsport

BOOK CREDITS

Excerpts, other than from newspapers, are from the following books:

8-9 British Boxing by Denzil Batchelor, published by Collins.

36-7 Golden Miller by Gregory Blaxland, published by Constable, 1972.

102-3 Great Moments in Sport: Soccer by Geoffrey Green, published by Pelham, 1972.

132-3 The Olympics 1972 by James Coote and John Goodbody, published by Robert Hale, 1972.

168-9 221 Peter Scudamore's Record Season by Dudley Doust, published by Hodder & Stoughton, 1989